FROM LITERATURE TO THEOLOGY
IN FORMATIVE JUDAISM
Three Preliminary Studies

Program in Judaic Studies
Brown University
BROWN JUDAIC STUDIES
Edited by
Jacob Neusner
Wendell S. Dietrich, Ernest S. Frerichs, William Scott Green,
Calvin Goldscheider, David Hirsch, Alan Zuckerman

Project Editors (Projects)

David Blumenthal, Emory University (Approaches to Medieval Judaism)
William Brinner (Studies in Judaism and Islam)
Ernest S. Frerichs, Brown University (Dissertations and Monographs)
Lenn Evan Goodman, University of Hawaii (Studies in Medieval Judaism)
William Scott Green, University of Rochester (Approaches to Ancient Judaism)
Norbert Samuelson, Temple University (Jewish Philosophy)
Jonathan Z. Smith, University of Chicago (Studia Philonica)

Number 199
FROM LITERATURE TO THEOLOGY
IN FORMATIVE JUDAISM
Three Preliminary Studies
by
Jacob Neusner

FROM LITERATURE TO THEOLOGY
IN FORMATIVE JUDAISM
Three Preliminary Studies

by

Jacob Neusner

Scholars Press
Atlanta, Georgia

BM
517
.M63
N48
1989

FROM LITERATURE TO THEOLOGY
IN FORMATIVE JUDAISM
Three Preliminary Studies

© 1989
Brown University

Library of Congress Cataloging in Publication Data

Neusner, Jacob, 1932-
  From literature to theology in formative Judaism : three
preliminary studies / Jacob Neusner
  p. cm. -- (Brown Judaic Studies ; no. 199)
  ISBN 1-55540-420-0 (alk. paper)
  1. Midrash rabbah--Criticism, interpretation, etc. 2. Rabbinical
literature--History and criticism. 3. Judaism--History--Talmudic
period. 10-425. I. Title. II. Series.
BM517.M63N48 1989
296.1'206--dc20
                                                89-24040
                                                CIP

Printed in the United States of America
on acid-free paper

IN MEMORY OF

MAX KADUSHIN

He was unique in his generation and the first of his line,
the most interesting mind in the study of
the theology of Judaism in its canonical writings,

the most inventive and reflective and articulate
intellect of his day in the study of Judaism
and with little competition in the past and present century.

Table of Contents

Preface xi

Introduction 1

PROLOGUE

1. Carrying Forward the Inquiry of Max Kadushin 13

Part One
THE QUEST FOR UNITY
IN THE MISHNAH'S PHILOSOPHY OF JUDAISM
AND IN THE MIDRASH COMPILATIONS' THEOLOGY OF
JUDAISM

2. The Mishnah's Philosophical Method: The Judaism of
   Hierarchical Classification in Greco-Roman Context 23

3. The Theological Method of Midrash Compilations:
   Saying One Thing Many Times and in Many Ways.
   Theology Expressed through Writing with Scripture and
   the Representation of the Moabite Messiah
   in Ruth Rabbah 45
   i.   The Religious System Faces Outward 45
   ii.   Writing with Scripture 46
   iii. Why Ruth Rabbah? A Document with a Message, or
         a Scrapbook for Collecting and Preserving Completed
         Writings? 50
   iv.   The Categories of the Topical Program 51
   v.   Israel and God 53
   vi.   Israel and the Nations 53
   vii. Israel on its Own [1]: The Outsider Becomes Insider,
         the Moabite Woman the Israelite Messiah, through
         the Torah 54
   viii. Israel on its Own [2]: The Documentary Message
         Viewed Whole 60
   ix.   Ruth in Particular 65
   x.   Passages with Propositions Not Relevant to the Book
         of Ruth 65
   xi.   The Message of Ruth Rabbah 67
   xii. Writing and Repeating with Scripture 68
   xiii. Writing with Scripture, Writing with Symbols:
         Rational Discourse and Emotional Transaction 69

Part Two
WHEN IS "ANOTHER THING" THE SAME THING?
THE THEOLOGICAL UNITY OF DISCRETE SYMBOLS

4. Cases of *Davar Aher* in Genesis Rabbah 73
    i. The Issue 73
    ii. Genesis Rabbah XXI:IX 74
    iii. Genesis Rabbah XXXII:I 76
    iv. Genesis Rabbah LXV:X-XI 77
    v. Genesis Rabbah LXX:VIII-IX 80

5. Cases of *Davar Aher* in Esther Rabbah I 85
    i. Chapter Two. Esther Rabbah I *Petihta* 2 85
    ii. Chapter Three. Esther Rabbah I *Petihta* 3 86
    iii. Chapter Eighteen. Esther Rabbah I Esther 1:9 87
    iv. Chapter Twenty-Three. Esther Rabbah I Esther 1:14 90
    v. Chapter Thirty-Two Esther Rabbah I Esther 2:1 93

6. Cases of *Davar Aher* in Ruth Rabbah 97
    i. Chapter Two. Ruth Rabbah *Petihta* 2 97
    ii. Chapter Three. Ruth Rabbah *Petihta* 3 100
    iii. Chapter Twenty. Ruth Rabbah to Ruth 1:16 101
    iv. Chapter Fifty-Six. Ruth Rabbah to Ruth 3:7 102

7. Cases of *Davar Aher* in Lamentations Rabbah 105
    i. *Petihta* 17 105
    ii. *Petihta* 20 106
    iii. *Petihta* 25 107
    iv. Chapter Thirty-Nine. Parashah I. Lamentations 1:5 109
    v. Chapter Sixty. Parashah II. Lamentations 2:4 109
    vi. Chapter Sixty-Nine. Parashah II. Lamentations 2:13 110
    vii. Chapter One Hundred and One. Parashah IV.
        Lamentations 4:1 111
    viii. Chapter One Hundred and Two. Parashah IV.
        Lamentations 4:2 112
    ix. Chapter One Hundred and Twenty-Three. Parashah
        V. Lamentations 5:1 116
    x. Chapter One Hundred and Thirty. Parashah V.
        Lamentations 5:8 117
    xi. Chapter One Hundred and Forty-Two. Parashah V.
        Lamentations 5:20 117

8. Cases of *Davar Aher* in Song of Songs Rabbah 119
    i. From Literature to Theology? 119
    ii. Chapter One. Song of Songs Rabbah to Song 1:1 120
    iii. Chapter Two. Song of Songs Rabbah to Song 1:2 124

iv. Chapter Five. Song of Songs Rabbah to Song 1:5............127
 v. Chapter Twenty-Three. Song of Songs Rabbah
      to Song 2:6..128
vi. Chapter Twenty-Five. Song of Songs Rabbah
      to Song 3:8..129
vii. Chapter Twenty-Six. Song of Songs Rabbah
      to Song 2:9..131
viii. Chapter Thirty. Song of Songs Rabbah to Song 2:13........135
ix. Chapter Eighty-Seven. Song of Songs Rabbah
      to Song 6:11 138

Part Three
FROM UNITY TO DIVERSITY

9. The Three Stages in the Formation of Rabbinic Writings 145
    i. The Correct Starting Point...............................146
   ii. Redaction and Writing: The Extreme Case
         of the Mishnah..147
  iii. When the Document Does Not Define the Literary
         Protocol: Stories Told But Not Compiled.................149
   iv. Pericopes Framed for the Purposes of the Particular
         Document in Which They Occur 151
    v. Pericopes Framed for the Purposes of a Particular
         Document, But Not of a Type We Now Possess 155
   vi. Pericopes Framed for Purposes Not Particular
         to a Type of Document Now in Our Hands..................157
  vii. The Three Stages of Literary Formation...................163
10. Documentary Hermeneutics and the Interpretation
     of Narrative in the Classics of Judaism....................167
    i. The Starting Point.......................................167
   ii. The Hypothesis: The Three Stages
         of Literary Formation...................................169
  iii. Our Case: Ruth Rabbah to Ruth 3:13......................174
   iv. What Is at Stake: The Three Stages of Literary
         Formation and the Formation of a New Hermeneutics 180
    v. The Priority of Documentary Hermeneutics 181
   vi. The Three Stages of Literary Formation Revisited........184
  vii. Itinerancy and Documentary Integrity: The Problem
         of the Peripatetic Composition..........................184
 viii. Theology and Hermeneutics: The Unacknowledged
         Participant in the Debate 187
   ix. Autonomy, Connection, Continuity 188
    x. The Next Stage...191

EPILOGUE

11. The Documentary History of Judaism. Or:
     Why Schechter, Moore, and Urbach are Irrelevant
     to Scholarship Today..197
Index 219

Preface

Describing the theology of the Judaism of the Dual Torah as the canon of that Judaism attests to a fundamental theological order and structure which has challenged a century of scholarship. In these pages I mean to begin to address that challenge and to explore ways of meeting it. I move outward from my literary-descriptive studies toward the description of theology; but the steps taken in these pages are halting and few. In the Introduction I specify what I mean to accomplish here and how the definition of the task of theological description defines, also, the problems of method on which in these pages I experiment. But if I start the work only reluctantly, after thirty years of evasion of the descriptive and analytical task of asking about structure, system, and order of a theological character, that does not mean others have not proposed to move in giant steps across the canon and attain the goal of a fully-exposed theological description; many have thought to do so, though, in my view, they got nowhere at all.

The work of theological description of the Judaism attested by the rabbinic writings of late antiquity is now more than a century old. It has extended back from the later nineteenth century in Germany and Britain, with Solomon Schechter's response to the German Evangelical (Lutheran) Protestant caricature of Judaism in their attack on Roman Catholicism, through the earlier part of this century in the USA, with George F. Moore's apologia for Judaism in response to a more general Christian onslaught, on through the State of Israel, with Ephraim E. Urbach's portrait of the sages and their beliefs, and, onward to our own day in Canada, with E. P. Sanders' renewal of the apologia against the Reformation churches' account of a Judaism of law, an apologia now framed in the language of covenantal nomism. Yet in my view, we have yet to discover an appropriate method for carrying out the descriptive task in the study of theology. The reason is that, with one exception, named presently, prior scholars have focused upon a program of theological issues framed out of relationship with the documentary structure and order of the canon under consideration. They selected sayings deemed relevant to theological taxa, rather than beginning with the data subject to theological description and allowing those data to dictate the course of inquiry. So while they claimed to let Judaism speak for itself, in its own terms and language, that is precisely what they did not do. But their intent was sound, and the only problem is how to realize it.

The answer lies in allowing the canonical literature to guide us. We have to begin with individual documents and work outward toward the far limits of the canonical boundary, moving not promiscuously anywhere we find a saying relevant to a topic of interest to us, but attempting to find the structure and order that a given document, or a given linguistic usage common to a number of documents but differentiated by document, may portray for us. That is the answer – to focus on linguistic usage, on the one side, and documentary structure, on the other – proposed by the one exception to the rather dreary rule, who is Max Kadushin. His critique of Schechter and Moore, which applies without any important variation to Urbach, who dismisses Kadushin virtually unread, and Sanders, who seems to have learned very little from Kadushin, provides an important corrective to their errors. His realization of the correct process, to be sure, proved deeply flawed, for even while he did read documents one by one, he repudiated his own initial method. That decision precipitated for him a chaos so paralyzing that in the end his inquiry into the theological language of the canonical writings of Judaism allowed everything to mean its opposite and nothing to mean anything in particular.

Then how to begin, after so many false starts and disappointing, truncated journeys? The answer is not in the pages of this book, but the beginnings of the question are. For, as I see it, we reach theology through hermeneutics, by which I mean, our study of the right way to read the documents must come before our description of the documents' theology (or any other traits of order and system). That explains the experiments, the results of which are presented in these pages. For all I can do, just now, is conduct experiments and present the results; but I think, in the end, in sustained learning that is all that is worth doing.

This book of three sets of studies of literary experiments including hermeneutical problems that yield consequences for the description of the theology of the Judaism of the Dual Torah is made up of experimental papers. The Introduction explains why I conceive the initial movement to the description of the theology of formative Judaism to begin with a literary problem, how I have formulated the experiments of this book to solve that problem and why I conceive that the solutions will guide us deeper into the theological structure of the

Judaism of the Dual Torah. The Prologue spells out why I insist that that Judaism, as set forth in its canonical writings, comprises not only a system of myth and ritual – way of life, world view, theory of the social entity that realizes the one and explains itself through the other – as I have insisted in a variety of prior studies. It comprises also a theology, a word I define in the Introduction.

To reach the correct method for the description of the theology of the Judaism of the Dual Torah as attested by its canonical writings, I contemplate preliminary studies, which in due course can make possible a single, coherent volume, *Judaism and Theology: The Evidence of...*, parallel to my earlier work, e.g., *Judaism in Society: The Evidence of the Yerushalmi. Toward the Natural History of a Religion.* Chicago, 1983: The University of Chicago Press; *Judaism and Scripture: The Evidence of Leviticus Rabbah.* Chicago, 1986: The University of Chicago Press; *Judaism: The Classical Statement. The Evidence of the Bavli.* Chicago, 1986: University of Chicago Press; *Judaism and Story: The Evidence of The Fathers According to Rabbi Nathan.* Chicago, 1990: University of Chicago Press. But at this time I do not know whether the results will justify such an encompassing account of a principal trait of this Judaism.

Still, these books show how in the past I have translated literary studies into a history-of-religions' account of a definitive aspect of the Judaism, the system of which is attested by the canonical writings I have mastered. They explain therefore why I propose to move from literary to theological problems of description, analysis, and interpretation. This approach to the formulation of a question and its solution is characteristic of all that I have done over the past three decades of sustained work. For I always begin with the fringes of a problem, its literary epiphenomena, moving out from literary evidence in slow and rather deliberate stages to problems of generalization and large-scale description.

For philosophy, for example, the work began with *The Philosophical Mishnah* (Atlanta, 1989: Scholars Press for Brown Judaic Studies) and only then yielded *The Philosophy of Judaism: The First Principles* (in press). Along these same lines, for systemic description, my forty-three volumes, *A History of the Mishnaic Law* (Leiden, 1974-1982: E. J. Brill), then produced *Judaism: The Evidence of the Mishnah* (Chicago, 1981: University of Chicago Press). On a smaller scale my sustained translation of Leviticus Rabbah led to *Judaism and Scripture*, and also, *Writing with Scripture* (cited below). And how many, and what sort of, literary studies will guide me toward the theology of this Judaism I cannot now predict. Judging from the modest sets of results provided here, I anticipate that the work will be prolonged; but then it is the most important work of all.

Accordingly, each of my sustained analysis of a block of the canonical literature in due course has produced a large-scale project in the history of religion. This volume, also, stands in such a line, several steps beyond translation and introduction, but a considerable space before systemic description, analysis, and interpretation. This book consists of three free-standing parts, though the essays in each part are quite cogent with one another.

In the Prologue I ask the question that preoccupies me here by rereading the program and method of a great figure in the study of Judaism, Max Kadushin, to whom this book is dedicated. I show how he asked precisely the question of method and result I take up here and explain why I think he failed. Had he not done the work he did, the beginnings would be all the more difficult than they are.

In Part One I differentiate philosophical from theological discourse and show the difference between a document that proposes an essentially philosophical exercise, one that, to be sure, bears profound implications for theology of the Judaism that canonizes that document, and one that proposes a fundamentally theological statement, one conveyed within the theological idiom of the Judaism of the Dual Torah. The two essays, written separately, form a striking contrast and so make a single point in two parts. They relate as do two distinct compositions formed into a *davar-aher* construction – an "another matter" composite – that forms the two into a whole larger than the sum of the parts.

In Part Two I set forth and illustrate in great detail the hypothesis that when the author of a composition, or the authorship of a composite, sets forth a sequence of autonomous statements ("paragraphs"), announcing at the head of each, "another matter," in point of fact each of these "other matters" turns out to say the same matter as was originally said; the "other thing" really is the "same thing." Why this rather humble fact of literary consequence bears considerable weight for theological description of the Judaism of the Dual Torah will be made clear in the Introduction and in the corresponding effort of Max Kadushin described in the Prologue.

In Part Three I revert to literary questions, but these shade over into hermeneutics, which I regard as both a door toward theological inquiry and also evidence concerning theological logic. But the hermeneutical route toward the theological description of the Judaism of the Dual Torah stretches far, far beyond the limits of these papers, and my theological observations at the end are at best murmurings of someone no longer asleep but not yet awake.

The Epilogue, like the Prologue, contrasts my results, aiming toward the description of (this) Judaism, with prior descriptions of the same Judaism on the basis of exactly the same sources. But here I spell out why, apart from episodically illuminating explanations of words and phrases, I do not think we have anything to learn about that Judaism from those descriptions. The fact that Kadushin's critique of these same figures and their methods was philosophical, rather than historical and religions-historical, should not be missed. And his critique of his predecessors underlines the excellence of intellect that led him to perceive the unhappy fact that, until his time, the study of the theology of this Judaism consisted of collecting and arranging sayings, within the pseudo-methodological claim that, after all, in doing so, all we are doing is allowing "the rabbis" to speak in their own terms and language. Since the categories of Schechter, Moore, Urbach, and Sanders derive from Protestant dogmatics, the first part of that claim is nonsense; since the work invariably involves both translation (Schechter, Moore, Sanders) and paraphrase (Urbach), the second part of that claim is absurd. But Kadushin saw that the self-serving allegation, as to method, that his predecessors in fact had no method worthy of the name, even while positing a method that determined their results no less than his method would determine his results, or my method mine, was to be dismissed, and by doing the work he did, he dismissed it.

I need hardly underline that these studies are preliminary and the several parts are not continuous and do not follow a single unfolding argument; the three parts of the work are merely juxtaposed, and I have not formed them into a single sustained composition, such as a proper book would entail: a well-crafted, and coherent statement of premise, method, argument, and result. I face the simple problem of how to study theology in a given kind of literature, and I have come up with some definitions of what and how to carry on that historical study of a particular theology. In due course, I expect, the three distinct initiatives undertaken in these pages will reach a more sophisticated stage in a single sustained and encompassing program of thought and inquiry. But I have come this far, and a reconsideration of the alternatives to my approach will remind readers that there is no going back.

The translations that make possible the analyses of these pages are as follows:

Genesis Rabbah. The Judaic Commentary on Genesis. A New American Translation. Atlanta, 1985: Scholars Press for Brown Judaic Studies. I. *Genesis Rabbah. The Judaic Commentary on Genesis. A*

New American Translation. Parashiyyot One through Thirty-Three. Genesis 1:1-8:14.

Genesis Rabbah. The Judaic Commentary on Genesis. A New American Translation. Atlanta, 1985: Scholars Press for Brown Judaic Studies. II. *Genesis Rabbah. The Judaic Commentary on Genesis. A New American Translation. Parashiyyot Thirty-Four through Sixty-Seven. Genesis 8:15-28:9.*

Genesis Rabbah. The Judaic Commentary on Genesis. A New American Translation. Atlanta, 1985: Scholars Press for Brown Judaic Studies. III. *Genesis Rabbah. The Judaic Commentary on Genesis. A New American Translation. Parashiyyot Sixty-Eight through One Hundred. Genesis 28:10-50:26.*

Lamentations Rabbah. An Analytical Translation. Atlanta, 1989: Scholars Press for Brown Judaic Studies.

Esther Rabbah I. An Analytical Translation. Atlanta, 1989: Scholars Press for Brown Judaic Studies.

Ruth Rabbah. An Analytical Translation. Atlanta, 1989: Scholars Press for Brown Judaic Studies.

Song of Songs Rabbah. An Analytical Translation. Volume One. *Song of Songs Rabbah to Song Chapters One through Two.* Atlanta, 1990: Scholars Press for Brown Judaic Studies.

Song of Songs Rabbah. An Analytical Translation. Volume Two. *Song of Songs Rabbah to Song Chapters Three through Eight.* Atlanta, 1990: Scholars Press for Brown Judaic Studies.

Note also the most recent systematic statement on the theory of translation behind my work:

Translating the Classics of Judaism. In Theory and in Practice. Atlanta, 1989: Scholars Press for Brown Judaic Studies.

The introductions behind this work are as follows:

The Midrash Compilations of the Sixth and Seventh Centuries. An Introduction to the Rhetorical, Logical, and Topical Program. I. Lamentations Rabbah. Atlanta, 1990: Scholars Press for Brown Judaic Studies.

The Midrash Compilations of the Sixth and Seventh Centuries: An Introduction to the Rhetorical, Logical, and Topical Program. II. Esther Rabbah I. Atlanta, 1990: Scholars Press for Brown Judaic Studies.

The Midrash Compilations of the Sixth and Seventh Centuries: An Introduction to the Rhetorical, Logical, and Topical Program. III. Ruth Rabbah. Atlanta, 1990: Scholars Press for Brown Judaic Studies.

The Midrash Compilations of the Sixth and Seventh Centuries: An Introduction to the Rhetorical, Logical, and Topical Program. IV. Song of Songs Rabbah. Atlanta, 1990: Scholars Press for Brown Judaic Studies.

Note also the following, which spells out what I believe to be the consequences for literary history of these introductions (summarized here in Part Three):

Making the Classics in Judaism: The Three Stages of Literary Formation. Atlanta, 1990: Scholars Press for Brown Judaic Studies.

Other works of mine that are fundamental in understanding how I have framed matters as I have in this one are as follows:

Writing with Scripture: The Authority and Uses of the Hebrew Bible in the Torah of Formative Judaism. Philadelphia, 1989: Fortress Press. [With William Scott Green]

The Making of the Mind of Judaism. Atlanta, 1987: Scholars Press for Brown Judaic Studies.

The Formation of the Jewish Intellect. Making Connections and Drawing Conclusions in the Traditional System of Judaism. Atlanta, 1988: Scholars Press for Brown Judaic Studies.

This study, marking my move from history of religion to descriptive theology (not the same thing, at all, as history of ideas) takes its leave from my general theory of the history of Judaism, which is contained in the following books:

The Foundations of Judaism. Method, Teleology, Doctrine. Philadelphia, 1983-5: Fortress Press. I-III. I. *Midrash in Context. Exegesis in Formative Judaism.* Second printing: Atlanta, 1988: Scholars Press for Brown Judaic Studies.

The Foundations of Judaism. Method, Teleology, Doctrine. Philadelphia, 1983-5: Fortress Press. I-III. II. *Messiah in Context. Israel's History and Destiny in Formative Judaism.* Second printing: Lanham, 1988: University Press of America. Studies in Judaism series.

The Foundations of Judaism. Method, Teleology, Doctrine. Philadelphia, 1983-5: Fortress Press. I-III. III.   *Torah: From Scroll to Symbol in Formative Judaism.* Second printing: Atlanta, 1988: Scholars Press for Brown Judaic Studies.

Vanquished Nation, Broken Spirit. The Virtues of the Heart in Formative Judaism. New York, 1987: Cambridge University Press. Jewish Book Club selection, 1987.

Judaisms and their Messiahs in the Beginning of Christianity. New York, 1987: Cambridge University Press. Edited by Jacob Neusner, William Scott Green and Ernest S. Frerichs.

Judaism in the Matrix of Christianity. Philadelphia, 1986: Fortress Press. British edition, Edinburgh, 1988: T. & T. Collins.

Judaism and Christianity in the Age of Constantine. Issues of the Initial Confrontation. Chicago, 1987: University of Chicago Press.

Death and Birth of Judaism. The Impact of Christianity, Secularism, and the Holocaust on Jewish Faith. New York, 1987: Basic Books.

Self-Fulfilling Prophecy: Exile and Return in the History of Judaism. Boston, 1987: Beacon Press.

Judaism and its Social Metaphors. Israel in the History of Jewish Thought. New York, 1988: Cambridge University Press.

The Incarnation of God: The Character of Divinity in Formative Judaism. Philadelphia, 1988: Fortress Press.

The Economics of the Mishnah. Chicago, 1989: The University of Chicago Press.

The Politics of Judaism. The Initial Structure and System. Submitted to University of Chicago Press. Sixth draft to be filed: 7.1.89.

The Christian and Judaic Invention of History. Atlanta, 1989: Scholars Press for American Academy of Religion. Studies in Religion series. Edited by Jacob Neusner and William Scott Green.

The Philosophy of Judaism. The First Principles.

Torah through the Ages. A Short History of Judaism. New York and London, 1990: Trinity Press International and SCM.

The next phase in my work on the history of the formation of the Judaism of the Dual Torah, beyond the work on philosophy, politics, and economics, will be in the following books:

From Philosophy to Theology: The Intellectual Reformation in the Formation of Judaism [1]. [The second stage in the formative process, focusing upon the Yerushalmi, Genesis Rabbah, and Leviticus Rabbah. The following items are parts of this same program.]

From King to Holy Man: The Politics of the Sacred and the Reconsideration of Power in the Formation of Judaism [2].

From Economics to Ethics: The Economics of the Supernatural and the Redefinition of Scarce Resources in the Formation of Judaism [3].

To accomplish the tasks of this book, I have relied to a still greater extent than usual upon the counsel of Professors Ernest S. Frerichs, Wendell S. Dietrich, and Calvin Goldscheider at Brown University and William Scott Green at the University of Rochester. Some of the work was completed after my arrival at The Institute for Advanced Study, to which I am happy to express thanks as well. Since my principal project here is to trace the movement from philosophical to theological formulation of the Judaic system of the Dual Torah, the pertinence, to the sustained research planned for the current year, of the present project hardly requires explanation.

JACOB NEUSNER
July 28, 1989
My fifty-seventh birthday

School of Historical Studies
The Institute for Advanced Study
Princeton, New Jersey

Introduction

When we propose to describe the theological system to which a piece of well-crafted writing testifies, our task is easy when the writing to begin with discusses in syllogistic logic and within an appropriate program of propositions what we conceive to be theological themes or problems. Hence – it is generally conceded – we may legitimately translate the topically theological writings of Paul, Augustine, or Luther into the systematic and coherent theologies of those three figures, respectively: finding order and structure in materials of a cogent theological character. But what about a literature that to begin with does not set forth theological propositions in philosophical form, even while using profoundly religious language for self-evidently religious purposes? Surely that literature testifies to an orderly structure or system of thought, for the alternative is to impute to the contents of those writings the status of mere episodic and unsystematic observations about this and that. True, profound expressions of piety may exhibit the traits of intellectual chaos and disorder, and holy simplicity may mask confusion. But such a description of the rabbinic literature of late antiquity, which I call the canon of the Judaism of the Dual Torah, defies the most definitive and indicative traits of the writings. These are order, system, cogency, coherence, proportion, fine and well-crafted thought.

The Mishnah, with which the writing begins, is a profoundly philosophical statement; the two Talmuds presuppose the harmony and unity of the conceptions of the Mishnah and their own conceptions; the various midrash compilations make statements that exhibit intellectual integrity; they do not show the marks of confusion and contradiction, only of variety and richness, and they assuredly do not merely compile ad hoc and episodic observations. The results of my introductions to Lamentations Rabbah, Ruth Rabbah, Esther Rabbah, and Song of Songs Rabbah I, showing that the compilers of each of these documents proposed to say one thing in a great many ways, hardly sustain the thesis that the midrash compilations cannot be read as expressions of orderly minds. So, by their own character, these writings point toward some sort of logic and order and structure that as a matter of fact find attestation in the writings themselves. And when we seek to articulate the principles of order and structure as these pertain to the fundamental characteristics of God, the Torah, and Israel, we set forth the theology of the canon of the Judaism of the Dual Torah.

Now that simple and everywhere-acknowledged fact of the yearning for order and structure characteristic of that Judaism leads us to the question of these essays: how to move from literature to the description of a theological system that gives sense, structure, and cogency to the literature's fundamental convictions? What is the theology, or what are the theologies, that make the literature what it is: coherent in sense and in meaning? That is the question that faces anyone who wants to know whether the canonical literature of the Judaism of the Dual Torah constitutes a mass of discrete observations about this and that or a well-crafted structure and system. For the canonical writings, appealing to God's revelation to Moses at Sinai, everywhere calling upon God and spelling out what God wants of Israel in quest of God and God's service, form one of the great religious writings of humanity. But do these writings yield theology, in addition to religion? That is to say, can we see them as system, structure, order, and not merely as a vast and confusing mass of half-coherent thoughts? And how are we to test the perception of order amid the appearance of chaos, such as these writings, this literature, creates?

To begin with, we have to justify the theological inquiry into literature that self-evidently does not conform to the conventions of theological discourse to which Western civilization in its Greco-Roman heritage and Christian (and, as a matter of fact, Muslim) civilization in its philosophical formulation has made us accustomed. The Muslim and Christian theological heritage, formulated within the conventions of philosophical argument, joined by a much smaller Judaic theological corpus to be sure, does not allow us to read as a theological statement a single canonical writing of the Judaism of the Dual Torah of late antiquity. So if the literary canons of Western theology are to govern, then to begin with the literature of Judaism in its formative age by definition can present no theological order and system at all.

But that proposition on the face of it hardly proves compelling. For it is difficult for us to imagine a mental universe so lacking in structure, form, and order as to permit everything and its opposite to be said about God, to imagine a God so confused and self-contradictory as to yield a revelation lacking all cogency and truly unintelligible.[1] The very premises of all theology – that there is order, structure, and composition, proportion, and form, in God's mind, which in fact is intelligible to us through the medium of revelation properly construed – a priori render improbable the hypothesis that the canonical writings of the Judaism of the Dual Torah violate every rule of intelligible discourse concerning the principal and foundation of all being. If, after all, we really cannot speak intelligibly about God, the Torah, holy Israel, and what God wants of us, then why write all those books to begin with?

The character of the literature, its rather hermetic modes of discourse, arcane language of thought, insistence upon speaking only about detail and rarely about the main point – these traits of discourse stand in the way of the description of theology because of their very unsyllogistic character. And yet, if we consider not the received modes of discourse of theology in our civilization but rather the problem and topic of theology – systematic and orderly thinking about God through the medium of revelation – we can hardly find a more substantial or suitable corpus of writing for theological analysis than the literature of the Judaism of the Dual Torah.

For while theology may comprise propositions well-crafted into a cogent structure, about fundamental questions of God and revelation, the

---

[1]As a matter of fact, the great Zoroastrian theologians of the ninth century criticized Judaism (and other religions) on just this point, see my "Zoroastrian Critique of Judaism," reprinted in my *History of the Jews in Babylonia* (Leiden, 1969: E. J. Brill) 4:403-423. But not a single Judaic thinker, whether a philosopher or a theologian, whether in the Islamic philosophical tradition or the Western theological and philosophical tradition, has ever entertained the proposition that the God who gave the Torah is confused and arbitrary; and why should anyone have thought so, when, after all, the entire dynamic of Judaic thought embodied within the great halakhic tradition from the Yerushalmi and Bavli forward has aimed at the systematization, harmonization and ordering of confusing, but never confused, facts of the Torah. There is, therefore, no possibility of finding in the Judaism of the Dual Torah the slightest hint of an unsystematic system, an a-theological corpus of thought. True, a fixed truth of the theological system known as *die Wissenschaft des Judenthums* has maintained that "Judaism has no theology," but that system knew precisely what it meant by "Judaism," even while never explaining what it might mean by the "theology" that that "Judaism" did not have. But that is a problem of description, analysis, and interpretation for those who take an interest in the system of thought that underpins "Jewish scholarship" and Reform Judaism in particular, that is, specialists in the history of ideas in the nineteenth century, and of the nineteenth century in the twentieth century. These are not statements of fact that must be taken into account in describing, analyzing, and interpreting documents of the Judaism of the Dual Torah.

social entity that realizes that revelation, the attitudes and deeds that God, through revelation, requires of humanity, there is another way entirely. Theology – the structure and system, the perception of order and meaning of God, in God, through God – these may make themselves known otherwise than through the media of thought and expression that yield belief that: theology can deliver its message to and through sentiment and emotion, heart as much as mind; it can be conviction as much as position, and conviction for its part also is orderly, proportioned, compelling of mind and intellect by reason of right attitude, rather than right proposition or position. That is to say, theology may set forth a system of thought in syllogistic arguments concerning the normative truths of the worldview, social entity, and way of life of a religious system. But theology may speak in other than dynamic and compelling argument, and theologians may accomplish their goal of speaking truth about God through other than the statements made by language and in conformity with the syntax of reasoned thought.

Theology may also address vision and speak in tactile ways; it may utilize a vocabulary of not proposition but opaque symbol (whether conveyed in visual or verbal media), and through portraying symbol, theology may affect attitude and emotion, speak its truth through other media than those of philosophy and proposition. From the time of Martin Buber's *Two Types of Faith*, now nearly four decades ago, people have understood that this other type of theology, the one that lives in attitude and sentiment and that evokes and demands trust, may coexist, or even compete, with the philosophical type to the discourse of which, in general, we are accustomed.

Since, as a matter of fact, in the canonical writings of the Judaism of the Dual Torah we do not have a single sustained theological treatise, while we do have a monument to a faith that is choate and subject to fully accessible expression, we must not find surprising the thesis of theological study that, for me, begins in the pages of the three free-standing parts of this book. My goal is to describe the theology of the Judaism of the Dual Torah out of its fully exposed and complete, systemic documents, the Talmud of Babylonia and the related writings of its age, Lamentations Rabbah, Song of Songs Rabbah, Ruth Rabbah, Esther Rabbah I, and some minor works of the same stratum.

My first task is to formulate and carry out those *Vorstudien* – preliminary studies – which will guide the work when it is fully and completely undertaken in a major systematic study. Over the past three decades, I have always worked from the parts toward the whole, from the details to the main point, inductively attained, and from literature through history to religion, or, in my system, from the (canonical) text through the (historical) context to the matrix defined by attitude and doctrine alike that we must call, the religion, in this case, (a) Judaism. So here I begin what I hope will bear fruit as *Judaism and Theology: The Evidence of the Late Midrash Compilations.* I hasten to add that the steps taken here are not only uncertain and preliminary, but may never lead beyond themselves; so I make no promises about what I shall do, only express a hope and an intention of what I should like to be able to achieve.

The first task, as is clear, is to return to our documents with the questions that animate the present inquiry. So I want to know, first propositionally, then in other media altogether, precisely what relationship I can discern between theology and literature, and how I am to proceed when I wish to uncover the deeper and more complex layers of theological reflection and expression within the canonical writings. For that purpose I return to the familiar realm of the Mishnah, where I always begin, whence I always move outward. What I want to know is whether, in the Mishnah, I am on firm ground in setting forth a proposition that bears theological implications. Since the Mishnah is a philosophical, and not a theological, document, the question has to be phrased in the way I do: "that bears...implications." The answer is that the philosophical quest of the authorship of the Mishnah indeed states, in philosophical (natural scientific and metaphysical) terms the fundamental theological affirmation of this Judaism (and every other one), which is that God is one. If we wished to state in this-worldly philosophical terms the proposition of the unity of all being, we could do no better than to do so in the medium and the message of the Mishnah.

For the authorship of that document demonstrates in stupefying detail the hierarchical unity of being, on the one side, and the complexity of the simple, the simplicity of the complex, on the other; putting these two principles of nature together permits us, in theological terms, to conclude: *Q.E.D. One God.* And that work, fully exposed in my *The Philosophical Mishnah* (Atlanta, 1989: Scholars Press for Brown Judaic Studies) I-IV, as well as in the consequent *The Philosophy of Judaism. The Initial System* (in press), allows me to proceed to the problem of theology studied in its own right.

But where to begin and how to proceed? And what kind of data will point me toward the structure and system that comprise theology in general, and that, consequently, also should comprise (a) theology of the Judaism of the Dual Torah in particular? I begin with a picture of someone who framed a method and explored the same documents that I find normative, the great philosopher of Judaism, Max Kadushin. He is the only scholar, writing in any language, who systematically attempted to bring order out of the chaos of the rabbinic writings by a sustained and articulated method that transcended mere collecting, arranging, paraphrasing, and free-associating.

For my part, as shown in Part One, I do not know a better way of starting than with documents, and, it must follow, I have to identify writings that will as a matter of theory or at least hypothesis yield (following Buber's definition of faith in Judaism) statements concerning attitudes and evocative symbols that, all together and in proper place and proportion, will constitute the theology of the Judaism for which those writings stand. The answer to the question, what kind of data, is not difficult to formulate. I clearly have to identify writings that, on the very surface, stand for theological truths, convey and argue and set forth theological convictions. Once readers have read Chapter Two they will know that I know the difference between writings that do, and also do not, represent theological discourse; for obviously the Mishnah does not.

Then what writings do? In Chapter Three, I answer that question in a simple way. I show what kind of writing will exhibit traits that permit me to identify and express a theological position – if not a proposition, then a theological attitude and a theological symbol that serve to attest to a theology of (this) Judaism. For that purpose I turn to certain midrash compilations, which exemplify the kinds of writings, and the sorts of discourse, that for this Judaism quite fully expose theological thought and constitute, in the suitable idiom of these authorships, theological expression. That is to say, I claim that certain documents carry out a clearly and distinctively theological purpose, make a theological statement in the manner in which their authorships have chosen, and so permit us to speak of a theology of (their) Judaism. I do not claim to know all the documents that fall into the category of theological discourse. But since I can here show what is not a document that presents a theological statement and also what is a document that does so, my goal for this book is accomplished.

To proceed, then: for preliminary studies, it suffices to say with finality that the late midrash compilations, Lamentations Rabbah, Esther Rabbah I, Ruth Rabbah, and Song of Songs Rabbah make theological statements. These statements are not episodic but systematically presented; they are repeated over and over again; to make these statements, the documents that make them are constituted. That justifies my claim to know the difference between a document that falls into the category of theological discourse and one that does not but is, rather, of philosophical genre, purpose, and character. These four compilations, all of them generally regarded as belonging in the same age as the Talmud of Babylonia, as a matter of simple fact make theological, and only theological, statements.

In my introductions to these documents, which are *The Midrash Compilations of the Sixth and Seventh Centuries. An Introduction to the Rhetorical, Logical, and Topical Program. I. Lamentations Rabbah.* Atlanta, 1990: Scholars Press for Brown Judaic Studies; *The Midrash Compilations of the Sixth and Seventh Centuries: An Introduction to the Rhetorical, Logical, and Topical Program. II. Esther Rabbah I.* Atlanta, 1990: Scholars Press for Brown Judaic Studies; *The Midrash Compilations of the Sixth and Seventh Centuries: An Introduction to the Rhetorical, Logical, and Topical Program. III. Ruth Rabbah.* Atlanta, 1990: Scholars Press for Brown Judaic Studies; and *The Midrash Compilations of the Sixth and Seventh Centuries: An Introduction to the Rhetorical, Logical, and Topical Program. IV. Song of Songs Rabbah.* Atlanta, 1990: Scholars Press for Brown Judaic Studies, I have shown that simple fact. I have furthermore made explicit what theological statement I think each authorship has made, and I justify my claim through a complete survey of the evidence that each of these documents makes the statement that I assign to it. Not only so, but each of the documents says one thing – that one thing and not much else – in a great many ways. In Chapter Three, I spell out how these documents make cogent statements – with stress on Ruth Rabbah – and specify of what three of those quintessentially theological statements consist. The contrast between the results of Chapters Two and Three completes the opening exercise.

Part Two builds on those results, but only agglutinatively. All I do in this part is a sequence of simple examinations of "another-matter" compositions, that is to say, I take up, for the four specified compilations, sizable abstracts in which we find sequences of "another interpretation of" a given clause or verse, or "another matter" to prove a given point, and similar matters. Here, then, I ask whether "another matter" is not the same matter said in other words, and I believe I establish through the sample at hand the hypothetical claim that "another matter" really is the same thing twice. It follows that I address a literary question with theological implications, carrying out a much more primitive experiment. I want to know one thing, and the results open the way to knowledge of many things. What I want to know is whether there is a fixed symbolic vocabulary, to which our authorships repeatedly appeal, and which we for our part can discover and define? If we can, then we shall have moved a long step toward the identification, through correct method, of the theology of the Judaism of the Dual Torah. For then we shall know precisely how to identify those symbols, whether expressed visually or conveyed in words, that for this Judaism constitute the theological language and therefore define the theological structure – the syntax of intellect, if not the grammar of speech – of this Judaism. In framing matters in terms of symbol, I am guided by the general method of Max Kadushin, as I explain at the beginning of Chapter Three.

The experiment at hand begins in an observation of William Scott Green, in Jacob Neusner with William Scott Green, *Writing with Scripture. The Authority and Uses of the Hebrew Bible in the Torah of Formative Judaism* (Minneapolis, 1989: Fortress Press), p. 19:

> Although the interpretations in this passage are formally distinguished from one another...by the disjunctive device *davar aher* ('another interpretation'), they operate within a limited conceptual sphere and a narrow thematic range. As is typical of most lists of *davar aher* comments in rabbinic literature, the three segments not only do not conflict but are mutually reinforcing. Taken together, B-C, D-G, and H-N claim that God's past wondrous acts in Israel's behalf will continue, and be even greater, in the future. Thus rather than 'endless multiple meanings,' they in fact ascribe to the words 'doing wonders' multiple variations of a single meaning...By gathering discrete verses from scripture's three divisions – the list form makes scripture itself seem naturally and ubiquitously to articulate a single message about God's persistent devotion to Israel. By providing multiple warrant for that message, the form effectively restricts the interpretive options...

First, we have now to ask whether or not Green's observation about the passage at hand is subject to generalization. If we may find a variety of passages that conform to the description he has accomplished for the passage at hand, then we may proceed to the theological question: of what does the cogent truth consist? And how does that truth come to expression? Now what I wish to know is, when we find *davar-aher* compositions, how in fact do they work, and precisely what is the theological discourse that is accomplished? Having justified, in Chapter Two, my insistence that the documents under discussion in fact constitute theological statements of a quite simple order – but not theological treatises in the propositional-philosophical mode of discourse that we in general expect in the West – I turn back to those same writings.

Accordingly in Part Two, through Chapters Four through Eight, I systematically examine the *davar-aher* passages, that is, those discussions that appear disjunctive but that, Green argues, in fact say one thing in many different ways. In surveying for a mere probe Genesis Rabbah, Lamentations Rabbah, Esther Rabbah I, Ruth Rabbah, and Song of Songs Rabbah, I ask three questions: [1] do *davar-aher* passages make a single statement in many ways? and [2] if so, precisely *how* do those passages make that statement, and [3] what is that statement? To answer these questions requires what is by now expected from me: a patient, thorough, line-by-line, exact and precise rereading of the documents, with the present program of inquiry in hand. That is what I do through Part Two.

Part Three proceeds to a third, and also free-standing but connected, inquiry. It concerns questions of historical study of the formation of the literature before us, on the one side, and the hermenutics yielded by my results in these pages, on the other. If I am right that we can undertake a theological reading of certain components of the canon of the Judaism of the Dual Torah, then what results, for the history of the formation of the theology of that Judaism, can we anticipate? Here I argue that certain types of writing in fact antedate the documents in which they occur, and, not only so (for the issue is not, is never, mere chronology), but those same types of writing represent not documentary authorships but a prior type of authorship and a prior social consensus. The meanings of these words, presently somewhat obscure, are spelled out in Chapter Nine.

Chapter Ten goes over the same points, but now with special reference to how I think we should read and interpret a specific kind of writing, narrative; and since I think narrative is a principal medium for theological expression – an expression concerning symbols, on the one side, an expression aiming at the shaping of emotions and attitudes, on the other side, I should claim to point toward a hermeneutic rich in theological promise that emerges from the literary conceptions I set forth here.

The Epilogue, Chapter Eleven, corresponds to the Prologue, but flows from Part Three in particular. What I explain is now negative: why there is nothing more to be learned about "Judaism," meaning, theology of Judaism, in the works of theology produced from Solomon Schechter's *Some Aspects of Rabbinic Theology* through George F. Moore's *Judaism* and Ephraim E. Urbach's *The Sages* to E. P. Sanders's *Paul and Palestinian Judaism* (with many stops, in French with Bonsirven, in German with a variety of genuinely malevolent caricatures of "Judaism," and other languages, in between). Since mine is a quite fresh and unfamiliar approach to historical study of theology, I owe it to readers to remind them of the conventional approach and to instruct them concerning what is wrong with that approach. That is what is done in the Epilogue.

I leave to the end these rather sad figures, since those of them who worked after Kadushin and never read him, or read him and obtusely dismissed him with an off-hand aside (Urbach's dismissal is characteristically contemptuous) turn out to have worked in vain;

Kadushin still requires close reading, while these lesser figures serve only for collections and arrangements of sayings on given topics. Since Schechter, Moore, Urbach, and the others (not to mention authors of innumerable articles and monographs on rabbinic concepts of various kinds) imagined that they were contributing more than mere anthologies with some episodic footnotes deriving, in the main, from free association, they are fairly called tragic.

It suffices to repeat at the end that these are three essentially free-standing experiments; I stand at a considerable distance from the position I seek, and I am not entirely certain that the methods explored here, particularly in Part Two, will carry me to my destination. Yet my conviction remains absolutely firm: the Judaism of the Dual Torah through its canon did make intelligible statements, of a fundamental order, about God, God's relationship with Israel, and God's plan and purpose for the world – that is to say, their Torah truly did set forth a theology – and when we grasp the logic of those writings, we shall also understand the structure and dynamic of those statements: their theology.

PROLOGUE

1

Carrying Forward the Inquiry of Max Kadushin

In such seminal works as *Organic Thinking. A Study in Rabbinic Thought* (New York, 1938: The Jewish Theological Seminary of America), *The Rabbinic Mind* (New York, 1952: The Jewish Theological Seminary of America), and *Worship and Ethics. A Study in Rabbinic Judaism* (Evanston, 1964: Northwestern University Press), not to mention the work on Leviticus Rabbah published in this series, Max Kadushin investigated the possibilities of showing the mode of thought of the documents I call the canon of the Judaism of the Dual Torah. He tried to show that within the rabbinic canon is present "an articulation of thought and values more complicated than that which can be devised by logic....This type of thinking...is universal, whilst local in content and individualistic in configuration. It is not logical but organismic: Each organismic pattern of thought or organic complex has its own distinctive individuality – each social pattern and each individual variation of it." He claimed, in particular, that rabbinic "thought is concerned with numerous rabbinic concepts...These concepts are certainly not united in logical fashion and their relationship with each other defies diagrammatic representation. Instead, every concept is related to every other concept because every concept is a constituent part of the complex as a whole. Conversely, the complex of concepts as a whole enters into the constitution of every concept; and thus every concept is in constant, dynamic relationship with every other concept. Rabbinic thought, hence, is organismic, for only in an organism are the whole and its parts mutually constitutive...."[1] In *Worship and Ethics*, moreover, Kadushin moved directly to define "rabbinic value concepts,"

---

[1] *Organic Thinking*, pp. v-vi.

such as Torah, religious duty, charity, holiness, repentance, man: "Such terms are noun forms, but they have a different character than other types of terms or concepts. These terms are connotative only, and hence are not amenable to formal definition. Again, they refer to matter which are not objects, qualities, or relations in sensory experience. Their function is to endow situations or events with significance. These value concepts are related to each other not logically but organismically. This means that the value concepts are not deduced from one another and that they cannot be placed in a logical order. Instead, the coherence or relatedness of the value concepts is such that they interweave dynamically."[2]

In making these statements, Kadushin intended to take up the study of the concepts of what I call the Judaism of the Dual Torah and he called "the Rabbis." His intent is to enter into "the great realm of awareness, the realm of ideas that endow life with significance." While, in general, Kadushin avoided the word "theology," e.g., "The values of Rabbinic Judaism consist of ideas,"[3] in fact, his inquiry, in its terms, aimed at elucidating that system and order, that coherence and proportion and composition and cogency, that the description of the theology of a document or a set of documents lays forth. Kadushin, for his part, insisted that we cannot define value-terms, over and over again maintaining that these are "undefined concepts," gaining their meaning in context: "We shall find that the value-concepts are not only undefined but non-definable, and that this accords with the dual nature of the task which is accomplished by them. Being non-definable, the value-concepts are extremely flexible, and they can, therefore, respond to and express the *differentia* of human personalities. At the same time, the value-term does convey an abstract, generalized idea of the concept it represents, and this generalized idea is common to all the members of the group."[4] Clearly, we have at the same time a definition of the theological task and a denial that it can be done. For Kadushin's acute concern for the social locus of thought, his interest in allowing for individual difference translate theological inquiry into sociological description of the uses, rather than the logic, of language; that would prove quite plausible, if, at the same time, he did not double back and insist that language has no meaning (merely) because different people use different words differently – but we can nonetheless impute to "the value-term" "an abstract, generalized idea of the concept it represents." But that statement sounds very much like

---

[2]*Worship and Ethics*, p. vii.
[3]*Rabbinic Mind*, p. 1.
[4]*Ibid.*, p. 2.

the claim that we know the "concept it represents" even though we cannot define any words that express or convey that concept, that is to say, a priori and intuitive definition.

What makes Kadushin interesting to me, as I reread his corpus, is that he addressed the question of descriptive theology of the Judaism of the Dual Torah that seems to me urgent. Not only so, but his interest lay in framing a viable method of description; he recognized, as have very few others who have proposed to do the same work, that prior to inquiry we have to solve the methodological problem of how to inquire. He understood full well the need for self-conscious definition of what we wish to know, how we propose to find it out, and why the methods we use in our study prove both congruent to the task and also appropriate to the sources. Thus he stated quite explicitly, "Every modern presentation of rabbinic thought is also an interpretation."[5] To those who claimed to give "just the facts," he countered that knowing what we mean by a fact, which is to say, defining taxa and utilizing them, itself represents much more than giving just the facts. He criticized Schechter for his pretentious claim, "I considered it advisable not to intrude too much interpretation or paraphrase upon the Rabbis. I let them have their own say in their own words" – as though we could translate into rabbi-talk such categories as "the Kingdom of God (Invisible)," "the Visible Kingdom (Universal)," "the Kingdom of God (National)," and on and on; Kadushin insisted in the face of Schechter's anti-intellectual nonsense: "they are interpretative terms."

Then how to proceed? Kadushin framed what he conceived to be a descriptive vocabulary, doing more than merely re-presenting or paraphrasing in translation rabbinic passages: "Once the rabbinic materials are subjected to analysis, an injustice is done if we reckon merely with this or that specific statement; such specific statements then stand unrelated to rabbinic thought as a whole."[6] But the issue then was, how to speak of the whole all together, all at once? And that, of course, forms the centerpiece of theological description: the claim to be able to say, "This is what it was, this is what it meant, and this is what held the whole together: what was important." To solve that problem, Kadushin called upon the concept of "rabbinic value-concepts," as we have already seen. In my judgment, he took a philosophical route to the solution of a theological problem, and that was both sensible and also unseemly. It was sensible because the ultimate goal of the study of a theological system or structure is to

---

[5] *Rabbinic Mind*, p. 8.
[6] *Ibid.*, p. 9.

describe the structure, which is choate and stable, rather than the system, which, in the nature of things, proves dialectical and dynamic and hence defies the low-level description of which, at this time, we may with much work prove capable. But it was unseemly because in order to speak of system and to work in an encompassing way, as we have seen, Kadushin defined out of existence the very thing he wished to describe, analyze, and interpret. His error lay in interpreting too soon, describing too little, analyzing altogether too much out of all context. He missed the specificities, but, alas, that is where God lives: only in the details. That simple fact after all is what defines the task to begin with: to find the theology in the literature, God in the details of words.

What did Kadushin do wrong? He lept directly into words and their definition, even while recognizing that documents matter (I believe the only scholar before this writer who took seriously the documentary boundaries of texts!). Thus he started with *The Theology of Seder Eliahu* (New York, 1932); he worked on "Aspects of the Rabbinic Concept of Israel in the Mekilta," *Hebrew Union College Annual* 1943-6, 19:57-96; he produced the posthumous book published in this series as well on Leviticus Rabbah. Accordingly, we cannot dismiss him as another routine lexical-theologian, imputing uniform meanings to words wherever and whenever they occur, at the same time assuming that lexical paraphrase sufficed to represent the logic, order, coherence, and structure of those sets of words, even comprising sentences, that represent (a) theology through description. This he did not do, but this still is what emerged. He identified four concepts of special interest, God's justice, love, Torah, and Israel, each with its own sub-concepts, e.g., "God's justice the subconcepts of chastisements, Merit of the Fathers, Merit of the Children, and 'measure for measure;' God's love the sub-concepts of prayer, repentance and atonement...," and so on. Each of these concepts with their sub-concepts he classified and organized and categorized, with this result: "The relation of a general concept to its sub-concepts...is one form of integration to be found then in the complex of the rabbinic value-concepts." Now to what end and what is at stake? That Kadushin proposed a theological description is beyond any doubt: "Ramified into sub-concepts and conceptual phrases, the four concepts...play a large role in integrating the entire complex of concepts."[7] The key word here is "integrating," and the main point clear.

Kadushin's result, repeated in all of his books, is that the concepts "combine or interweave with *every* value-concept of the rabbinic

---

[7]*Rabbinic Mind*, p. 18.

complex of concepts." Lest readers suppose that I have imputed to him this confession of the indeterminacy of all language, I point out that the italics of "every" are his, not mine. Kadushin produces an utter chaos with such hermeneutical positions as this one: "In like manner the four concepts also interweave with each other and with all their sub-concepts and conceptual phases....Apparent now is an all-embracing principle of coherence, making by and large for the organization of the rabbinic value-complex, for, since the four concepts combine with one another and with the rest of the concepts, every concept can interweave with every other concept in the complex...."[8] The upshot is that we can never know what anything means in general, because all language is specific to its setting: "The process of integration has enormous bearing on the meaning of the individual concepts. The conceptual term is only suggestive of the meaning of the value-concept. The idea-content of any particular rabbinic value-concept is a function of the entire complex of concepts as a whole, more specifically, of the process of the integration of the particular concept with the rest of the concepts of the complex. Depending on how we view the process, we can say, therefore, either that a value-concept takes on idea-content, or that its idea-content becomes explicit only as it interweaves with other concepts of the complex."[9] Again and again Kadushin insists that fixed combinations will not serve to impute the meaning of a value-concept: "There is no way to predict, on the basis of the particular concepts involved, precisely what idea any given combination of concepts may be made to express." Then what of coherence, logic, order? Kadushin answers that question, and with this answer we conclude our survey of his method:

> What is the principle of coherence or order which governs the concepts? We have to do here not with a fixed, static form of unity but with a dynamic process. It is a process of integration, on the one hand, in which the four fundamental concepts combine with each other and with the rest of the concepts so that each individual concept is always free to combine with any other concept of the complex; and it is also a process of individuation, on the other hand, in which any particular concept takes on meaning or character in the very process whereby it combines with the other concepts of the complex....The rabbinic complex of value-concepts is an organism...The rabbinic value-complex, since it is composed of concepts and ideas, is a mental organism....[10]
>
> The organization of the rabbinic value-concepts is...a highly complicated affair, complex enough because of the constant interweaving of all the concepts in their organismal relationship and

---

[8] *Ibid.*, p. 22.
[9] *Ibid.*, p. 23.
[10] *Ibid.*, p. 24f.

made still more complex because of further, supplementary types of relationship permitted by the organismic integration...the rabbinic value-complex functions easily, simply, often almost casually...The rabbinic value-concept is not a meaning added or applied to objective facts or situations but inherent in the situations and as easily apprehended...[11]

It now suffices to repeat that Kadushin has taken a philosophical route to the solution of what is, to begin with, a literary problem – even while, as I said, identifying the importance of the literary evidence read *in situ*. He has taken the language of the rabbinic writings as the probative evidence, the meanings of words read at one and the same time essentially out of all specific context and also wholly and only in discrete and specific context alone. In my view, the result is wholly negative. Kadushin did not succeed in describing the theology of the Judaism of the Dual Torah, because he identified as the appropriate evidence the wrong data, words read pretty much every which way, and furthermore having focused upon the right question – the character of documents and the message of documents – he turned away from his own results.

Kadushin most certainly identified as his quest a theological description problem, so he knew precisely the problem he wished to solve. What makes me sure it was the problem of the description of theology? I find ample justification in his own words (even while he did not like the word theology at all):

The problem of the coherence of rabbinic theology [to which he appends the footnote, p. 267, n. 2: "the term 'rabbinic theology' is not an appropriate designation for rabbinic thought"] appears to be precisely that which we have just raised with regard to values in general. Any representation of rabbinic theology as a logical system...is bound to be a distortion. Careful scholars agree with Schechter who says, 'that any attempt at an orderly and complete system of Rabbinic theology is an impossible task.' Instead they aim at 'letting Judaism speak for itself in its own way,' to use Moore's words, and therefore, for the most part, merely offer collected data on rabbinic concepts or attitudes in the form of centos of rabbinic passages on these themes drawn from various sources. The very fact however that disparate passages drawn from rabbinic sources that were composed at different periods and under divergent circumstances can yet be brought together so as to elucidate a rabbinic concept – that fact is proof positive that rabbinic theology possessed some kind of unity, some sort of coherence.[12]

---

[11]*Ibid.*, p. 30.
[12] *Organic Thinking,* p. 2.

There we have it: what is the logic of this logical system? How is it systemic at all? Not only so, but Kadushin points out, all those who have worked in the Western academic idiom have concurred that we may ask such a question of consensus, logic, order, and coherence. He points out, for instance, that Schechter insisted on the presence of "consensus of opinion," and points to remarkable agreement in doctrine; Bacher in his time stressed that both in method and content (in Kadushin's words) "haggadic literature was already well developed at a very early period and that therefore it is more correct to speak of the enlargement rather than the development of the Haggadah." From this, Kadushin concluded, "The principle of coherence of rabbinic theology...must have been such as made for unity of thought over great stretches of time and still gave room for differences due to changing circumstances and to the divergent proclivities of individuals."[13] And that ends up with his organismic thinking, in which we cannot define anything, but know what everything means.

While among philosophically engaged colleagues, Kadushin quite justifiably retains more than antiquarian interest, for the study of religion, his *ouevre* marks only an experiment that failed. He asked the right question; his criticism of his predecessors (which applies with even greater force to those who followed him in time but learned nothing from him, as the concluding chapter of this book shows in the case of E. E. Urbach and others of the now-passed generation) hit the mark. But in asking questions of coherence and logic, he denied that these questions could be answered; that is, I think, because he did not know how to answer them. He tried to cover everything all at once, even while correctly working through specific documents in concrete ways; it was, then, a failure of nerve. He wanted too much too soon, and he did not do the detailed work that would have yielded results commensurate to the inquiry: what holds the whole together is a question he never in the end answered at all, and the answers that he did give underlined his own failure.

And yet – and yet, for the sheer wit and intelligence, the effort, and the courage and the nobility of the enterprise as he undertook to realize it, Kadushin stands pretty much all by himself. He is the only scholar who has forthrightly and articulately asked the theological question of Judaism in the correct, academic mode.[14] He is the only scholar who

---

[13] *Ibid.*, pp. 2-3.

[14]Theologians who have offered normative statements of course are not subject to judgment here. True, I cannot point to theologies of Judaism that have exhibited profound grasp and appreciation of the rabbinic corpus, which commonly serves only to supply undifferentiated prooftexts for propositions

has undertaken to set forth a well-crafted method. And he is the only scholar who has provided sustained and well-articulated results. That is why I have dedicated this book to him. It is not because I think I have solved the problem he could not solve; it is because I wish to continue to work on the problem that, in my view, is the single most interesting question now confronting anyone interested in the description, analysis, and interpretation of the Judaism of the Dual Torah. I cannot (yet) describe "the rabbinic mind," but, like Kadushin, I am confident that unless and until we can make sense of that mind (I should prefer the word "theology"), we shall have attained only a very partial, and not a very persuasive or compelling, description of Judaism.

---

formulated not within the Dual Torah but within other realms of thought and discourse entirely; to the discourse of theology of Judaism, therefore, the canonical books, while authoritative and critical, prove peripheral and ancillary. The sole exception in any language is Abraham J. Heschel, but his *Torah min hashshamayim*, on the theology of revelation of the sages, Ishmael and Aqiba, the one immanental, the other transcendental (and for Heschel these words bear rather particular and possibly idiosyncratic meanings) cast in merely descriptive language what is, in fact, a prescriptive and normative theory of revelation in the Judaism of the Dual Torah; he mixed academic scholarship with theology, and whether the result was theology, as I should claim, certainly it was not scholarship. But beyond Heschel, the theological scene proves barren indeed to those who take their sight by the fixed star of the Dual Torah. And, it goes without saying, when the theologizing of avatars of "the tradition," that is, people educated in the Yeshiva-world, gets translated into English, we are presented with either confused meanderings (J. B. Soloveichik's *Halakhic Man* is the outstanding example) of a pseudo-philosophical order or sheer platitude and banality (the cult figure, Adin Steinsaltz, provides the best instance among a great many).

Part One

THE QUEST FOR UNITY IN THE MISHNAH'S PHILOSOPHY OF JUDAISM AND IN THE MIDRASH COMPILATIONS' THEOLOGY OF JUDAISM

2

The Mishnah's Philosophical Method: The Judaism of Hierarchical Classification in Greco-Roman Context

The Mishnah, seen whole, presents a profoundly philosophical system, one that employs numerous cases to make a single general point. That proposition is that all things are one, complex things yield uniform and similar components, and, rightly understood, there is a hierarchy of being, to be discovered through the proper classification of all things. That philosophical representation of the theology of the one and singular God, from whom all being comes, comes to full expression in the Mishnah's massive and detailed account of the realm of nature: the rules that govern the ordering of all things in a cogent, ascending structure.

What marks the Mishnah's system as philosophical – and not theological – is its focus upon not merely how things are, but why they are the way they are, that is, upon the question of what it means that things are this way, rather than some other. The Mishnah's philosophical method derives from the natural history of Aristotle and aims at the hierarchical classification of all things. It follows that the Mishnah's systemic statement, its philosophy of Judaism demonstrates that all things in place, in proper rank and position in the hierarchy of being, point to, stand for, one thing. I suppose that, in the context of Scripture, with its insistence that Israel's God is one and unique, we may take as the unarticulated premise a theological position, and, it would follow, identify as premise that fundamental and ancient affirmation of Israel.

But we deal with a composition that is everywhere systematically philosophical and only rarely, and then episodically, theological. Two-thirds of all tractates focus upon issues of philosophy, and scarcely a line of the Mishnah invokes the word "God" or calls upon the active presence of God. More to the point, the philosophy never addresses in philosophical terms such theological questions as the meaning and end of history, the nature of prophecy, nature and supernature, the being of God, miracles, and the like.[1] True, answers to these questions assuredly lie at, or even lay, the foundations for the philosophical structure. But the system and structure ask the questions philosophers ask, concerning the nature of things, and answer them in the way the philosophers answer them, through orderly sifting of data in the process of natural philosophy. The only point of difference is subject matter, but, after all, philosophers in the great tradition took up multiple questions; some worked on this, some on the other thing, and no single question predominated.

To identify we turn to the telos of thought in the Mishnah, I state the generative proposition of the Mishnah very simply: in the Mishnah, many things are made to say one thing, which concerns the nature of being: telologically hierarchized, to state matters in simple terms. The system of the Mishnah registers these two contrary propositions: many things are one, one thing is many. These propositions of course complement each other, because, in forming matched opposites, the two provide a complete and final judgment of the whole. The philosophy of Judaism must be deemed ontological, for it is a statement of an ontological order that the system makes when it claims that all things are not only orderly, but ordered in such wise that many things fall into one classification, and one thing may hold together many things of a single classification.

For this philosophy rationality consists in the hierarchy of the order of things. That rationality is revealed by the possibility always of effecting the hierarchical classification of all things: each thing in its taxon, all taxa in correct sequence, from least to greatest. And showing that all things can be ordered, and that all orders can be set into relationship with one another, we transform method into message. The message of hierarchical classification is that many things really form a single thing, the many species a single genus, the many genera an encompassing and well-crafted, cogent whole. Every time we speciate, we affirm that position; each successful labor of forming relationships among species, e.g., making them into a genus, or identifying the hierarchy of the species, proves it again. Not only so, but when we can show that many things are really one, or that one thing yields many

---

[1]The suspicious attitude toward miracles, expressed at M. Ta. 3:8 in the famous story about Honi the Circle-drawer, forms a very minor footnote. Silences testify far more eloquently than occasional observations or pointed stories.

(the reverse and confirmation of the former), we say in a fresh way a single immutable truth, the one of this philosophy concerning the unity of all being in an orderly composition of all things within a single taxon.

To show how this works, I turn to a very brief sample of the Mishnah's authorship's sustained effort to demonstrate how many classes of things – actions, relationships, circumstances, persons, places – really form one class. This supererogatory work of classification then works its way through the potentialities of chaos to explicit order. It is classification transformed from the how of intellection to the why and the what for and, above all, the what does it all mean. Recognition that one thing may fall into several categories and many things into a single one comes to expression, for the authorship of the Mishnah, in diverse ways. One of the interesting ones is the analysis of the several taxa into which a single action may fall, with an account of the multiple consequences, e.g., as to sanctions that are called into play, for a single action. The right taxonomy of persons, actions, and things will show the unity of all being by finding many things in one thing, and that forms the first of the two components of what I take to be the philosophy's teleology.

Mishnah-tractate Keritot 3:9

A. There is one who ploughs a single furrow and is liable on eight counts of violating a negative commandment:

B. [specifically, it is] he who (1) ploughs with an ox and an ass [Deut. 22:10], which are (2,3) both Holy Things, in the case of (4) [ploughing] Mixed Seeds in a vineyard [Deut. 22:9], (5) in the Seventh Year [Lev. 25:4], (6) on a festival [Lev. 23:7] and who was both a (7) priest [Lev. 21:1] and (8) a Nazirite [Num. 6:6] [ploughing] in a grave-yard.

C. Hanania b. Hakhinai says, "Also: He is [ploughing while] wearing a garment of diverse kinds" [Lev. 19:19, Deut. 22:11].

D. They said to him, "This is not within the same class."

E. He said to them, "Also the Nazir [B8] is not within the same class [as the other transgressions]."

Here is a case in which more than a single set of flogging is called for. B's felon is liable to 312 stripes, on the listed counts. The ox is sanctified to the altar, the ass to the upkeep of the house (B2,3). Hanania's contribution is rejected since it has nothing to do with ploughing, and sages' position is equally flawed. The main point, for our inquiry, is simple. The one action draws in its wake multiple consequences. Classifying a single thing as a mixture of many things then forms a part of the larger intellectual address to the nature of mixtures. But it yields a result that, in the analysis of an action, far transcends the metaphysical problem of mixtures, because it moves us toward the ontological solution of the unity of being.

The real interest in demonstrating the unity of being lies not in things but in abstractions, and, among abstractions *types* of actions take the center stage. Mishnah-tractate Keritot works out how many things are really one thing. This is accomplished by showing that the end or consequence of diverse actions to be always one and the same. The issue of the tractate is the definition of occasions on which one is obligated to bring a sin-offering and a suspensive guilt-offering. The tractate lists those sins that are classified together by the differentiating criterion of intention. If one deliberately commits those sins, he is punished through extirpation. If it is done inadvertently, he brings a sin-offering. In case of doubt as to whether or not a sin has been committed (hence: inadvertently), he brings a suspensive guilt-offering. Lev. 5:17-19 specifies that if one sins but does not know it, he brings a sin-offering or a guilt-offering. Then if he does, a different penalty is invoked, with the suspensive guilt-offering at stake as well. While we have a sustained exposition of implications of facts that Scripture has provided, the tractate also covers problems of classification of many things as one thing, in the form of a single sin-offering for multiple sins, and that problem fills the bulk of the tractate.

Mishnah-tractate Keritot 1:1, 2, 7, 3:2, 4

1:1

A.   Thirty-six transgressions subject to extirpation are in the Torah...

1:2

A.   For those [transgressions] are people liable, for deliberately doing them, to the punishment of extirpation,

B.   and for accidentally doing them, to the bringing of a sin-offering,

C.   and for not being certain of whether or not one has done them, to a suspensive guilt-offering [Lev. 5:17] –

D.   "except for the one who imparts uncleanness to the sanctuary and its Holy Things,

E.   "because he is subject to bringing a sliding-scale offering (Lev. 5:6-7, 11)," the words of R. Meir.

F.   And sages say, "Also: [except for] the one who blasphemes, as it is said, 'You shall have one law for him that does anything unwittingly' (Num. 15:29) – excluding the blasphemer, who does no concrete deed."

1:7

A.   The woman who is subject to a doubt concerning [the appearance of] five fluxes,

B.   or the one who is subject to a doubt concerning five miscarriages

C.   brings a single offering.

D.   And she [then is deemed clean so that she] eats animal sacrifices.

E. And the remainder [of the offerings, A, B] are not an obligation for her.

F. [If she is subject to] five confirmed miscarriages,

G. or five confirmed fluxes,

H. she brings a single offering.

I. And she eats animal sacrifices.

J. But the rest [of the offerings, the other four] remain as an obligation for her [to bring at some later time] –

K. M'SH S: A pair of birds in Jerusalem went up in price to a golden *denar*.

L. Said Rabban Simeon b. Gamaliel, "By this sanctuary! I shall not rest tonight until they shall be at [silver] *denars*."

M. He entered the court and taught [the following law]:

N. "The woman who is subject to five confirmed miscarriages [or] five confirmed fluxes brings a single offering.

O. "And she eats animal sacrifices.

P. "And the rest [of the offerings] do not remain as an obligation for her."

Q. And pairs of birds stood on that very day at a quarter-*denar* each [one one-hundredth of the former price].

3:2

A. [If] he ate [forbidden] fat and [again ate] fat in a single spell of inadvertence, he is liable only for a single sin-offering,

B. [If] he ate forbidden fat and blood and remnant and refuse [of an offering] in a single spell of inadvertence, he is liable for each and every one of them.

C. This rule is more strict in the case of many kinds [of forbidden food] than of one kind.

D. And more strict is the rule in [the case of] one kind than in many kinds:

E. For if he ate a half-olive's bulk and went and ate a half-olive's bulk of a single kind, he is liable.

F. [But if he ate two half-olive's bulks] of two [different] kinds, he is exempt.

3:4

A. There is he who carries out a single act of eating and is liable on its account for four sin-offerings and one guilt-offering:

B. An unclean [lay] person who ate (1) forbidden fat, and it was (2) remnant (3) of Holy Things, and (4) it was on the Day of Atonement.

C. R. Meir says, "If it was the Sabbath and he took it out [from one domain to another] in his mouth, he is liable [for another sin-offering]."

D. They said to him, "That is not of the same sort [of transgression of which we have spoken heretofore since it is not caused by eating (A)]."

M. Ker. 1:7 introduces the case of classifying several incidents within a single taxon, so that one incident encompasses a variety of cases and therefore one penalty or sanction covers a variety of instances. That same conception is much more amply set forth in Chapter Two. There we have lists of five who bring a single offering for many transgressions, five who bring a sliding-scale offering for many incidents, and the like, so M. Ker. 2:3-6. Then M. Ker. 3:1-3 we deal with diverse situations in which a man is accused of having eaten forbidden fat and therefore of owing a sin-offering. At M. Ker. 3:1 the issue is one of disjoined testimony. Do we treat as one the evidence of two witnesses? The debate concerns whether two cases form a single category. Sages hold that the cases are hardly the same, because there are differentiating traits. M. Ker. 3:2-3 show us how we differentiate or unify several acts. We have several acts of transgression in a single spell of inadvertence; we classify them all as one action for purposes of the penalty. That at stake is the problem of classification and how we invoke diverse taxic indicators is shown vividly at M. Ker. 3:2 in particular. Along these same lines are the issues of M. Ker. 3:3, 4-6: "There is he who carries out a single act of eating and is liable on its account for four sin-offerings and one guilt-offering; there is he who carries out a single act of sexual intercourse and becomes liable on its account for six sin-offerings," with the first shown at M. Ker. 3:4.

The recognition that one thing becomes many does not challenge the philosophy of the unity of all being, but confirms the main point. Why do I insist on that proposition? The reason is simple. If we can show that differentiation flows from within what is differentiated – that is, from the intrinsic or inherent traits of things – then we confirm that at the heart of things is a fundamental ontological being, single, cogent, simple, that is capable of diversification, yielding complexity and diversity. The upshot is to be stated with emphasis. *That diversity in species or diversification in actions follows orderly lines confirms the claim that there is that single point from which many lines come forth.* Carried out in proper order – [1] the many form one thing, and [2] one thing yields many – the demonstration then leaves no doubt as to the truth of the matter. Ideally, therefore, we shall argue from the simple to the complex, showing that the one yields the many, one thing, many things, two, four.

Mishnah-tractate Shabbat 1:1

1:1

A.		[Acts of] transporting objects from one domain to another, [which violate] the Sabbath, (1) are two, which [indeed] are four [for one who is] inside, (2) and two which are four [for one who is] outside,
B.		How so?
C.		[If on the Sabbath] the beggar stands outside and the householder inside,

D.	[and] the beggar stuck his hand inside and put [a beggar's bowl] into the hand of the householder,
E.	or if he took [something] from inside it and brought it out,
F.	the beggar is liable, the householder is exempt.
G.	[If] the householder stuck his hand outside and put [something] into the hand of the beggar,
H.	or if he took [something] from it and brought it inside,
I.	the householder is liable, and the beggar is exempt.
J.	[If] the beggar stuck his hand inside, and the householder took [something] from it,
K.	or if [the householder] put something in it and he [the beggar] removed
L.	both of them are exempt.
M.	[If] the householder put his hand outside and the beggar took [something] from it,
N.	or if [the beggar] put something into it and [the householder] brought it back inside,
O.	both of them are exempt.

M. Shab. 1:1 classifies diverse circumstances of transporting objects from private to public domain. The purpose is to assess the rules that classify as culpable or exempt from culpability diverse arrangements. The operative point is that a prohibited action is culpable only if one and the same person commits the whole of the violation of the law. If two or more people share in the single action, neither of them is subject to punishment. At stake therefore is the conception that one thing may be many things, and if that is the case, then culpability is not incurred by any one actor. The Sabbath exposition appears so apt and perfect for the present proposition that readers may wonder whether the authorship of the Mishnah could accomplish that same wonder of concision of complex thought more than a single time. Joining rhetoric, logic, and specific proposition transforms thought into not merely expository prose but poetry.

Have I given a proof consisting of one case? Quite to the contrary, the document contains a plethora of exercises of the same kind. My final demonstration of the power of speciation in demonstrating the opposite, namely, the generic unity of species and the hierarchy that orders them, derives from the treatment of oaths, to which we now turn. The basic topical program of Mishnah-tractate Shabuot responds systematically to the potpourri of subjects covered by Leviticus Chapters Five and Six within the (to the priestly author) unifying rubric of those who bring a guilt-offering. Lev. 5:1-6 concerns oaths, an oath of testimony, and one who touches something unclean in connection with the Temple cult, and finally, one who utters a rash oath.

Mishnah-tractate Shabuot 1:1-2, 2:1

1:1

A.   Oaths are of two sorts, which yield four subdivisions.

B.   Awareness of [having sinned through] uncleanness is of two sorts, which yield four subdivisions.

C.   Transportation [of objects from one domain to the other] on the Sabbath is of two sorts, which yield four subdivisions.

D.   The symptoms of *negas* are of two sorts, which yield four subdivisions.

1:2

A.   In any case in which there is awareness of uncleanness at the outset and awareness [of uncleanness] at the end but unawareness in the meantime – lo, this one is subject to bringing an offering of variable value.

B.   [If] there is awareness [of uncleanness] at the outset but no apprehension [of uncleanness] at the end, a goat which [yields blood to be sprinkled] within [in the Holy of Holies], and the Day of Atonement suspend [the punishment],

C.   until it will be made known to the person, so that he may bring an offering of variable value.

2:1

A.   Awareness of uncleanness is of two sorts, which yield four subdivisions [M. 1:lB].

B.   (1) [If] one was made unclean and knew about it, then the uncleanness left his mind, but he knew [that the food he had eaten was] Holy Things,

C.   (2) the fact that the food he had eaten was Holy Things left his mind, but he knew about [his having contracted] uncleanness,

D.   (3) both this and that left his mind, but he ate Holy Things without knowing it and after he ate them, he realized it –

E.   lo, this one is liable to bring an offering of variable value.

F.   (1) [If] he was made unclean and knew about it, and the uncleanness left his mind, but he remembered that he was in the sanctuary;

G.   (2) the fact that he was in the sanctuary left his mind, but he remembered that he was unclean,

H.   (3) both this and that left his mind, and he entered the sanctuary without realizing it, and then when he had left the sanctuary, he realized it – lo, this one is liable to bring an offering of variable value.

M. Shabuot 1:1-7, 2:1-5 accomplishes the speciation of oaths, on the one side, and uncleanness in regard to the cult, on the other. That work of speciation then joins two utterly disparate subjects, oaths and uncleanness, so showing a unity of structure that forms a metaphysical argument for the systemic proposition on the unity of being. We do so in a way that is now to be predicted. It is by showing that many things are one thing, now, as I said, oaths, uncleanness. When the priestly author joined the same subjects, it was because a single offering was involved for diverse and distinct sins or crimes. When the mishnaic author does, it is because a single inner structure sustains these same diverse and distinct sins or crimes. Comparing the priestly with the Mishnah's strategy of exposition underlines the remarkable shift accomplished by our philosophers. Their power of formulation – rhetoric, logic together – of course, works to demonstrate through the medium the message that these enormously diverse subjects in fact can be classified within a simple taxonomic principle. It is that there are two species to a genus, and two subspecies to each species, and these are readily determined by appeal to fixed taxic indicators. An abstract statement of the rule of classification (and, it must follow, also hierarchization) will have yielded less useful intellectual experience than the remarkably well-balanced concrete exemplification of the rule, and that is precisely what we have in Mishnah-tractate Shabuot Chapters One and Two.

The main point of differentiation – the taxic indicator – derives from the intersecting issues of a divided sequence of time frames and of awareness. If one knows something at one point in a differentiated process ("the outset," "the meantime," "the end") but does not know that thing at some other point, then we have a grid in two dimensions: sequence of time, sequence of spells of awareness or unawareness. And then the taxic indicators are in place, so the process of speciation and subspeciation is routine. At stake is the power of the taxic indicator. What is stunning is that the same process of speciation and subspeciation is explicitly applied to utterly unrelated matters, which demonstrates for all to see that the foundations of knowledge lie in method, which makes sense of chaos, and method means correct knowledge of the classification of things and the ability to identify the taxic indicators that make classification possible. All of this prepares the way for the treatment of oaths, Mishnah-tractate Shabuot 3:1-8:6, that is, the entire tractate.

The upshot may be stated very simply. The species point to the genus, all classes to one class, all taxa properly hierarchized then rise to the top of the structure and the system forming one taxon. So all things ascend to, reach, one thing. All that remains is for the theologian to define that one thing: God. But that is a step that the philosophers of the Mishnah did not take. Perhaps it was because they did not think they had to. But I think there is a different reason altogether. It is because, as a matter of fact, they were philosophers. And to philosophers, as I said at the outset, God serves as premise and principle (and whether or not it is one God or many gods, a unique being or a being that finds a place in a class of similar beings hardly is germane!), and philosophy serves not to demonstrate principles or to explore premises, but to analyze the unknown, to answer important questions.

In such an enterprise the premise, God, turns out to be merely instrumental, and the given principle, so to be merely interesting. But for philosophers, intellectuals, God can live not in the details, but in the unknowns, in the as-yet-unsolved problem and the unresolved dilemma. So, I think, in the philosophy of Judaism, God lives, so to speak, in the excluded middle. God is revealed in the interstitial case. God is made known through the phenomena that form a single phenomenon. God is perceived in the one that is many. God is encountered in the many that are one. For that is the dimension of being – that, so I claim, immanental and sacramental dimension of being – that defines for this philosophy its statement of ultimate concern, its recurrent point of tension, its generative problematic.

That then is the urgent question, the ineluctable and self-evidently truthful answer: God in the form, God in the order, God in the structure, God in the heights, God at the head of the great chain of hierarchical being. True, God is premise, scarcely mentioned. But it is because God's name does not have to be mentioned when the whole of the order of being says that name, and only that name, and always that name, the Name unspoken because it is always in the echo, the silent, thin voice, the numinous in all phenomena.

What next? As we shall now see, among the philosophers of that time and place, which is to say, within important components of the philosophical tradition that sustained the Greco-Roman world, however arcane the subject matter of the philosophy of Judaism, the philosophers of Judaism can claim a rightful, and honored, place. I shall now show that among the philosophers, Judaism's philosophy can and should have been perceived not merely as philosophical, but, indeed, as philosophy. The basis for that claim is simple: whether or not philosophers can have understood a line of the document (and I doubt that they would have cared to try), the method and the message of the philosophy of Judaism fall into the classification of philosophical methods and messages of the Greco-Roman philosophical tradition. The method is like that of Aristotle, the message, congruent to that of neo-Platonism.[2] To state the upshot of the proposition at hand, Judaism's first system, the Mishnah's, finds its

---

[2]But here I restrict my presentation to the issue of the method of hierarchical classification. Elsewhere I treat the message, to which I merely allude in the present context.

natural place within philosophy first because it appeals to the Aristotelian methods of natural philosophy – classification, comparison and contrast – and the media of expression of philosophy – *Listenwissenschaft* – to register its position.[3]

As to method, can we classify the taxonomic method – premises and rules – of the sages in the same category as the method of Aristotle? This is the question that yields answers on the methodological context in which the philosophy of Judaism is to be located. And in this setting by "context" we mean something piquantly appropriate to our results: the classification of the philosophy. For, as I shall now show, our back-country philosophers in a fairly primitive way replicated the method of Aristotle in setting forth the single paramount proposition of neo-Platonism.[4]

Having said that, I hasten to add this qualification. The issue is not one of direct connection. None conjures the fantasy and anachronism of the Mishnah's authorship's tramping down a Galilean hill from their yeshiva to the academy in a nearby Greek-speaking town, Caesarea or Sepphoris, for example, there studying elementary Aristotle and listening to the earliest discourses of neo-Platonism, then climbing back up the hill and writing it all up in their crabbed back-country idiom made up of the cases and examples of the Mishnah.

But as a matter of fact, in its indicative traits of message and method, the Mishnah's philosophical system is a version of one critical proposition of neo-Platonism, set forth and demonstrated

---

[3] That proposition, on the essential unity of the hierarchical nature of all being, falls into the classification of philosophy, since it forms one important, generative premise of neo-Platonism. But here I concentrate on the issue of method, and the theological implications of the choices made by the Mishnah's philosophers.

[4] I leave for Philonic scholarship the comparison of the Mishnah's neo-Platonism with that of Philo. Philo's mode of writing, his presentation of his ideas, seems to me so different from the mode and method of the Mishnah that I am not sure how we can classify as Aristotelian (in the taxonomic framework of natural philosophy, which seems to me the correct framework for the Mishnah's philosophical method) the principal methodological traits of Philo's thought. But others are most welcome to correct what is only a superficial impression. I think the selection for comparison and contrast of Aristotle and neo-Platonism, first method, then proposition, is a preferable strategy of analysis (and exposition, as a matter of fact), and I willingly accept the onus of criticism for not comparing and contrasting the method and message of Philo with those of the Mishnah. I mean only to suggest that the questions Wolfson's *Philo* raised may well be reopened, but within an entirely fresh set of premises and in accord with what I conceive to be a more properly differentiated and therefore critical reading of the data.

through a standard Aristotelian method.[5]   And that is what an
examination of the philosophical context will show us. But – I cannot
overstress – these judgments rest upon not a claim of direct connection but
an exercise of simple, inductive comparison and contrast, that is to say,
of mere classification.[6]   I propose now only in an entirely inductive
manner to classify the system by the indicative traits of philosophical
systems.   In that simple way I shall show that in one of the two
fundamental aspects – method, message – this system shares traits
important to systems all deem to be philosophical.   Therefore this
system by the criteria of philosophy and in the specific and explicit
context of philosophy must be classified as philosophical.   That is my

---

[5]And I need hardly add that the very eclecticism of the philosophy of Judaism
places it squarely within the philosophical mode of its time. See J. M. Dillon
and A. A. Long, eds., *The Question of "Eclecticism." Studies in Later Greek
Philosophy* (Berkeley and Los Angeles, 1988: University of California Press).

[6]But I hasten to add that further studies of the Mishnah's philosophical context
are bound to make much more precise any judgment about the philosophical
context of the document and its system. For this initial account, it seems
unnecessary to do more than argue, as I do, that the Mishnah's fundamental
intellectual structure in its method and message fall into the classification,
defined by circumstance and context, of philosophy. The method, I shall show,
is standard for natural philosophy, exemplified by Aristotle, and the
proposition proves entirely congruent to one principal conception of Middle
Platonism, exemplified by Plotinus.   At the same time, I point out, the
components of congruence, method and message alike, yield far more specific
results. If we ask, does the Mishnah's theory of mixtures coincide with that of a
specific philosophy of the larger tradition, the answer is, indeed so: the Stoic.
But do other components of the Mishnah's metaphysics fit together with the
rest of Stoic physics, e.g., theories of space and time? So too, if Middle
Platonism will have found entirely familiar the Mishnah's keen interest in
showing how one thing yields many things, in demonstrating a hierarchical
unity of being through the ordering of all classes of things (that is to say, the
ontological unity of things proven on the basis of the natural world), does that
make the Mishnah's philosophy in general a form of Middle Platonism? If we
ask about the concept of space or place, we look in vain for a familiar
conception; cf. S. Samburnsky, *The Concept of Place in Late Neoplatonism*
(Jerusalem, 1982: The Israel Academy of Sciences and Humanities).   My
general impression is that when all is said and done, the philosophy of Judaism
is far less abstract, even at its most abstract level, than other philosophy of the
same tradition and temporal setting; as to the issue of space or place, my sense
is that the Judaic philosophers were deeply concerned with *what* things are, not
where they are; Jerusalem, for instance, is a profoundly abstract, taxic indicator.
That conforms to the larger Aristotelianism of the system. Here, as I stress, I
prove only that by the synchronic and even diachronic standards of philosophy,
Judaism – method, message, if not medium – in this system is philosophical.
These preliminary remarks are meant only to point the way toward a further
range of inquiry into the philosophy of Judaism: the comparison and contrast in
detail of that philosophy with other philosophies of the Greco-Roman tradition.

simple argument. But it is fundamental to my purpose, which is to show that in the Mishnah's system, both as to mode of thought and as to message, we deal with a philosophy – philosophy in an odd idiom to be sure, but philosophy nonetheless.[7]

Let me ask the question in its simplest form: by appeal to the paramount taxic traits of Aristotelian method, can we classify the method as Aristotelian? If we can, then my purpose, which is to demonstrate that the Judaism of the Mishnah is a philosophy, will have been accomplished. That is as far as we can go: no further. But it suffices to accomplish the goal of demonstrating that, as to the method of classification, the Mishnah's is philosophical, in the way in which Greco-Roman philosophy, exemplified by Aristotle, is philosophical. True, we cannot show, and therefore do not know, that the Mishnah's philosophers read Aristotle's work on natural history or his reflections on scientific method, e.g., the *Posterior Analytics*,[8] but we can compare our philosophers' method with that of Aristotle, who also, as a matter of fact, set forth a system that, in part, appealed to the right ordering of things through classification by correct rules.[9]

Now to the specific task at hand. A brief account, based upon the standard textbook picture, of the taxonomic method of Aristotle permits us to compare the philosophical method of the philosophy of Judaism with that of the methodologically paramount natural philosophy of the Greco-Roman world.[10] We begin with the simple

---

[7]And no less than Philo's philosophy was a philosophy. My sense is that these results when properly digested and refined as already noted must reopen the questions addressed by the great Harry A. Wolfson in his *Philo*.

[8]I consulted Jonathan Barnes, *Aristotle's Posterior Analytics* (Oxford, 1975: Clarendon Press).

[9]And, as to proposition about the hierarchical ordering of all things in a single way, the unity of all being in right order, while we cannot show and surely do not know that the Mishnah's philosophers knew anything about Plato, let alone Plotinus's neo-Platonism (which came to expression only in the century after the closure of the Mishnah!), we can compare our philosophers' proposition with that of neo-Platonism. For that philosophy, as we shall see, did seek to give full and rich expression to the proposition that all things emerge from one thing, and one thing encompasses all things, and that constitutes the single proposition that animates the system as a whole.

[10]For this section I consulted the following:

Adkins, A. W. H., *From the Many to the One. A Study of Personality and Views of Human Nature in the Context of Ancient Greek Society, Values, and Beliefs* (Ithaca, 1970: Cornell University Press).

Allan, D. J., *The Philosophy of Aristotle* (London, New York, Toronto, 1952: Oxford University Press/Geoffrey Cumberlege).

Armstrong, A. H., "Platonism and Neoplatonism," *Encyclopaedia Britannica* (Chicago, 1975) 14:539-545.

observation that the distinction between genus and species lies at the foundation of all knowledge. Adkins states the matter in the most accessible way, "Aristotle, a systematic biologist, uses his method of classification by genera and species, itself developed from the classificatory interests of the later Plato, to place man among other animals...The classification must be based on the final development of the creature...."[11] But to classify, we have to take as our premise that things are subject to classification, and that means that they have traits that are essential and indicative, on the one side, but also shared with other things, on the other. The point of direct contact and intersection between the Judaism's philosophy of hierarchical classification and the natural philosophy of Aristotle lies in the shared, and critical, conviction concerning the true nature or character of things. Both parties concur that there *is* such a true definition – a commonplace for philosophers, generative of interesting problems, e.g., about Ideas, or Form and Substance, Actual and Potential, and the like – of what things really are.[12]

Armstrong, A. H., "Plotinus," *Encyclopaedia Britannica* (Chicago, 1975) 14:573-4.

Bréhier, Émile, *The History of Philosophy. The Hellenistic and Roman Age* (Chicago and London, 1965: The University of Chicago Press). Translated by Wade Baskin.

Cherniss, Harold, *Selected Papers* (Leiden, 1977: E. J. Brill). Edited by Leonardo Tarán.

Feldman, Louis H., "Philo," *Encyclopaedia Britannica* (Chicago, 1975) 14:245-247.

Goodenough, Erwin R., *An Introduction to Philo Judaeus. Second Edition* (Lanham, 1986: University Press of America Brown Classics in Judaica).

Merlan, P., "Greek Philosophy from Plato to Plotinus," in A. H. Armstrong, ed., *The Cambridge History of Later Greek and Early Medieval Philosophy* (Cambridge, 1967: Cambridge University Press), pp. 14-136.

Minio-Paluello, Lorenzo, "Aristotelianism," *Encyclopaedia Britannica* 1:1155-1161.

Owens, Joseph, *A History of Ancient Western Philosophy* (New York, 1959: Appleton, Century, Crofts Inc.)

Parker G. F., *A Short History of Greek Philosophy from Thales to Epicurus* (London, 1967: Edward Arnold (Publishers) Ltd.).

Reale, Giovanni, *A History of Ancient Philosophy. III. The Systems of the Hellenistic Age* (Albany,1985: State University of New York Press). Edited and translated from the third Italian edition by John R. Catan.

[11]Adkins, A. W. H., *From the Many to the One. A Study of Personality and Views of Human Nature in the Context of Ancient Greek Society, Values, and Beliefs* (Ithaca, 1970: Cornell University Press), pp. 170-171.

[12]But only Aristotle and the Mishnah carry into the material details of economics that conviction about the true character or essence of definition of things. The economics of the Mishnah and the economics of Aristotle begin in the conception of "true value," and the distributive economics proposed by

But how are we to know the essential traits that allow us to define the true character of, e.g., to classify, things? And this is the point at which our comparison becomes particular, since what we need to find out is whether there are between Aristotle's and Judaism's philosophies only shared convictions about the genus and the species or particular conceptions as to how these are to be identified and organized. The basic conviction on both sides is this: objects are not random but fall into classes and so may be described, analyzed, and explained by appeal to general traits or rules.

The component of Aristotelianism that pertains here is "the use of deductive reasoning proceeding from self-evident principles or discovered general truths to conclusions of a more limited import; and syllogistic forms of demonstrative or persuasive arguments."[13] The goal is the classification of things, which is to say, the discovery of general rules that apply to discrete data or instances. Minio-Paluello states,

> In epistemology...Aristotelianism includes a concentration on knowledge accessible by natural means or accountable for by reason; an inductive, analytical empiricism, or stress on experience in the study of nature...leading from the perception of contingent individual occurrences to the discovery of permanent, universal patterns; and the primacy of the universal, that which is expressed by common or general terms. In metaphysics, or the theory of Being, Aristotelianism involves belief in the primacy of the individual in the realm of existence; in correlated conceptions allowing an articulate account of reality (e.g., 10 categories; genus-species-individual, matter-form, potentiality-actuality, essential-accidental; the four material elements and their basic qualities; and the four causes-formal, material, efficient and final); in the soul as the inseparable form of each living body in the vegetable and animal kingdoms; in activity as the essence of things; and in the primacy of speculative over practical activity.

The manner in which we accomplish this work is to establish categories of traits, and these will yield the besought rules or generalizations that make possible both classification, and, in the nature of things, therefore also hierarchization.

Clearly, when we review some of the more obvious characteristics of Aristotle's logical and taxonomic principles, in specific terms we find only occasional points of contact with the principles we uncover in the Mishnah's philosophical structure. Only in general does the manner in

---

each philosophy then develops that fundamental notion. The principle is so fundamental to each system that comparison of one system to the other in those terms alone is justified.
[13]Minio-Paluello, Lorenzo, "Aristotelianism," *Encyclopaedia Britannica* 1:1155-1161, p. 1155.

which Aristotle does the work of definition through classification also characterize the way in which sages do the same work. But there are points of intersection. For instance, while the actual and the potential form critical taxic categories for Aristotle, they prove subsidiary, though pertinent, in the Mishnah. While for the Mishnah, the matter of mixtures defines a central and generative problematic, for Aristotle, the same matter is subsumed into other compositions altogether. It constitutes a chapter in the story of change, which is explained by the passage of elements into one another. That will help us to account for the destruction of one element and the creation of another. In this connection Allan says:

> Aristotle does not mean by 'mixture' a mere shuffling of primary particles, as if the seeds of wheat and barley were mixed in a heap, but genuine change of quality resulting in a new 'form,' towards which each component has made a contribution.[14]

The consideration of the classes of mixtures plays its role in Aristotle's account of the sublunary region; it is not – as represented by Allan – a point at which Aristotle repeatedly uncovers problems that require solution, in the way in which the issue of mixtures forms the source for the Mishnah's solution of urgent problems.

Enough has been said to justify comparing Aristotle's and Judaism's philosophies, but I have yet to specify what I conceive to be the generative point of comparison. It lies in two matters: first, the paramount one of the shared principles of formal logic, which I find blatant in the Mishnah and which all presentations of Aristotle's philosophy identify as emblematic. The second, as is clear, is the taxonomic method, viewed from afar. Let us turn only briefly to the former. When we follow a simple account of the way in which we attain new truth, we find ourselves quite at home. Allan's account follows:[15]

> Induction...is the advance from the particular to the general. By the inspection of examples...in which one characteristic appears conjoined with another, we are led to propound a general rule which we suppose to be valid for cases not yet examined. Since the rule is of higher generality than the instances, this is an advance from a truth 'prior for us' toward a truth 'prior in nature.'

My representation of the mishnaic mode of presentation of cases that, with our participation, yield a general rule, accords with this logic, which is inductive.

---

[14]Allan, D. J., *The Philosophy of Aristotle* (London, New York, Toronto, 1952: Oxford University Press/Geoffrey Cumberlege), p. 60.
[15]*Op. cit.*, pp. 126ff.

The more important of the two principles of sound intellectual method, is the taxonomic interest in defining through classification. This definitive trait of natural philosophy is what we find in common between Aristotle's and the Mishnah's philosophical method, and the points in common prove far more than those yielded by the general observation that both systems appeal to the identification of genera out of species. In fact, what philosophers call the dialectical approach in Aristotle proves the same approach to the discovery or demonstration of truth as that we find in the Mishnah. Owens sets the matter forth in the following language:[16]

> Since a theoretical science proceeds from first principles that are found within the thing under investigation, the initial task of the philosophy of nature will be to discover its primary principles in the sensible thing themselves.

I cannot imagine a formulation more suited to the method of the Mishnah than that simple statement. For the Mishnah's philosophers compose their taxonomy by appeal to the indicative traits of things, rather than to extrinsic considerations of imposed classification, e.g., by reference to Scripture.[17] The philosophers whose system is set forth in the Mishnah appeal to the traits of things, deriving their genera from the comparison and contrast of those inherent or intrinsic traits. This I take to be precisely what is stated here.

> In accordance with the general directives of the Aristotelian logic, the process of their discovery will be dialectical, not demonstrative.

This distinction is between genuine reasoning and demonstration.

If the parallels in method are clear, where do we find the difference between Aristotle's system and the Mishnah's? It is that the goal of Aristotle's system, the teleological argument in favor of the unmoved mover, and the goal of Judaism's system, the demonstration of the unity of being, are essentially contradictory, marking utterly opposed positions on the fundamental character of God and the traits of the created world that carries us upward to God. So we establish the philosophical character of the method of the Mishnah's system, only at the cost of uncovering a major contradiction: the proposition that animates the one system stands in direct opposition, as to its premises, implications, and explicit results, with the results of the other. Aristotle's God attained through teleological demonstration

---

[16]Joseph Owens, *A History of Ancient Western Philosophy*, pp. 309ff.

[17]And for that decision they are criticized by all their successors, chief among them, the authorship of Sifra. See my *Uniting the Dual Torah: Sifra and the Problem of the Mishnah* (Cambridge, 1990: Cambridge University Press).

accomplished through the right classification of all things and the Mishnah's God, whose workings in the world derive from the demonstration of the ontological unity of all things, cannot recognize one another. And that is the case even though they are assuredly one.

Accordingly, we must ask ourselves, *cui bono*? Or more precisely, not to whose advantage, but rather, *against* whose position, did the Judaic philosophical system propose to argue? When we realize that at stake is a particular means for demonstrating the unity of God, we readily identify as the principal focus the pagan reading of the revealed world of the here and the now, and, it must follow, Judaism as a philosophy stood over against the pagan philosophy of the world of its time and place. The fundamental argument in favor of the unity of God in the philosophy of Judaism is by showing the hierarchical order, therefore the unity, of the world. The world therefore is made to testify to the unity of being, and – to say the obvious with very heavy emphasis – *the power of the philosophy derives from its capacity for hierarchical classification.* When we compare the pagan and the Christian philosophical ontology of God, we see that it is the pagan position, and not the Christian one, that forms the target of this system. The Christian position is simply not perceived and not considered.

The comparison of the Judaic, Christian, and pagan systems of Middle Platonism seems to me made possible, in a very preliminary way to be sure, by Armstrong:

> The difference here between pagans and Christians...is a difference about the degree of religious relevance of the material cosmos, and, closely connected with this, about the relative importance of general, natural, and special, supernatural, divine self-manifestation and self-communication. On the one side, the pagan, there is the conviction that a multiple self-communication and self-revelation of divinity takes place always and everywhere in the world, and that good and wise men everywhere...have been able to find the way to God and the truth about God in and through rational reflection on themselves and on the world, not only the heavens but the earth, and the living unity of the whole. On the other side, the Christian, there is indeed a readiness to see the goodness and beauty of the visible cosmos as a testimony to God's creation...but the religious emphasis lies elsewhere. Saving truth and the self-communication of the life of God come through the Incarnation of God as a man and through the human...society of which the God-Man is the head, the Church...It is only in the Church that material things become means of revelation and salvation through being understood in the light of Scripture and Church tradition and used by God's human ministers in the celebration of the Church's sacraments. It is the ecclesiastical

cosmos, not the natural cosmos, which appears to be of primary religious importance for the Christian.[18]

If God is revealed in the artifacts of the world, then, so pagans in general considered, God must be multiple. No, the philosophy of Judaism is here seen to respond. Here we find a Judaic argument, within the premises of paganism, against paganism. To state with emphasis what I conceive to be that argument: *the very artifacts that* appear *multiple in fact form classes of things, and, moreover, these classes themselves are subject to a reasoned ordering, by appeal to this-worldly characteristics signified by properties and indicative traits.* Monotheism hence is to be demonstrated by appeal to those very same data that for paganism prove the opposite.

The medium of hierarchical classification, which is Aristotle's, conveys the message of the unity of being[19] in the this-worldly mode of discourse formed by the framers of the Mishnah. The way to one God, ground of being and ontological unity of the world, lies through "rational reflection on themselves and on the world," this world, which yields a living unity encompassing the whole. That claim, conducted in an argument covering overwhelming detail in the Mishnah, directly faces the issue as framed by paganism. Immanent in its medium, it is transcendent in its message. And I hardly need spell out the simple reasons, self-evident in Armstrong's words, for dismissing as irrelevant to their interests the Christian reading of the cosmos. To the Mishnah's sages, it is not (merely) wrong, it is insufficient.

And yet, that is not the whole story. For the Mishnah's sages reach into Scripture for their generative categories, and, in doing so, they address head-on a Christianity that Armstrong centers, with entire soundness, upon the life of the Church of Jesus Christ, God-Man.[20] We do well here to review Armstrong's language: "It is only in the Church that material things become means of revelation and salvation through being understood in the light of Scripture and

---

[18]"Man in the Cosmos," A. Hilary Armstrong, *Plotinian and Christian Studies* (London, 1979: Variorum Reprints) No. XVII, p. 11.

[19]Which is Plato's and Plotinus's.

[20]That judgment does not contradict the argument of my *Uniting the Dual Torah: Sifra and the Problem of the Mishnah* (Cambridge, 1990: Cambridge University Press) concerning the Sifra's authorship's critique of the Mishnah's philosophers' stress upon classification through intrinsic traits of things as against through classes set forth solely by the Torah. I mean only to stress the contrast between appeal to Scripture and to nature, which I find in the philosophy of Judaism, and appeal to the eccleisial cosmos. This point registers immediately.

Church tradition and used by God's human ministers in the celebration of the Church's sacraments."

The framers of the Mishnah will have responded, "*It is in the Torah that material things are identified and set forth as a means of revelation.*"

Again Armstrong: "It is the ecclesiastical cosmos, not the natural cosmos, which appears to be of primary religious importance for the Christian."

To this the philosophers of Judaism reply, "*It is the scriptural account of the cosmos that forms our generative categories, which, by the power of intellect, we show to constitute an ordered, hierarchical unity of being.*"

So the power of this identification of "the ecclesiastical cosmos" is revealed when we frame the cosmos of the Mishnah by appeal to its persistent response to the classification and categories of Scripture. If the Church as Armstrong portrays matters worked out an ecclesiastical cosmos, only later on producing the Bible as it did, for its part the philosophy of Judaism framed a scriptural cosmos – and then read it philosophically in the way in which I have explained matters. We may therefore identify three distinct positions on the reading of the natural world: the pagan, the Christian, and the Judaic. The one reads nature as a source of revelation. The other two insist on a medium of mediation between nature and intellect. For Christianity it is, as Armstrong says, ecclesiastical, and, as I claim, for Judaism, the medium of mediation of nature lies through revelation, the Torah.

Why the difference? There is a philosophical reason, which I deem paramount, and which explains my insistence that this Judaism is a philosophy – not a theology – in its message and its mode of thought. It is that by not merely appealing to the authority of Scripture, but by themselves analyzing the revealed truths of Scripture, that the intellects at hand accomplished their purposes. By themselves showing the order and unity inherent within Scripture's list of topics, the philosophers on their own power meant to penetrate into the ground of being as God has revealed matters. This they did by working their way back from the epiphenomena of creation to the phenomenon of Creation – then to the numinous, that is, the Creator. That self-assigned challenge forms an intellectual vocation worthy of a particular kind of philosopher, an Israelite one. And, in my view, it explains also why in the Mishnah philosophers produced their philosophy in the form that they chose.

For the form, so superficially unphilosophical in its crabbed and obsessive mode of discourse, proves in the end to form a philosophy. Judaism in the system of the Mishnah is philosophical in medium, method, and message. But then philosophy also is represented as, and within, the Torah in topic and authority. The union then of the Torah's classifications and topics, philosophy's modes of thought and propositions – that marriage produced as its first fruits a philosophical Judaism, a Judaic philosophy: the Torah as Moses would have written it at God's instructions, were Moses a philosopher. But the offspring of the happy marriage was not to live long, and the philosophy of Judaism would soon give way to the theology of Judaism: theology, not philosophy, dictated the future for a thousand years.

3

The Theological Method of Midrash Compilations: Saying One Thing Many Times and in Many Ways

Theology Expressed through Writing with Scripture and the Representation of the Moabite Messiah in Ruth Rabbah

i. The Religious System Faces Outward

A religious system explains not only why people should stay within but also how people gain entry. In a well-crafted and cogent system, moreover, which says one thing in many ways, the answer to the question of how to get in will repeat the principal systemic message to all situations and judgment upon all matters. How shall we know what that repeated message is? When we can identify a religious system's mode of joining opposites, its generative symbol and how the symbol unites what should be incompatible, then we may form the hypothesis that here, in this message and symbol, the system says its simple statement. Endlessly reworked, susceptible to any number of fresh and novel restylings, in the end the message is always uniform; complex in its media of expression, the message is always simple. Discerning how the opposites unite, whether in Christ Jesus for Paul's slave and free person, gentiles and Jews, women and men, or – as we shall see – in the Torah of the Judaism of the Dual Torah for the outsider and the insider, the woman and the man, we know whatever it is that the system at hand wishes to say. In the case at hand, the opposites will be gentile and Israelite, woman and man. It is not sufficient for the system of the Dual Torah to show how they are made one – the gentile into Israelite, the abnormal (woman) into the normal (man). The system must place that union of opposites at the apex and pinnacle of its structure: that shows the power of the Torah to sanctify and to normalize what is ordinary and abnormal. When a Moabite woman can be changed into the Israelite Messiah, the system makes its statement with remarkable force, as the complex and multiplex becomes simple and uniform. Just how does this miracle take place?

ii. Writing with Scripture

In the Judaism of the Dual Torah, quite naturally, miracles are worked through the Torah. That means that appealing to the Written Torah will form the medium by which the message will be set forth. But how to make one's own statement through Scripture? It is through a combination of paraphrase, which establishes authenticity and compels assent, and parabolic reading, which effects the transformation of Scripture into that other, that fresh message, that an authorship wishes to set forth. A claim that, when sages wrote with Scripture, they merely paraphrased or set forth a fictive "plain meaning" must be relegated to the dustbin of anachronistic theologizing, on the one side, and dull-witted apologetics, on the other. True, the founders of Judaism engaged in dialogue with the Scriptures of ancient Israel. But of what that exchange consisted remains to be specified. For there are many ways in which to receive, read, and respond to Scripture.

In Ruth Rabbah, upon which we focus attention in our search for the power of the Torah to unite the opposites, outsider and insider, Moabite and Israelite, woman and man, they defined that relationship as one in which authors and authorships wrote with Scripture. Scripture provided the language, the vocabulary, the metaphors. But the authors supplied the syntax, the reference point, the experience that formed the subject of the writing. So by writing with Scripture, our sages in a profoundly classical formulation of their thought set forth propositions of their own in language of their own through constant appeal to a writing not their own. They made a statement in their own behalf by making Scripture their own, and that is what I mean by writing with Scripture.

For, as sages conducted their discourse through and dialogue with Scripture, Scripture raised questions, set forth rules of thought, premises of fact and argument. Scripture constituted that faithful record of the facts, rules, and meaning of humanity's, and Israel's, history that, for natural philosophy, derived from the facts of physics or astronomy. Whether or not their statement accorded with the position of Scripture on a given point, merely said the simple and obvious sense of Scripture, found ample support in prooftexts – none of these considerations bears material consequence.[1] What matters in the interpretation of the document is the document's own problem: how and why did those who compiled these materials consider that they made a statement, not of their own but of truth? And the answer, as we shall now see, is that they so selected and arranged what they inherited, they so framed and shaped what they themselves made up for their document, as to say in their own words and in Scripture's words a single proposition that they – with complete justification – identified with both themselves and with Scripture.

Sages' authorships made use of Scripture by making Scripture their own, and making themselves into the possession of Scripture as well, a reciprocal process in which both were changed, each into the likeness and image of the other. This they did by effecting their own selections, shaping a distinctive idiom of discourse, all the while citing, responding to, reflecting upon, Scripture's own words in Scripture's own context and for Scripture's own purpose: the here and now of eternal truth.

In the case of our document, the issue of the book of Ruth was their issue: the nature of leadership, the leader from the periphery, the Messiah from Moab – in all, Israel on its own terms. All contemporary scholarship reads the Book of Ruth as a powerful statement on that very issue: the Messiah from Moab. Yet, who could read the Ruth Rabbah and imagine that all we have in hand is a mere reprise, paraphrase and recapitulation, of the received writing? Quite to the contrary, in all its strange and determined program of exegesis and collage, arrangement and collection and restatement, the document bears no literary or rhetorical resemblance to Scripture, even while its

---

[1] To be sure, they form part of the massive system of theological apologetics created for Judaism by *Wissenschaft des Judenthums* and its continuators. But the history of modern and contemporary thought of Judaism is not at issue in this book. Nor is the question of whether or not sages set forth the plain meaning of Scripture relevant at all. The concept of a plain, historical and inherent meaning, as distinct from the fanciful ones invented by the Midrash exegetes, is purely anachronistic. See Raphael Loewe, "The 'Plain' Meaning of Scripture in Early Jewish Exegesis," in J. G. Weiss, ed., *Papers of the Institute of Jewish Studies, London. Volume I* (Repr. Lanham, 1989: University Press of America/Brown Classics in Judaica Series), pp. 140-185.

propositional program seems so profoundly to capture the message of Scripture in not only generalities but acute detail. For the message of Scripture, as contemporary scholarship has framed it, has condemned ethnocentrism and favored a religious, and not an ethnic, definition of who is Israel. The distinction of the religious from the ethnic forms a generative conception in modern and contemporary Old Testament scholarship; it is systemic and particular to the framework of thought in which that scholarship goes forward. We need not be detained by that reading of the document, yet another (interesting) mode of writing with Scripture.

It suffices to observe very simply that for the framers of our document, the categories are quite other; they did not understand Ruth as a denial but as an affirmation, and what the document affirmed, as we shall now see, is their own system. So to conclude that our sages have simply restated in their own terms the message of Scripture, paraphrasing and parroting what they found there, only in their own words, is profoundly to misconstrue how they wrote with Scripture. Indeed, among all the midrash compilations, I can find none that gives us a better view of what it means to write with Scripture than Ruth Rabbah.

Essentially, to write with Scripture, sages wrote about Scripture, but they also made their statement on Scripture and through Scripture. That dual mode of discourse accounts for the mixture, in rhetoric, of exegetical and syllogistic forms, and, in logic, of fixed associative and propositional logics. Writing with Scripture, for one thing sages referred to verses of Scripture. These required analysis and exposition. But they also provided facts and supplied proofs of propositions much as data of natural science proved propositions of natural philosophy. Writing with Scripture meant appealing to the facts that Scripture provided to prove propositions that the authorships at hand wished to prove. As a mode of discourse it required forming, out of Scripture, the systems these writers proposed to construct. Accordingly, in dialogue with Scripture, they made important statements, some of them paraphrases of lesson of Scripture, others entirely their own. In the aggregate, our authorship turned to Scripture not principally for prooftexts, let alone for pretexts, to say whatever they wanted, anyhow, to say. They read Scripture because they wanted to know what it said, but they took for granted that it spoke to them in particular. No other premise of the focus of scriptural discourse was possible; none was ever entertained.

Sages rather used Scripture as an artist uses the colors on the palette, expressing ideas through and with Scripture as the artist paints with those colors and no others. The colors remain always what they were before the artist and beside the artist. But the artist has made with them what is particular to the artist. Midrash exegetes did not not turn Scripture into a mere source of interesting facts or a set of propositions. The ancient rabbis read Scripture as God's personal letter to them. In the rabbis who produced the midrash compilations laid out in these pages, we find an example of how faced with challenge from without and crisis from within, sages found in Scripture the wisdom and the truth that guided them. No wonder, then, that these same figures undertook to answer the letter with a letter of their own.

And what was the topic of their letter? The Judaic sages saw the everyday as a recapitulation of Scripture in the here and the now. Witnessing an event in the street, they perceived a rehearsal of an event in Scripture. Or they understood the event and its meaning in the model of what they deemed to be Scripture's counterpart and parable. So they formed a single eternity out of disparate time, their present and the past of history. Through scriptural study they accomplished that recasting of the here and the now into the model of eternity. So they approached Scripture to help them see the everyday as recapitulation of Scripture, – but also, and I think of equal consequence, Scripture as the matrix for the everyday. They took the position that we understand Scripture better than did a generation before us, as they understood matters better than did their predecessors, for each succeeding age knows more than the one before about God's plan for all time and all humanity. If I may express what I conceive to be their conception of matters: we are not wiser because we know more, but in the pages of Scripture we may become wiser by understanding better what we know. All of this is meant to be captured by the phrase, "writing with Scripture."

When we contemplate the result of writing with Scripture – here, the messages our authorship presented in the setting of an encounter with the book of Ruth – we see work of considerable originality and striking cogency. But we should err if we maintained that our authorship, among many, merely said in their own words and in the words of Scripture what Scripture said anyhow. Nothing could be further from the point. Once a process of selection commences and a labor of system construction begins, then the materials at hand are relegated to merely that: the raw materials of building what is the work, in the end, of the architects, engineers, and laborers. As soon as an authorship does more than repeat what it finds in Scripture – and that authorship that merely apes or copies is no authorship at all – we enter the realm of those who write with Scripture.

Sages in the canonical writings of the Judaism of the Dual Torah appealed to Scripture not merely for prooftexts as part of an apologia but for a far more original and sustained mode of discourse. In constant interchange with Scripture, they found ways of delivering their own message, in their own idiom, and in diverse ways. Verses of Scripture therefore served not merely to prove but to instruct. Israelite Scripture constituted not merely a source of validation but a powerful instrument of profound inquiry. And the propositions that could be proposed, the statements that could be made, prove diverse. Scripture served as a kind of syntax, limiting the arrangement of words but making possible an infinity of statements. The upshot is that the received Scriptures formed an instrumentality for the expression of an authorship responsible for a writing bearing its own integrity and cogency, an authorship appealing to its own conventions of intelligibility, and, above all, making its own points. Our authorship did not write *about* Scripture, creating, e.g., a literature of commentary and exegesis essentially within the program of Scripture. Rather, they wrote *with* Scripture. And that they did in many ways.

iii. Why Ruth Rabbah? A Document with a Message, or a Scrapbook for Collecting and Preserving Completed Writings?

Before proceeding, I have to address the question that the established reading of midrash compilations must provoke: how can I maintain that we should read this document as though it were a document? For ordinarily people open midrash compilations looking for Midrash exegeses on given verses; they rarely propose to state what the compilers of the whole have wished to state in putting together this and that into a complete book. For commonly the various midrash compilations are read as mere scrapbooks, and the contents are seen as compositions that may float hither and yon, finding a perfectly comfortable place nowhere, because they fit in, somehow, everywhere. Accordingly, my claim that Ruth Rabbah addresses a particular problem, makes a systemic statement in its own cogent way, conflicts with the received and established hermeneutic of midrash compilations. Before I can set forth what I conceive to be the systemic message as Ruth Rabbah casts that common message, I have therefore to validate my approach, which is documentary and not discrete.

The question before us may be phrased in a simple way: which came first, the compositions or the conception of the document? What I want to know is whether people decided to make the compilation and then collected whatever they might, or whether they were in process of assembling this and that among ready-made writings on the book of Ruth. To frame the question more explicitly: Did our compilers have in hand a sizable corpus of completed writings on the book of Ruth, which they wished to assemble into a compilation? Or did they determine to make a compilation and only then go in search of whatever might be available concerning the book of Ruth among materials currently in circulation? The data that will permit us to answer the question consist in the character of the document as a whole.

The answer to this question derives from a survey of the document as a whole. When we simply review the proportions and dimensions of the compilation, we see very quickly that the compilers worked out rich materials for some verses and chapters, particularly the earlier ones, but had very little in hand for the later chapters and verses; there are sequences of verses on which our sages had nothing to say. It is not merely that the compilation tends to peter out in the end. These simple facts strongly suggest that the decision to compile Ruth Rabbah did not respond to the accumulation of a vast corpus of materials, evenly divided across the whole of the book. Rather, the compilers determined to produce a midrash compilation on the Book of Ruth, and then, and only then, did they collect, borrow, and also determine to make up appropriate materials. So the document comes prior to the formation of materials whether suitable for it or merely useful in accomplishing its framers' goals. And that means the physiognomy of the whole comes prior to the assessment of the parts.

The simple fact that the conception of the document came prior to the execution of the document through the selection and compilation of materials or through the composition of fresh writing points to our task. It is to ask whether the compositors wished to say some one thing in response to the one book they have selected for their agglutinative pretext. Or is their interest the book itself: exposition of Ruth wherever it may lead. What we shall now see, through results that, when I first reached them, I found amazing, is that there really is a single theme and a single message concerning them. Let us now proceed to consider the categories that, in the abstract and in theory, define the possible themes, then find out what one theme is addressed in many ways, and what one thing is said, in dull detail and merciless repetition, about that one theme.

iv. The Categories of the Topical Program

Then precisely what is the message of the compilation, which I claim constitutes a document with integrity, purpose, plan, and program? To describe the shape and structure of the document viewed all together and all at once ("the physiognomy of the whole"), I now reread every passage with an interest in its topical and even its propositional program. For that purpose my categories no longer derive

from inductive sifting of evidence, as evidence piece by piece coalesces
in accord with a given taxic trait, such as governed the formulation of
the studies of the rhetorical and logical traits of Ruth Rabbah. I have
now to impose my own categories, shaped essentially in the abstract,
upon the writing. For what I need to find out is whether, viewed all
together, the various components that have been collected coalesce to
say some few things, and, in the nature of this kind of inquiry, I have to
frame in my own mind the few topics that I think in general must form
the program of a compilation through which sages write with
Scripture. These concern God and Israel, the nations and Israel, and
Israel viewed in its own terms: the three dimensions of the existence of
the social entity that defined sages' inquiry and Scripture's frame of
reference alike.

Let us now survey the messages that they presented in this dialogue
with Scripture. In the abstract I see four principal topics on which our
authorship presents its propositions, of which the first three
correspond to the three relationships into which, in the sages' world,
that is, Israel, entered: with heaven, on earth, and within its own
existence. These yield, for our rubrics, systematic statements that
concern the relationships between: [1] Israel and God, with special
reference to the covenant, the Torah, and the land; [2] Israel and the
nations, with interest in Israel's history, past, present, and future, and
how that cyclical is to be known; [3] Israel on its own terms, with focus
upon Israel's distinctive leadership. We shall see that nearly the
whole of the propositional substrate of the document deals with the
nature of leadership, on the one side, and the definition of Israel, on
the other.

The final one addresses [4] the book of Ruth in particular. This
rubric encompasses not specific ad hoc propositions, that form
aggregates of proofs of large truths, but rather, prevailing modes of
thought, demonstrating the inner structure of intellect, in our document
yielding the formation, out of the cases of Scripture, of encompassing
rules. As I shall point out, this fourth classification of recurrent
proposition – predictably, utilizing the logic of fixed association –
forms the distinctive contribution of our authorship. There is, further,
a body of completed units of thought in which I am able to discern no
message subject to classification and generalization; or none particular
to our book of the Written Torah and its thematic interests; these latter
entries ordinarily appear in more than one midrash compilation, being
suitable anywhere but necessary nowhere. We proceed to catalogue
units of completed thought that make the specified points of the
systematic statements given at the head of each list.

v. Israel and God

Israel's relationship with God encompasses the matter of the covenant, the Torah, and the Land of Israel, all of which bring to concrete and material expression the nature and standing of that relationship. This is a topic treated only casually by our compilers. They make a perfectly standard point. It is that Israel suffers because of sin (I:i). The famine in the time of the judges was because of Israel's rebellion: "My children are in rebellion. But as to exterminating them, that is not possible, and to bring them back to Egypt is not possible, and to trade them for some other nation is something I cannot do. But this shall I do for them: lo, I shall torment them with suffering and afflict them with famine in the days when the judges judge" (III:i). This was because they got overconfident (III:ii).

Sometimes God saves Israel on account of its merit, sometimes for his own name's sake (X:i). God's punishment of Israel is always proportionate and appropriate, so LXXIV:i: "Just as in the beginning, Israel gave praise for the redemption: 'This is my God and I will glorify him' (Ex. 15:2), now it is for the substitution [of false gods for God]: 'Thus they exchanged their glory for the likeness of an ox that eats grass' (Ps. 106:20). You have nothing so repulsive and disgusting and strange as an ox when it is eating grass. In the beginning they would effect acquisition through the removal of the sandal, as it is said, 'Now this was the custom in former times in Israel concerning redeeming and exchanging: to confirm a transaction, the one drew off his sandal and gave it to the other, and this was the manner of attesting in Israel.' But now it is by means of the rite of cutting off." None of this forms a centerpiece of interest, and all of it complements the principal points of the writing.

vi Israel and the Nations

Israel's relationship with the nations is treated with interest in Israel's history, past, present, and future, and how that cyclical pattern is to be known. This topic is not addressed at all. Only one nation figures in a consequential way, and that is Moab. Under these circumstances we can hardly generalize and say that Moab stands for everybody outside of Israel. That is precisely the opposite of the fact. Moab stands for a problem within Israel, the Messiah from the periphery; and the solution to the problem lies within Israel and not in its relationships to the other, the nations.

vii. Israel on its Own [1]: The Outsider Becomes Insider, the Moabite Woman the Israelite Messiah, through the Torah

And, more to the point (for ours is not an accusatory document), how is the excluded included? And in what way do peripheral figures find their way to the center? Phrased in this way, the question yields the obvious answer, and the answer guides us to the center of the system. Let me state the answer with appropriate emphasis.

It is through the Torah as embodied by the sage, anybody can become Israel, and any Israelite can find his way to the center.

Even more – since it is through Ruth that the Moabite becomes the Israelite, and since (for our sages) the mother's status dictates the child's, we may go so far as to say that it is through the Torah that the woman may become a man (at least, in theory). But in stating matters in this way, I have gone beyond my representation of the topical and propositional program. Before proceeding to the account of the whole, let me give one stunning statement of what I conceive to be the systemic message as framed in this document. It involves David, the Messiah-sage, who is David the grandson of the Moabite woman, that is, a woman is identified as the mother of the Messiah, a Moabite as the progenitor of the sage. Only Torah can hold all this together, and it is made explicit. Let me give three concrete statements of the matter. The first concerns Ruth 4:18, "Now these are the descendants of Perez: Perez was the father of Hezron." What is important for my argument is simple. Here we see how David, the Messiah-sage, has to confront the fact that he comes from an outsider and derives his personal status from a Moabite woman. The leader from the periphery becomes the Messiah in only one way: through the Torah. This is in two parts. First, knowledge of the Torah allows David to justify himself. Second, mastery of and conformity to the Torah imparts to David that status that he enjoys, just as, in a passage cited presently, Ruth herself is instructed by Boaz on how to transform her status through conformity with the Torah.

LXXXV:i.

1. A ["Now these are the descendants of Perez: Perez was the father of Hezron":]

 B. R. Abba b. Kahana commenced by citing the following verse: "'Rage and do not sin; [commune with your own heart upon your bed and shut up]' (Ps. 4:5).

 C. "Said David before the Holy One, blessed be He, 'How long will they rage against me and say, "Is his family not invalid [for marriage into Israel]? Is he not descended from Ruth the Moabitess?"'

> D.   "'commune with your own heart upon your bed': [David continues,] 'You too have you not descended from two sisters?
>
> E.   "'You look at your own origins "and shut up."
>
> F.   "'So Tamar who married your ancestor Judah – is she not of an invalid family?
>
> G.   "'But she was only a descendant of Shem, son of Noah. So do you come from such impressive genealogy?'"

The form of the intersecting verse/base verse is not fully worked out at No. 1, since the intervention of the base verse is only by allusion. But the point is well developed, that the Messiah's family, from Ruth, is not genealogically inferior to the descendants of Judah via Tamar. David solves his problem through his knowledge of the Torah. What about his grandmother, the Moabite woman? She too is instructed in the Torah. The base verse is Ruth 2:8: Then Boaz said to Ruth, "Now listen, my daughter, do not go to glean in another field or leave this one, but keep close to my maidens."

XXXIV:i.

> 1. A.   "Then Boaz said to Ruth, 'Now listen, my daughter, do not go to glean in another field'":
>
> B.   This is on the strength of the verse, "You shall have no other gods before me" (Ex. 20:3).
>
> C.   "'or leave this one'":
>
> D.   This is on the strength of the verse, "This is my God and I will glorify him" (Ex. 15:2).
>
> E.   "'but keep close to my maidens'":
>
> F.   This speaks of the righteous, who are called maidens: "Will you play with him as with a bird, or will you bind him for your maidens" (Job 40:29).

The glosses invest the statement with a vast tapestry of meaning. Boaz speaks to Ruth as a Jew by choice, and the entire exchange is now typological. But the rich rereading of Ruth by our sages of blessed memory deals not only with details. Rather, it encompasses vast stretches of Israel's life, treating as metanomic and metaphorical every figure pertinent to the tapestry that is woven. Here is how the entire story will be represented in detail through the exposition of Ruth 2:14: "And at mealtime Boaz said to her, 'Come here and eat some bread, and dip your morsel in the wine.' So she sat beside the reapers, and he passed to her parched grain; and she ate until she was satisfied, and she had some left over."

XL:i.

> 1. A.   "And at mealtime Boaz said to her, 'Come here and eat some bread, and dip your morsel in the wine.' So she sat beside the reapers, and he passed to her parched grain; and she ate until she was satisfied, and she had some left over":

B.   R. Yohanan interpreted the phrase "come here" in six ways:

C.   "The first speaks of David.

D.   "'Come here': means, to the throne: 'That you have brought me here' (2 Sam. 7:18).

E.   "'and eat some bread': the bread of the throne.

F.   "'and dip your morsel in vinegar': this speaks of his sufferings: 'O Lord, do not rebuke me in your anger' (Ps. 6:2).

G.   "'So she sat beside the reapers': for the throne was taken from him for a time."

H.   As R. Huna said, "The entire six months that David fled from Absalom are not counted in his reign, for he atoned for his sins with a she-goat, like an ordinary person [rather than with a he-goat, as does the king]."

I.   [Resuming from G:] "'and he passed to her parched grain': he was restored to the throne: 'Now I know that the Lord saves his anointed' (Ps. 20:7).

J.   "'and she ate and was satisfied and left some over': this indicates that he would eat in this world, in the days of the messiah, and in the age to come.

2. A.   "The second interpretation refers to Solomon: 'Come here': means, to the throne.

B.   "'and eat some bread': this is the bread of the throne: 'And Solomon's provision for one day was thirty measures of fine flour and three score measures of meal' (1 Kgs. 5:2).

C.   "'and dip your morsel in vinegar': this refers to the dirt of the deeds [that he did].

D.   "'So she sat beside the reapers': for the throne was taken from him for a time."

E.   For R. Yohai b. R. Hanina said, "An angel came down in the form of Solomon and sat on the throne, but he made the rounds of the doors throughout Israel and said, 'I, Qohelet, have been king over Israel in Jerusalem' (Qoh. 1:12).

F.   "What did one of them do? She set before him a plate of pounded beans and hit him on the head with a stick, saying, 'Doesn't Solomon sit on the throne? How can you say, "I am Solomon, king of Israel"?'"

G.   [Reverting to D:] "'and he passed to her parched grain': for he was restored to the throne.

H.   "'and she ate and was satisfied and left some over': this indicates that he would eat in this world, in the days of the messiah, and in the age to come.

3. A.   "The third interpretation speaks of Hezekiah: 'Come here': means, to the throne.

B.   "'and eat some bread': this is the bread of the throne.

C.   "'and dip your morsel in vinegar': this refers to sufferings [Isa. 5:1]: 'And Isaiah said, Let them take a cake of figs' (Isa. 38:21).

D.   "'So she sat beside the reapers': for the throne was taken from him for a time: 'Thus says Hezekiah, This day is a day of trouble and rebuke' (Isa. 37:3).

E. "'and he passed to her parched grain': for he was restored to the throne: 'So that he was exalted in the sight of all nations from then on' (2 Chr. 32:23).

F. "'and she ate and was satisfied and left some over': this indicates that he would eat in this world, in the days of the messiah, and in the age to come.

4. A. "The fourth interpretation refers to Manasseh: 'Come here': means, to the throne.

B. "'and eat some bread': this is the bread of the throne.

C. "'and dip your morsel in vinegar': for his dirty deeds were like vinegar, on account of wicked actions.

D. "'So she sat beside the reapers': for the throne was taken from him for a time: 'And the Lord spoke to Manasseh and to his people, but they did not listen. So the Lord brought them the captains of the host of the king of Assyria, who took Manasseh with hooks' (2 Chr. 33:10-11)."

E. R. Abba b. R. Kahana said, "With manacles."

F. Said R. Levi bar Hayyata, "They made him a bronze mule and put him on it and lit a fire underneath it, and he cried out, 'Idol thus-and-so, idol thus-and-so, save me!' When he realized that it did him no good at all, he said, 'I remember that Father would read in Scripture for me, "In your distress, when all these things have come upon you...he will not fail you" (Dt. 4:30). I will call on him. If he answers me, well and good, and if he does not answer me, then it's all the same. "Every face is like every other face."'

G. "At that moment the ministering angels went and shut all the windows above. They said before him, 'Lord of the world, a man who put up an idol in the holy temple will you accept back in repentance?'

H. "He said to them, 'If I don't take him back, lo, I will be locking the door against all those who return in repentance.'

I. "What did the Holy One, blessed be He, do? He dug a hole for him under the throne of his glory, in a place in which no angel can reach: 'And he prayed to him, and he was entreated by him and heard his supplication' (2 Chr. 33:13)."

J. Said R. Levi, "In Arabia they call a hole [by the same letters as are used in the word 'entreat']."

K. [Reverting to D:] "'and he passed to her parched grain': for he was restored to the throne: 'And brought him back to Jerusalem to his kingdom' (2 Chr. 33:13)."

L. How did he restore him?

M. R. Samuel in the name of R. Aha: "He brought him back with a wind, in line with the usage, 'who causes the wind to blow' [the letters for the word restore and blowing of the wind being the same]."

N. "'and she ate and was satisfied and left some over': this indicates that he would eat in this world, in the days of the messiah, and in the age to come.

5. A. "The fifth interpretation refers to the Messiah: 'Come here': means, to the throne.

B. "'and eat some bread': this is the bread of the throne.

C.   "'and dip your morsel in vinegar': this refers to suffering: 'But he
      was wounded because of our transgressions' (Isa. 53:5).

D.   "'So she sat beside the reapers': for the throne is destined to be
      taken from him for a time: 'For I will gather all nations against
      Jerusalem to battle and the city shall be taken' (Zech. 14:2).

E.   "'and he passed to her parched grain': for he will be restored to
      the throne: 'And he shall smite the land with the rod of his mouth'
      (Isa. 11:4)."

F.   R. Berekhiah in the name of R. Levi: "As was the first redeemer, so
      is the last redeemer:

G.   "Just as the first redeemer was revealed and then hidden from
      them –"

H.   And how long was he hidden? Three months: "And they met
      Moses and Aaron" (Ex. 5:20),

I.   [reverting to G:] "so the last redeemer will be revealed to them
      and then hidden from them."

J.   How long will he be hidden?

K.   R. Tanhuma in the name of rabbis: "Forty-five days: 'And from the
      time that the continual burnt-offering shall be taken away...there
      shall be a thousand two hundred and ninety days. Happy is the
      one who waits and comes to the thousand three hundred and
      thirty-five days' (Dan. 12:11-12)."

L.   What are the extra days?

M.   R. Isaac b. Qaseratah in the name of R. Jonah: "These are the
      forty-five days in which the Israelites will harvest [Rabinowitz, p.
      65:] saltwort and eat it: 'They pluck saltwort with wormwood' (Job
      30:45)."

N.   Where will he lead them?

O.   From the [holy] land to the wilderness of Judah: "Behold, I will
      entice her and bring her into the wilderness" (Hos. 2:16).

P.   Some say, "To the wilderness of Sihon and Og: 'I will yet again
      make you dwell in tents as in the days of the appointed season'
      (Hos. 12:10)."

Q.   And whoever believes in him will live.

R.   But whoever does not believe in him will go to the nations of
      idolatry, who will kill him.

S.   [Supply: "and she ate and was satisfied and left some over":] Said
      R. Isaac b. R. Merion, "In the end the Holy One, blessed be He,
      will be revealed upon them and bring down manna for them: 'And
      there is nothing new under the sun' (Qoh. 1:9)."

T.   "'and she ate and was satisfied and left some over':

6. A.   "The sixth interpretation refers to Boaz: 'Come here': [supply:]
          means, to the throne.

    B.   "'and eat some bread': this refers to the bread of the reapers.

    C.   "'and dip your morsel in vinegar': it is the practice of reapers to
          dip their bread in vinegar."

    D.   Said R. Jonathan, "On this basis we derive the rule that people
          bring out various kinds of [dishes made with] vinegar to the
          granaries."

    E.   [Reverting to C:] "'So she sat beside the reapers': this is meant
          literally.

F.	"'and he passed to her parched grain': a pinch between his two fingers."
G.	Said R. Isaac, "One might derive from this passage two rules:
H.	"either that a blessing [Rabinowitz, p. 66:] reposed between the fingers of that righteous man,
I.	"or that a blessing reposed between the fingers of that righteous woman.
J	"However, since Scripture states, 'and she ate and was satisfied and left some over,' it appears that the blessed reposed in the belly of that righteous woman."
7. A.	R. Isaac b. Marion said, "The verse ['and he passed to her parched grain; and she ate until she was satisfied, and she had some left over'] teaches you that if one carries out a religious duty, he should do it with a whole heart.
B.	"For had Reuben known that the Holy One, blessed be He, would have written concerning him, 'And Reuben heard it and delivered him out of their hand' (Gen. 37:21), he would have brought him on his shoulder back to his father.
C.	"And if Aaron had known that the Holy One, blessed be He, would have written concerning him, 'And also behold, he comes forth to meet you' (Ex. 4:14), he would have gone out to meet him with timbrels and dances.
D.	"And if Boaz had known that the Holy One, blessed be He, would have written concerning him, 'and he passed to her parched grain; and she ate until she was satisfied, and she had some left over,' he would have fed her with fatted calves."
8. A.	R. Kohen and R. Joshua of Sikhnin in the name of R. Levi: "In the past a person would do a religious duty and a prophet would inscribe it, but now when a person does a religious duty, who writes it down?
B.	"It is Elijah who writes it down, and the Messiah and the Holy One, blessed be He, affix their seals with their own hands:
C.	"'Then they who feared the Lord spoke with one another, and the Lord listened and heard and a book of remembrance was written before him' (Mal. 3:16)."

Nos. 1-6 form a beautifully crafted and utterly unitary composition, assigned to Yohanan, interpreting the base verse in six ways: David, Solomon, Hezekiah, Manasseh, the Messiah, and Boaz. The last, of course, is quite out of phase in the exegetical side, but fits beautifully in the redactional framework; Boaz of course produced the Messiah. His passage comes last solely for redactional reasons. In an autonomous setting, the Messiah would come at the end. But then Boaz is the only one whose reading of the verse is literal, and that marks the No. 6 as independent of the foregoing. While Nos. 1-6 then focus upon our base verse, for the framer of No. 7 it is simply one fact among a variety of facts that prove his main proposition. It is that if people knew the full value assigned to their deeds by Heaven, they would carry out those deeds with greater enthusiasm than they do ("a whole heart"). No. 8

is tacked on to No. 7 prior to insertion here; it makes no contribution to the interpretation of our base verse and is out of place except as a complement to No. 7. That of course is a commonplace component of the history of a composition: [1] composition joined to [2] a matched or pertinent or somehow-intersecting composition and [3] the whole then inserted where one or another of the parts makes a place for it, now without revision for the purposes of the larger composite in which it is included. We should not lose the main point in the quite natural engagement with this wonderful composition. It is that through the Torah, the Moabite woman has become an Israelite, imparting her character as originally a stranger and a woman upon what is now the center and heart of the life of holy Israel, the Messiah – all through mastery of the Torah. The plethora of details should not obscure the simple and repeated message of the Judaism of the Dual Torah: it is Torah alone that matters; here Torah unites opposites, makes the outsider an insider, allows the insider to retain the status of a woman – David's grandmother – and yet places him at the center of the system. Have I represented the document's message, or merely given some examples of a commonplace message that happens to come up in this document too? The answer derives from the following survey of the way in which, in the document seen whole, the same statement is repeated in one detail after another.

viii. Israel on its Own [2]: The Documentary Message Viewed Whole

Israel on its own concerns the holy nation's understanding of itself: who is Israel, who is not? Within the same rubric we find consideration of Israel's capacity to naturalize the outsider, so to define itself as to extend its own limits, and other questions of self-definition. And, finally, when Israel considers itself, a principal concern is the nature of leadership, for the leader stands for and embodies the people. Therein lies the paradox of the base document and the midrash compilation alike: how can the leader most wanted, the Messiah, come, as a matter of fact, from the excluded people and not from the holy people? Let us review it from the beginning to the end.

The sin of Israel, which caused the famine, was that it was judging its own judges. "He further said to the Israelites, 'So God says to Israel, "I have given a share of glory to the judges and I have called them gods, and they humiliate them. Woe to a generation that judges its judges"'" (I:i). The Israelites were slothful in burying Joshua, and that showed disrespect to their leader (II:i). They were slothful about repentance in the time of the judges, and that is what caused the famine; excess of commitment to one's own affairs leads to sin. The

Israelites did not honor the prophets (III:iii). The old have to bear with the young, and the young with the old, or Israel will go into exile (IV:i). The generation that judges its leadership ("judges") will be penalized (V:i). Arrogance to the authority of the Torah is penalized (V:i). Elimelech was punished because he broke the penalized heart; everyone depended upon him, and he proved undependable (V:iii); so bad leadership will destroy Israel. Why was Elimelech punished? It is because he broke the Israelites' heart. When the years of drought came, his maid went out into the marketplace, with her basket in her hand. So the people of the town said, "Is this the one on whom we depended, that he can provide for the whole town with ten years of food? Lo, his maid is standing in the marketplace with her basket in her hand!" So Elimelech was one of the great men of the town and one of those who sustained the generation. But when the years of famine came, he said, "Now all the Israelites are going to come knocking on my door, each with his basket." The leadership of a community is its glory: "The great man of a town – he is its splendor, he is its glory, he is its praise. When he has turned from there, so too have turned its splendor, glory, and praise" (XI:i.1C).

A distinct but fundamental component of the theory of Israel in its own terms concerns who is Israel and how one becomes a part of Israel. That theme, of course, proves fundamental to our document, so much of which is preoccupied with how Ruth can be the progenitor of the Messiah, deriving as she does not only from gentile but from Moabite stock. Israel's history follows rules that are to be learned in Scripture; nothing is random and all things are connected (IV:ii). The fact that the king of Moab honored God explains why God raised up from Moab "a son who will sit on the throne of the Lord" (VIII:i.3). The proselyte is discouraged but then accepted. Thus XVI:i..2B: "People are to turn a proselyte away. But if he is insistent beyond that point, he is accepted. A person should always push away with the left hand while offering encouragement with the right." Orpah, who left Naomi, was rewarded for the little that she did for her, but she was raped when she left her (XVIII:i.1-3). When Orpah went back to her people, she went back to her gods (XIX:i).

Ruth's intention to convert was absolutely firm, and Naomi laid out all the problems for her, but she acceded to every condition (XX:i). Thus she said, "Under all circumstances I intend to convert, but it is better that it be through your action and not through that of another." When Naomi heard her say this, she began laying out for her the laws that govern proselytes. She said to her, "My daughter, it is not the way of Israelite women to go to theaters and circuses put on by idolators." She said to her, "Where you go I will go." She said to her,

"My daughter, it is not the way of Israelite women to live in a house that lacks a *mezuzah.*" She said to her, "Where you lodge I will lodge." "Your people shall be my people": This refers to the penalties and admonitions against sinning. "And your God my God": This refers to the other religious duties. And so onward: "for where you go I will go": to the tent of meeting, Gilgal, Shiloh, Nob, Gibeon, and the eternal house. "And where you lodge I will lodge": "I shall spend the night concerned about the offerings." "Your people shall be my people": "so nullifying my idol." "And your God my God": "to pay a full recompense for my action." I find here the centerpiece of the compilation and its principal purpose. The same message is at XXI:i.1-3.

Proselytes are respected by God, so XXII:i: "And when Naomi saw that she was determined to go with her, [she said no more]": Said R. Judah b. R. Simon, "Notice how precious are proselytes before the Omnipresent. Once she had decided to convert, the Scripture treats her as equivalent to Naomi." Boaz, for his part, was equally virtuous and free of sins (XXVI:i). The law provided for the conversion of Ammonite and Moabite women, but not Ammonite and Moabite men, so the acceptance of Ruth the Moabite was fully in accord with the law, and anyone who did not know that fact was an ignoramus (XXVI:i.4, among many passages). An Israelite hero who came from Ruth and Boaz was David, who was a great master of the Torah, thus he was "Skillful in playing, and a mighty man of war, prudent in affairs, good-looking, and the Lord is with him" (1 Sam. 16:18): "Skillful in playing" in Scripture; "...and a mighty man of valor" in Mishnah; "...a man of war" who knows the give and take of the war of the Torah; "...prudent in affairs" in good deeds; "...good-looking" in Talmud; "...prudent in affairs" able to reason deductively; "...good-looking" enlightened in law; "...and the Lord is with him" the law accords with his opinions.

Ruth truly accepted Judaism upon the instruction, also, of Boaz (XXXIV:i), thus: "Then Boaz said to Ruth, 'Now listen, my daughter, do not go to glean in another field": This is on the strength of the verse, "You shall have no other gods before me" (Ex. 20:3). "'or leave this one'": This is on the strength of the verse, "This is my God and I will glorify him" (Ex. 15:2). "But keep close to my maidens": This speaks of the righteous, who are called maidens: "Will you play with him as with a bird, or will you bind him for your maidens" (Job 40:29). The glosses invest the statement with a vast tapestry of meaning. Boaz speaks to Ruth as a Jew by choice, and the entire exchange is now typological. Note also the typological meanings imputed at XXXV:i.1-5. Ruth had prophetic power (XXXVI:ii). Ruth was rewarded for her sincere conversion by Solomon (XXXVIII:i.1).

Taking shelter under the wings of the Presence of God, which is what the convert does, is the greatest merit accorded to all who do deeds of grace, thus: So notice the power of the righteous and the power of righteousness, the power of those who do deeds of grace. For they take shelter not in the shadow of the dawn, nor in the shadow of the wings of the earth, nor in the shadow of the wings of the sun, nor in the shadow of the wings of the hayyot, nor in the shadow of the wings of the cherubim or the seraphim. But under whose wings do they take shelter? "They take shelter under the shadow of the One at whose word the world was created: 'How precious is your loving kindness O God, and the children of men take refuge in the shadow of your wings' (Ps. 36:8)." The language that Boaz used to Ruth, "Come here," – as we saw above – bore with it deeper reference to six: David, Solomon, the throne as held by the Davidic monarchy, and ultimately, the Messiah, e.g., in the following instance: "The fifth interpretation refers to the Messiah: 'Come here': means, to the throne. "'And eat some bread': this is the bread of the throne. "'And dip your morsel in vinegar': this refers to suffering: 'But he was wounded because of our transgressions' (Isa. 53:5). "'So she sat beside the reapers': for the throne is destined to be taken from him for a time: For I will gather all nations against Jerusalem to battle and the city shall be taken' (Zech. 14:2). "'And he passed to her parched grain': for he will be restored to the throne: 'And he shall smite the land with the rod of his mouth' (Isa. 11:4)." R. Berekhiah in the name of R. Levi: "As was the first redeemer, so is the last redeemer: "Just as the first redeemer was revealed and then hidden from them, so the last redeemer will be revealed to them and then hidden from them" (XL:i.1ff.).

Boaz instructed Ruth on how to be a proper Israelite woman, so LIII:i: "Wash yourself": from the filth of idolatry that is yours. "And anoint yourself": this refers to the religious deeds and acts of righteousness [that are required of an Israelite]. "And put on your best clothes": this refers to her Sabbath clothing. So did Naomi encompass Ruth within Israel: "and go down to the threshing floor": She said to her, "My merit will go down there with you." Moab, hence Ruth came, was conceived not for the sake of fornication but for the sake of Heaven (LV:i.1B). Boaz, for his part, was a master of the Torah and when he ate and drank, that formed a typology for his study of the Torah (LVI:i). His was a life of grace, Torah study, and marriage for holy purposes. Whoever trusts in God is exalted, and that refers to Ruth and Boaz; God put it in his heart to bless her (LVII:i).

The role of the grandmother, the Moabite Ruth, is underlined, emphasized, celebrated. For example, David sang psalms to thank God for his grandmother, Ruth, so LIX:i.5, "[At midnight I will rise to give thanks to you] because of your righteous judgments" (Ps. 119:62): [David speaks,] "The acts of judgment that you brought upon the Ammonites and Moabites. And the righteous deeds that you carried out for my grandfather and my grandmother [Boaz, Ruth, of whom David speaks here]. For had he hastily cursed her but once, where should I have come from? But you put in his heart the will to bless her: 'And he said, "May you be blessed by the Lord." Because of the merit of the six measures that Boaz gave Ruth, six righteous persons came forth from him, each with six virtues: David, Hezekiah, Josiah, Hananiah, Mishael, Azariah, Daniel and the royal Messiah.'"

God facilitated the union of Ruth and Boaz (LXVIII:i). Boaz's relative was ignorant for not knowing that while a male Moabite was excluded, a female one was acceptable for marriage. The blessing of Boaz was, "May all the children you have come from this righteous woman" (LXXIX:i), and that is precisely the blessing accorded to Isaac and to Elkanah. God made Ruth an ovary, which she had lacked (LXXX:i). Naomi was blessed with messianic blessings (LXXXI:i), thus: "Then the women said to Naomi, 'Blessed be the Lord, who has not left you this day without next of kin; and may his name be renowned in Israel'": Just as "this day" rules dominion in the firmament, so will your descendants rule and govern Israel forever. On account of the blessings of the women, the line of David was not wholly exterminated in the time of Athaliah.

David was ridiculed because he was descended from Ruth, the Moabitess, so LXXXV:i. But many other distinguished families derived from humble origins. "Said David before the Holy One, blessed be He, 'How long will they rage against me and say, "Is his family not invalid [for marriage into Israel]? Is he not descended from Ruth the Moabitess?"' '"Commune with your own heart upon your bed': [David continues,]. 'You too have you not descended from two sisters? You look at your own origins and shut up.'" '"So Tamar who married your ancestor Judah – is she not of an invalid family? 'But she was only a descendant of Shem, son of Noah. So do you come from such impressive genealogy?'" David referred to and defended his Moabite origins, so LXXXIX:i: "Then I said, Lo, I have come [in the roll of the book it is written of me]' (Ps. 40:8). "[David says,] 'Then I had to recite a song when I came, for the word "then" refers only to a song, as it is said, "Then sang Moses" (Ex. 15:1). '"I was covered by the verse, 'An Ammonite and a Moabite shall not come into the assembly of the Lord' (Dt. 23:4),, but I have come "in the roll of the book it is written of me" (Ps. 40:8). "in the roll": this refers to the verse, [David continues], "concerning whom you commanded that they should not enter into your congregation" (Lam. 1:10). '""of the book it is written of me": "An

Ammonite and a Moabite shall not enter into the assembly of the Lord" (Dt. 23:4). "'It is not enough that I have come, but in the roll and the book it is written concerning me: ""'In the roll": Perez, Hezron, Ram, Amminadab, Nahshon, Salmon, Boaz, Obed, Jesse, David. ""'In the book": "And the Lord said, Arise, anoint him, for this is he'" (1 Sam. 16:12)."

ix Ruth in Particular

I should misrepresent the character of the document if I did not take note, also, of many passages that are exegetical in a narrow sense: explain, paraphrase, amplify words and phrases. In these entries that concern the exposition of verses of the book of Ruth I find no messages that I can frame in a propositional way, though of course throughout there are implicit meanings that cohere with the propositions I have just now catalogued. A fair sample of such passages, catalogued below, rely – predictably – on fixed associative logic and commentary form. It is true that we might simply impute to these passages whatever the intention of the verse of Scripture may be, but even the (from this viewpoint) banalities of Scripture are not expressed. The focus in what follows is solely the amplification of the words of the book of Ruth. The numerous phrase-by-phrase exegeses seem to me not to coalesce into a few fundamental propositions, endlessly illustrated or repeated. In the items listed here, I find nothing more than ad hoc and episodic clarifications of this and that: VI:ii, VIII:i, XII:i.1-6, XIII:i, XV:i, XVII:i, ii, iii, XXII:i.1-5, XXIV:i, XXV:i, XXVIII:i, XXIX:i, XXXI:i.1, XXXII:i, XXXIII:i, XXXVII:i, XLIII:i, XLVI:i, XLVII:i, XLIX:i, LIII:i, LVIII:i, LXI:i, LXII:i, LXIII:i, LXIV:i, LXV:i, LXXI:i, LXXVIII:i, LXXXII:i, LXXXVI:i, LXXXVII:i. These do not form a very large portion of the whole.

x. Passages with Propositions Not Relevant to the Book of Ruth

Various other passages also have either no clear proposition, or none pertinent to our book in particular. In the following I catalogue the philological-propositional and the sustained-exegetical passages not pertinent to the book of Ruth. These too do not form a large proportion of the whole.[2]

---

[2]It is noteworthy that these items commonly occur in more than a single document, which is quite natural, since they belong in particular nowhere. One of the marks of the itinerant compositions is that they ordinarily stand autonomous of every document in which they occur. In my *Making the Classics in Judaism: The Three Stages of Literary Formation.* (Atlanta, 1990:

IV:ii	The meaning of the word "and it came to pass."
V:ii	There were ten famines that affected the world. One will take place in the world to come.
VI:i	The purpose of the book of Chronicles is only for interpretation and not for a literal reading.
VII:i	People die in cohorts; happy is the person who leaves this world with a good name.
IX:i	God injures property, then persons, so as to give people a chance to repent. This proposition has no bearing upon the theme of the book of Ruth in particular.
XVIII:i.4	Every act of kissing is frivolous except for three: meeting, departing, and inauguration.
XXI:i.4	After death, one cannot repent. It is best to live well in this life because later on there is no rewriting the record. A long series of stories illustrates this point.
XXVII:i.5	The name of the wicked is given before Scripture gives the name, and the name of the righteous is given afterward.
XXX:i	There were three decrees that the earthly court issued, and the heavenly court concurred in their decision. And these are the ones: [1] to give greetings using the name of God; [2] the scroll of Esther; [3] and tithing."
XXXI:i.2-3	A virtuous person always signals virtue through his deeds.
XXXVI:i	The interpretation of 1 Chr. 11:13-14 occupies the entire composition, reading the biblical story typologically as an account of Torah study.
XXXIX:i	The peculiarity of spelling is interpreted.
XLII:i	
XLV:i	More than the householder does for the poor, the poor does for the householder. How people treat the poor determines the destiny of the nation. There are various propositions on poverty and on helping the poor.
LIX:i	David would study the Torah.
LXII:ii	
LXII:iii	There were three who were tempted by their inclination to do evil, but who strengthened themselves against it by taking an oath, Joseph, David, and Boaz.
LXVI:i	"In every place in which the Israelites came, they did not go forth empty-handed. From the spoil of Egypt they did not go forth empty-handed. From the spoil of Sihon and Og they did not go forth empty-handed. From the spoil of the thirty-one kings they did not go forth empty-handed."
LXVII:i	"The yes said by a righteous person is yes, their no is a no."
LXIX:i	An unimportant person has not got the right to take his seat before the more important person invites him to do so. This ruling house [David's, hence the patriarch's at this time] appoints elders [to the governing body, even] in their banquet

---

Scholars Press for Brown Judaic Studies) I have explained what is at stake in these remarks.

halls!"] The blessing of the bridegroom requires a quorum of ten.

LXXV:i.1-4   The mode of solving the problem of an obscure antecedent of a pronoun.

xi. The Message of Ruth Rabbah

To speak of "messages" in the midrash compilation, Ruth Rabbah, simply is misleading. Our document has only one message, which is expressed in a variety of components but is single and cogent. It concerns the outsider who becomes the principal, the Messiah out of Moab, and this miracle is accomplished through mastery of the Torah. I find these points:

[1] Israel's fate depends upon its proper conduct toward its leaders.

[2] The leaders must not be arrogant.

[3] The admission of the outsider depends upon the rules of the Torah. These differentiate among outsiders. Those who know the rules are able to apply them accurately and mercifully.

[4] The proselyte is accepted because the Torah makes it possible to do so, and the condition of acceptance is complete and total submission to the Torah. Boaz taught Ruth the rules of the Torah, and she obeyed them carefully.

[5] Those proselytes who are accepted are respected by God and are completely equal to all other Israelites. Those who marry them are masters of the Torah, and their descendants are masters of the Torah, typified by David. Boaz in his day and David in his day were the same in this regard.

[6] What the proselyte therefore accomplishes is to take shelter under the wings of God's presence, and the proselyte who does so stands in the royal line of David, Solomon, and the Messiah. Over and over again, we see, the point is made that Ruth the Moabitess, perceived by the ignorant as an outsider, enjoyed complete equality with all other Israelites, because she had accepted the yoke of the Torah, married a great sage, and produced the Messiah-sage, David.

Scripture has provided everything but the main point: the story, the irritant: the Moabite Messiah. But our sages impose upon the whole their distinctive message, which is the priority of the Torah, the extraordinary power of the Torah to join the opposites – Messiah, utter outsider – into a single figure, and, as I said, to accomplish this union of opposites through a woman. The femininity of Ruth seems to me as critical to the whole, therefore, as the Moabite origin: the two modes of the (from the Israelite perspective) abnormal, outsider as against Israelite, woman as against man, therefore are invoked, and both for the same purpose, to show how, through the Torah, all things become one. That is the message of the document, and, I think, seen whole, the principal message, to which all other messages prove peripheral.

xii. Writing and Repeating with Scripture

We began with the observation that through Scripture the sages accomplished their writing, and we have further noted throughout that it is not so much by writing fresh discourses as by compiling and arranging materials that the framers of the document accomplished that writing. It would be difficult to find a less promising mode of writing than merely collecting and arranging available compositions and turning them into a composite. But that in the aggregate is the predominant trait of this writing. That our compilers were equally interested in the exposition of the book of Ruth as in the execution of their paramount proposition through their compilation is clear. For we have a large number of entries that contain no more elaborate proposition than the exposition through paraphrase of the sense of a given clause or verse.

Indeed, Ruth Rabbah proves nearly as much a commentary in the narrowest sense – verse by verse amplification, paraphrase, exposition – as it is a compilation in the working definition of this inquiry of mine. What holds the document together and gives it, if not coherence, then at least flow and movement, after all, are the successive passages of (mere) exposition. All the more stunning, therefore, is the simple fact that, when all has been set forth and completed, there really is that simple message that the Torah (as exemplified by the sage) makes the outsider into an insider, the Moabite into an Israelite, the offspring of the outsider into the Messiah: all on the condition, the only condition, that the Torah govern. This is a document about one thing, and it makes a single statement, and that statement is coherent.

As a matter of fact, Lamentations Rabbah likewise deals with one topic, which is God's unique relationship with Israel. It makes a single statement about that topic, which is that the relationship of God to Israel is unique among the nations, that relationship works itself out even now, in a time of despair and disappointment. The resentment of the present condition, recapitulating the calamity of the destruction of the Temple, finds its resolution and remission in the redemption that will follow Israel's regeneration through the Torah – that is the program, that is the proposition, and in this compilation, there is no other. And, it goes without saying, I also have been able to identify the single topic and message of Esther Rabbah I. It concerns Israel among the nations. It is that the nations are swine, their rulers fools, and Israel is subjugated to them, though it should not be, because of its own sins. But just as God saved Israel in the past, so the salvation that Israel can attain will recapitulate the former ones. The theme, then, is Israel among the nations; on that theme, the sages propose a proposition entirely familiar from the books of Deuteronomy through Kings, on the one side, and much of prophetic literature, on the other.

The proposition is familiar, and so is the theme; but since the book of Esther can hardly be characterized as "deuteronomic," lacking all interest in the covenant, the land, and issues of atonement (beyond the conventional sackcloth, ashes, and fasting, hardly the fodder for prophetic regeneration and renewal!), the sages' distinctive viewpoint in the document must be deemed an original and interesting contribution of their own. The compilers of Esther Rabbah I, who, like the compilers of Ruth Rabbah, really constituted an authorship, a single, single-minded and determined group (whether of one or ten or two hundred workers hardly matters) set forth their variation on a very old and profoundly rooted theology. If I have to identify one recurrent motif that captures that theology, it is the critical role of Esther and Mordecai, particularly Mordecai, who, as sage, emerges in the position of messiah. Here again the theme of the sage-Messiah proves paramount, now through the figure of Mordecai alongside Esther, as much as, in Ruth Rabbah, the theme is worked out through David alongside Ruth.

xiii. Writing with Scripture, Writing with Symbols: Rational Discourse and Emotional Transaction

What that now-demonstrated fact of description of the compilation means is simple. Our authorship decided to compose a document concerning the book of Ruth in order to make a single point. Everything else was subordinated to that definitive intention. Once the work got underway, the task was one of not exposition so much as repetition, not unpacking and exploring a complex conception, but restating the point, on the one side, and eliciting or evoking the proper attitude that was congruent with that point, on the other. The decision, viewed after the fact, was to make one statement in an enormous number of ways. This highly restricted program of thought resorted to a singularly varied vocabulary. Indeed, some might call it a symbolic vocabulary, in that messages are conveyed not through propositions but through images, whether visual or verbal.

Since, as they responded to it, Scripture supplied a highly restricted vocabulary, the message was singular, the meanings were few and to be repeated, not many and to be cast aside promiscuously. When we find the "another-interpretation" sequences, we see how this works: a great many ways are found to say some one thing. That is why we do not find endless multiple meanings[3] but a highly limited repertoire of a few cogent and wholly coherent meanings, to be replayed again and again. It is the repetitious character of discourse, in which people say the same thing in a great many different ways, that characterizes this document. The reason for the repetition is simple: it is through a re-presentation of the simple symbolic vocabulary that the messages emerge.

So through propositional discourse on the one side and through narrative on the other – the one aiming at the intellect, the other at the emotions – our compilers set forth their variation. What was new to them was not the message but the medium. It was one thing to write with Scripture; that had been done before. It was quite another to write by collecting and arranging verses of Scripture in such a way that many things were made to say one thing. In Ruth Rabbah, many things do say one thing, and here, we see, God lives not only in the details, but in the repetition of details, always in the same way, always with the same message. Everything says one thing, and that one thing is, the Torah dictates Israel's fate, if you want to know what that fate will be, study the Torah, and if you want to control that fate, follow the model of the sage-Messiah, in whom are formed the perfect unions of outsider, woman, Moabite and insider, man, Israelite, all one in the Torah of Moses our rabbi.

---

[3]Cf. William Scott Green, "Romancing the Tome: Rabbinic Hermeneutics and the Theory of Literature," *Semeia* 1987, 40:147-169, *Text and Textuality*, ed. Charles Winquist, with special reference to p. 163: "If it is doubtful that rabbis ascribed 'endless multiple meanings' to scripture, it is no less so that rabbinic hermeneutics encouraged and routinely tolerated the metonymical coexistence of different meanings of scripture that did not, and could not, annul one another."

Part Two

WHEN IS "ANOTHER THING" THE SAME THING? THE THEOLOGICAL UNITY OF DISCRETE SYMBOLS

4

Cases of *Davar Aher* in Genesis Rabbah

i. The Issue

Our initial task is to ask whether, when we find "another matter," that is, *davar aher*, what follows says something different from the preceding composition, or says the same thing in other words, or says something complementary and necessary to make some larger point. It suffices for the present stage in the inquiry to examine a variety of cases, both those in which *davar aher* is explicit, as well as those in which that formula, which can be contributed by a scribe and is hardly demanded by the requirements of rhetoric, is left implicit but necessary. Further, we shall want to know whether the use of the formula in one document differs from the function served by it in another; specifically, do the *davar-aher* compositions in a given compilation differ in any important way from those in another. In the nature of things, all I offer at this point is a preliminary probe, with an equally provisional hypothesis under consideration. The hypothesis derives from Green's observation, cited earlier:

> Although the interpretations in this passage are formally distinguished from one another...by the disjunctive device *davar aher* ('another interpretation'), they operate within a limited conceptual sphere and a narrow thematic range....Thus rather than 'endless multiple meanings,' they in fact ascribe to the words 'doing wonders' multiple variations of a single meaning....By providing multiple warrant for that message, the form effectively restricts the interpretive options...

My hypothesis is that when we have a sequence of *davar aher*s, the message is cumulative and forms a sum greater than that of the parts; it

73

will then be that accumulation that guides us to what is if implicit yet fundamental in the exact sense: at the foundation of matters; there is where we should find that system, order, proportion, cogency that all together we expect a theology to impart to discrete observations about holy matters. In contemporary language, God may live in the details, but only when the details highlight the structure of which they are part. In a well-crafted system, as I have argued time and again, the entire systemic statement should be accessible in any detail of the system (in the context of the Moabite Messiah, as we noted, the generative symbol, Torah, is ubiquitous).

To begin with, we simply survey evidence and examine its overall traits. In this and the next four chapters, we consider more or less random samples of the usages, ordinarily explicit, sometimes not, of "another matter." We note that the single routine venue for the incidence of the formula is in the intersecting-verse/base-verse construction, in which a variety of readings of an intersecting verse is meant to clarify the message and meaning of the base verse. Thus a verse in Psalms will be asked to impart its meaning to a verse in Genesis, or of Chronicles to one in Esther. Here the chain of alternative readings of that intersecting verse of Psalms or Chronicles will prove, time and again, to say one thing many times. But *davar-aher* compositions are by no means limited to that form. Not only so, but our quest for a method of theological description would scarcely have reached its goal with that limited observation.

For even if we conclude that *davar-aher* compositions in general say the same thing in different ways, that one thing need not be a theological statement at all. When we come to Song of Songs Rabbah, however, we shall see why the theological inquiry proves well conceived when we focus upon that one thing that is said through many things.

The method throughout what follows is simple. We shall *simply review composites of compositions* in situ *and see how the davar-aher* materials appear and what they mean to say, in the discrete compositions, in the complex composites, through five compilations: Genesis Rabbah, Esther Rabbah I, Ruth Rabbah, Song of Songs Rabbah, and Lamentations Rabbah.

ii. Genesis Rabbah XXI:IX

XXI:IX.

1.   A   "And at the east [of the garden of Eden he placed the cherubim and a flaming sword which turned every way, to guard the way to the tree of life]" (Gen. 3:24):

B.   Rab said, "Under all circumstances the east provides refuge.

C.   "As to the first man: 'He drove out the man, and caused him to dwell at the east of the garden of Eden' (Gen. 3:24).

D.   "Cain: 'And Cain went out from the presence of the Lord and dwelt in the land of Nod, on the east of Eden' (Gen. 4:16).

E.   "The one guilty of manslaughter: 'Then Moses set aside three cities on the other side of the Jordan towards the sunrise' (Deut. 4:41), that is, on the east."

2.   A.   Another interpretation of "at the east":

B.   The consonants of the word for "east" bear the meaning, "prior."

C.   Before the garden of Eden, the angels were created, in line with this verse: "This is the living creature that I saw under the God of Israel by the river Chebar, and I knew that they were cherubim" (Ezek. 10:20).

3.   A.   "[He placed the cherubim] and a flaming sword which turned every way]" (Gen. 3:24):

B.   This is in line with the following verse: "His ministers are as flaming fire" (Ps. 104:4).

4.   A.   "...which turned every way..." (Gen. 3:24):

B.   Which turn from one thing to something else, sometimes appearing as men, sometimes as women, sometimes as spirits, sometimes as angels.

5.   A.   Another interpretation of "at the east":

B.   The consonants of the word for "east" bear the meaning, "prior."

C.   Before the garden of Eden, Gehenna was created.

D.   Gehenna was created on the second day of the week of creation, and the Garden of Eden on the third.

6.   A.   "...and a flaming sword...":

B.   This is in line with the verse, "And the day that comes shall set them aflame" (Mal. 3:19).

7.   A.   "...that turned every way...":

B.   For it turns around a man and burns him up from his head to his feet.

C.   Said man, "Who will save my descendants from this burning flame?"

8.   A.   R. Huna in the name of R. Abba: "The 'sword' speaks of circumcision in line with the verse that follows: 'Make yourselves knives of flint and circumcise again' (Josh. 5:2)."

B.   Rabbis say, "The sword refers to Torah: 'And a two edged sword in their hand' (Ps. 149:6).

C.   "When the first man saw that his descendants were destined to burn in Gehenna, he refrained from having sexual relations. But when he saw that after twenty-six generations, Israel was destined to accept the Torah, he determined to produce offspring.

D.   "'Now Adam knew Eve his wife...' (Gen. 4:1)."

Here we do not find "another matter" made explicit, but we do have a sequence of carefully matched compositions formed into a composite. I see two groups before us, Nos. 1-4, dealing with the family above, namely, angels, and Nos. 5-8, dealing with the family below, namely, Israel. The former set, beginning with Rab's comment, sees the

point of the passage as the establishment of a protection and refuge for
man near the Garden of Eden. God set up the sword and the cherubim to
protect man. The first set, then emphasizes that angels were created
prior to the fall. The second set places its stress on the creation of
Gehenna, symbolized by the flaming sword. Then comes the climax:
"Who will save my descendants," with the answer that circumcision,
which stands for the commandments, an appropriate symbol because
circumcision makes use of a knife, hence, the sword. That commandment
and receiving the Torah through study of Torah are what will save
man. The conclusion then is reached at the reference to Sinai. The
revelation of the Torah will mark the redemption of man from the fall.
Then the first man is willing to produce descendants because he foresaw
that, twenty-six generations later, the Torah would come and save
man's descendants. It is a strikingly homogeneous construction
throughout, with two matching pairs, each making a necessary point.
Normally, the supernatural and heavenly dimension will be stated
first, then the historical and this-worldly one, involving Israel, and
that, of course, is the sequence before us. When I claim that *davar-aher*
compositions say one thing in several ways, this is a good example of
what I mean.

iii. Genesis Rabbah XXXII:I

XXXII:I.

1. A   "Then the Lord said to Noah, 'Go into the ark, you and all your household, for I have seen that you are righteous before me in this generation'" (Gen. 7:1):

    B.   "You destroy those who speak lies, [the Lord abhors bloodthirsty and deceitful men. But I through the abundance of your steadfast love will enter your house]" (Ps. 5:6-7):

    C.   This ["You destroy those who speak lies"], refers to Doeg and Ahitophel.

    D   "Those that speak falsehood" refers to them and what they have to say.

    E.   R. Phineas said, "To them and their allies."

    F.   "Blood thirsty and deceitful men": This one [Doeg] permitted fornication and murder, and that one [Ahitophel] permitted fornication and murder.

    G.   "This one [Ahitophel] permitted fornication and murder": [For he advised Absalom, "Go in unto your father's concubines" (2 Sam. 16:21).

    H.   "That one [Doeg] permitted fornication and murder": Said R. Nahman b. Samuel b. Nahman, "He took away the civil rights [of David] and made him an outlaw, as one who was dead, so that it was permitted to shed his blood, and his wife was made available to anyone."

    I.   "The Lord abhors" (Ps. 5:6):

J.   For those two will not live in the resurrection of the dead nor be subjected to judgment.

K.   "But I": [David points out,] "What they did I did too, so what is the difference between me and them? But you had mercy on me and said to me, 'The Lord also has put away your sin, you shall not die'" (2 Sam. 12:13).

2 A.   ["You destroy those who speak lies, the Lord abhors bloodthirsty and deceitful men. But I through the abundance of your steadfast love will enter your house" (Ps. 5:6-7]: This verse speaks of the generation of the flood.

B.   "You destroy those who speak lies" means, both they and what they say.

C.   "Bloodthirsty [and deceitful men]": "The murderer rises with the light" (Job 24:14).

D.   "And deceitful": "For the earth is filled with violence" (Gen. 6:13).

E.   "The Lord abhors": For they will neither live [at the resurrection of the dead] nor be judged.

F.   "[But I through the abundance of your steadfast love will enter your house" (Ps. 5:7).] "But I": [Noah points out,] "What they did I did too, so what is the difference between me and them? But you had mercy on me and said to me, 'Go into the ark, you and all your household' (Gen. 7:1)."

We now compare two salvific figures, David and Noah. Neither one has any independent claim, both relying on God's grace. Neither one was much better than his adversaries. Each differed from his enemies in his submission to God's will. No. 1 has David speak the intersecting verse, No. 2, Noah. The sense of the verse in both compositions is the same, but the application differs. The net effect is to point again to the counterpart between the history of humanity and the history of Israel, with Noah now serving as the nations' equivalent to David.

iv. Genesis Rabbah LXV:X-XI

LXV:X.

1. A.   "[When Isaac was old, and his eyes were dim,] so that he could not see, [he called Esau his older son, and said to him, 'My son,' and he answered, 'Here I am']" (Gen. 27:1):

B.   R. Eleazar b. Azariah said, "'...so that he could not see' the wickedness of the wicked person.

C.   "Said the Holy One, blessed be He, 'Should Isaac go out to the market and have people say, "Here is the father of that wicked man."

D.   "'It is better that I make his eyes dim, so he will stay home.'

E.   "So it is written, 'When the wicked rise, men hide themselves' (Prov. 28:28).

F.   "On the basis of this verse, they have said, 'Whoever raises a wicked son or a wicked disciple will have his eyes grow dim.'

G.   "The case of the wicked disciple derives from Ahijah the Shilonite, who raised up Jeroboam, so his eyes grew dim: 'Now Ahijah could not see, for his eyes were set by reason of his old age' (1 Kgs. 14:4). It was because he had produced Jeroboam, the wicked disciple.

H.   "As for a wicked son, that is shown by the case of Isaac."

2. A.   Another matter: "So that he could not see..."

B.   It was on account of that spectacle [at Moriah].

C.   Now at the moment at which our father, Abraham, bound Isaac his son, the ministering angels wept. That is in line with this verse: "Behold, their valiant ones cry outside" (Isa. 33:7).

D.   The tears fell from their eyes into his and made a mark on them, so when he got old, his eyes dimmed: "When Isaac was old, and his eyes were dim, so that he could not see..."

3. A.   Another matter: "So that he could not see...."

B.   It was on account of that spectacle.

C.   Now at the moment at which our father, Abraham, bound Isaac his son, he looked upward and gazed upon the Presence of God.

D.   They made a parable. The case may be compared to that of a king who was strolling in the gate of his palace, and he looked up and saw the son of his ally peeking in and gazing at him through a window. He said, "If I put him to death, I shall alienate my ally. But I shall give a decree that his windows be stopped up [so he will not do this again].

E.   Now at the moment at which our father, Abraham, bound Isaac his son, he looked upward and gazed upon the Presence of God. Said the Holy One, blessed be He, "If I put him to death, I shall alienate Abraham, my ally. But I shall give a decree that his eyes should be stopped up [so he will not do this again]."

F.   "When Isaac was old, and his eyes were dim, so that he could not see...."

LXV:XI.

1. A.   "When Isaac was old, and his eyes were dim, so that he could not see, he called Esau his older son, and said to him, 'My son,' and he answered, 'Here I am'" (Gen. 27:1):

B.   Said R. Eleazar b. R. Simeon, "The matter may be compared to the case of a town that was collecting a bodyguard for the king. There was a woman there, whose son was a dwarf. She called him 'Tallswift' [Freedman]. She said, 'My son is "Tallswift," so why do you not take him?'

C.   "They said to her, 'If in your eyes he is "Tallswift," in our eyes he is a dwarf.'

D.   "So his father called him 'great': '...he called Esau his great son.' So too his mother called him 'great': 'Then Rebecca took the best garments of Esau, her great son.'

E.   "Said the Holy One, blessed be He, to them, 'If in your eyes he is great, in my eyes he is small: "Behold, I make you small among the nations"' (Obad. 1:2) [speaking of Edom/Esau/Rome]."

2. A.   Said R. Abbahu said R. Berekhiah, "In accord with the size of the ox is the stature of the slaughter.

B. "That is in line with the following verse: 'For the Lord has a sacrifice in Bozrah, and a great slaughter in the land of Edom' (Isa. 34:6)."

C. Said R. Berekhiah, "The sense is, 'There will be a great slaughter in the land of Edom.' [Freedman, p. 587, n. 2: Since Esau is called great, his slaughterer, God, will likewise be great.]"

3. A. "...he called Esau his older son, and said to him, 'My son,' and he answered, 'Here I am'" (Gen. 27:1):

B. That [credulity on the part of Isaac] is in line with this verse: "When he speaks fair, do not believe him [for there are seven abominations in his heart]" (Prov. 26:25). [Isaac should never have believed Esau.]

C. Hezekiah the translator said, "'For there are seven abominations in his heart' (Prov. 26:25).

D. "You find that while the Torah speaks of a single abomination, in point of fact ten abominations are stated in that connection.

E. "It is written, 'There shall not be found among you any one who makes his son or his daughter pass through the fire...or a charmer or one who consults a ghost or a familiar spirit or a necromancer. For whoever does these things is an abomination to the Lord' (Deut. 18:11).

F. "Here is a case [referring to Esau, as stated above] in which seven are mentioned, how much the more so is it the case: 'For there are seven abominations in his heart' (Prov. 26:25) means that in fact there are seventy abominations in his heart."

LXV:X No. 1 explains Isaac's blindness in the familiar framework; he tolerated Esau's wicked ways or at least had to be protected from them. Nos. 2, 3 then link the blindness to something he saw when he was bound on the altar. The parable is striking, since it presents the blindness as an act of mercy on God's part. The union of the several "another matters" is seen in a simple statement: he could not see the wickedness of the wicked person; he could not see because he had lost his eyesight at Moriah; this was God's action. The parable immediately following restates the same point, which is that Isaac's blindness was moral, not merely physical. Ordinarily, parables bear no autonomous message but restate in narrative form a message that has already been expressed and spelled out. The remainder goes its own way. I include it to show how the *davar-aher* compositions really hold together conceptually and stand apart from their context fore and aft. The parable of XLV:IXI powerfully makes the point of the exegete: only in the parents' eyes was Esau "great." Thus at No. 1 the reference to the older son is explained away. In no way was Esau the elder, and Jacob's action was justified. No. 2 works out a different meaning for the same reference. No. 3 moves on to the exchange in which Esau responds faithfully to Isaac, making the point that Isaac should never have believed Esau on any terms, as Scripture says.

v. Genesis Rabbah LXX:VIII-IX

Thus far all we have seen is cogency. What makes me claim that the cogency is implicitly systemic, not merely thematic? The following seems to me to constitute nothing less than a theological statement of a systemic and orderly character. The six ways in which the base verse is read – all of them thus "another matter" – coalesce into a complete "Judaism," that is, an account of a worldview, a way of life, and a social entity that understands itself by reference to the one and that realizes the other in its life.

LXX:VIII.

2   A.   "As he looked, he saw a well in the field":

    B.   R. Hama bar Hanina interpreted the verse in six ways [that is, he divides the verse into six clauses and systematically reads each of the clauses in light of the others and in line with an overriding theme:

    C.   "'As he looked, he saw a well in the field': this refers to the well [of water in the wilderness, Num. 21:17].

    D.   "'...and lo, three flocks of sheep lying beside it': specifically, Moses, Aaron, and Miriam.

    E.   "'...for out of that well the flocks were watered': from there each one drew water for his standard, tribe, and family."

    F.   "And the stone upon the well's mouth was great":

    G.   Said R. Hanina, "It was only the size of a little sieve."

    H.   [Reverting to Hama's statement:] "'...and put the stone back in its place upon the mouth of the well': for the coming journeys. [Thus the first interpretation applies the passage at hand to the life of Israel in the wilderness.]

3.   A   "'As he looked, he saw a well in the field': refers to Zion.

    B.   "'...and lo, three flocks of sheep lying beside it': refers to the three festivals.

    C.   "'....for out of that well the flocks were watered': from there they drank of the holy spirit.

    D.   "'...The stone on the well's mouth was large': this refers to the rejoicing of the house of the water-drawing."

    E.   Said R. Hoshaiah, "Why is it called 'the house of the water drawing'? Because from there they drink of the Holy Spirit."

    F.   [Resuming Hama b. Hanina's discourse:] "'...and when all the flocks were gathered there': coming from 'the entrance of Hamath to the brook of Egypt' (1 Kgs. 8:66).

    G.   "'...the shepherds would roll the stone from the mouth of the well and water the sheep': for from there they would drink of the Holy Spirit.

    H.   "'...and put the stone back in its place upon the mouth of the well': leaving it in place until the coming festival. [Thus the second interpretation reads the verse in light of the Temple celebration of the Festival of Tabernacles.]

4.   A   "'...As he looked, he saw a well in the field': this refers to Zion.

B. "'...and lo, three flocks of sheep lying beside it': this refers to the three courts, concerning which we have learned in the Mishnah: **There were three courts there, one at the gateway of the Temple mount, one at the gateway of the courtyard, and one in the chamber of the hewn stones [M. San. 11:2].**

C. "'...for out of that well the flocks were watered': for from there they would hear the ruling.

D. "The stone on the well's mouth was large': this refers to the high court that was in the chamber of the hewn stones.

E. "'...and when all the flocks were gathered there': this refers to the courts in session in the Land of Israel.

F. "'...the shepherds would roll the stone from the mouth of the well and water the sheep': for from there they would hear the ruling.

G. "'...and put the stone back in its place upon the mouth of the well': for they would give and take until they had produced the ruling in all the required clarity." [The third interpretation reads the verse in light of the Israelite institution of justice and administration.]

5. A. "'As he looked, he saw a well in the field': this refers to Zion.

B. "'...and lo, three flocks of sheep lying beside it': this refers to the first three kingdoms [Babylonia, Media, Greece].

C. "'...for out of that well the flocks were watered': for they enriched the treasures that were laid upon up in the chambers of the Temple.

D. "'...The stone on the well's mouth was large': this refers to the merit attained by the patriarchs.

E. "'...and when all the flocks were gathered there': this refers to the wicked kingdom, which collects troops through levies over all the nations of the world.

F. "'...the shepherds would roll the stone from the mouth of the well and water the sheep': for they enriched the treasures that were laid upon up in the chambers of the Temple.

G. "'...and put the stone back in its place upon the mouth of the well': in the age to come the merit attained by the patriarchs will stand [in defense of Israel]." [So the fourth interpretation interweaves the themes of the Temple cult and the domination of the four monarchies.]

6. A. "'As he looked, he saw a well in the field': this refers to the sanhedrin.

B. "'...and lo, three flocks of sheep lying beside it': this alludes to the three rows of disciples of sages that would go into session in their presence.

C. "'for out of that well the flocks were watered': for from there they would listen to the ruling of the law.

D. "'...The stone on the well's mouth was large': this refers to the most distinguished member of the court, who determines the law-decision.

E. "'...and when all the flocks were gathered there': this refers to disciples of the sages in the Land of Israel.

F. "'...the shepherds would roll the stone from the mouth of the well and water the sheep': for from there they would listen to the ruling of the law.

G.   "'...and put the stone back in its place upon the mouth of the well': for they would give and take until they had produced the ruling in all the required clarity." [The fifth interpretation again reads the verse in light of the Israelite institution of legal education and justice.]

7. A. "'As he looked, he saw a well in the field': this refers to the synagogue.

B.   "'...and lo, three flocks of sheep lying beside it': this refers to the three who are called to the reading of the Torah on weekdays.

C.   "'...for out of that well the flocks were watered': for from there they hear the reading of the Torah.

D.   "'...The stone on the well's mouth was large': this refers to the impulse to do evil.

E.   "'...and when all the flocks were gathered there': this refers to the congregation.

F.   "'...the shepherds would roll the stone from the mouth of the well and water the sheep': for from there they hear the reading of the Torah.

G.   "'...and put the stone back in its place upon the mouth of the well': for once they go forth [from the hearing of the reading of the Torah] the impulse to do evil reverts to its place." [The sixth and last interpretation turns to the twin themes of the reading of the Torah in the synagogue and the evil impulse, temporarily driven off through the hearing of the Torah.]

LXX:IX.

1. A. R. Yohanan interpreted the statement in terms of Sinai:

B.   "'As he looked, he saw a well in the field': this refers to Sinai.

C.   "'...and lo, three flocks of sheep lying beside it': these stand for the priests, Levites, and Israelites.

D.   "'...for out of that well the flocks were watered': for from there they heard the Ten Commandments.

E.   "'...The stone on the well's mouth was large': this refers to the Presence of God."

F.   "...and when all the flocks were gathered there":

G.   R. Simeon b. Judah of Kefar Akum in the name of R. Simeon: "All of the flocks of Israel had to be present, for if any one of them had been lacking, they would not have been worthy of receiving the Torah."

H.   [Returning to Yohanan's exposition:] "'...the shepherds would roll the stone from the mouth of the well and water the sheep': for from there they heard the Ten Commandments.

I.   "'...and put the stone back in its place upon the mouth of the well': 'You yourselves have seen that I have talked with you from heaven' (Ex. 20:19)."

What makes me claim that our *davar-aher* composite forms a systemic statement? It is because of the systematic and orderly repertoire of cogent references. These points of reference seen together comprise a picture of the formation of Israel, its holy way of life, its social institutions, its history past and present – in our language,

Judaism. We do not find doctrines, e.g., a set of propositions that are made explicit, unpacked, argued and proved. Rather we find a set of allusions or references, that is, set-piece items. These items are capable of expression in more than words; they can be visualized, for instance. Indeed, putting them into words does not expand their meaning or supply them with a cutting edge of a syllogistic character. What we have then is a tableau, set-piece items that can be arranged on a stage to provide a complete picture of a static reality – that is the best language I can provide to describe what is before us. The word "symbol," while weighty with difficulty, seems to me to serve. The composite compiles a variety of symbolic matters – events captured in a word, actions captured in a word, institutions captured in a word; and the words then convey a reality that evokes much more than is said. When we come to the Song of Songs Rabbah's "another-matter" compositions, we shall see explicit use of the required formula; but the substance is the same.

The six themes read in response to the verse cover (1) Israel in the wilderness, (2) the Temple cult on festivals with special reference to Tabernacles, (3) the judiciary and government, (4) the history of Israel under the four kingdoms, (5) the life of sages, and (6) the ordinary folk and the synagogue. The whole is an astonishing repertoire of fundamental themes of the life of the nation, Israel: at its origins in the wilderness, in its cult, in its institutions based on the cult, in the history of the nations, and, finally, in the twin social estates of sages and ordinary folk, matched by the institutions of the master-disciple circle and the synagogue. The vision of Jacob at the well thus encompassed the whole of the social reality of Jacob's people, Israel. Yohanan's exposition adds what was left out, namely, reference to the revelation of the Torah at Sinai.

5

Cases of *Davar Aher* in Esther Rabbah I

i. Chapter Two. Esther Rabbah I *Petihta* 2

II:i.

1. A. Samuel commenced by citing the following verse of Scripture: "'Yet for all that, when they are in the land of their enemies, I will not spurn them, neither will I abhor them so as to destroy them utterly and break my covenant with them, for I am the Lord their God; but I will for their sake remember the covenant with their forefathers, whom I brought forth out of the land of Egypt in the sight of the nations, that I might be their God: I am the Lord" (Lev. 26:44-45):

   B. "'I will not spurn them': in Babylonia.

   C. "'neither will I abhor them': in Media.

   D. "'so as to destroy them utterly': under Greek rule.

   E. "'and break my covenant with them: under the wicked kingdom.

   F. "'for I am the Lord their God': in the age to come."

   G. Taught R. Hiyya, "'I will not spurn them': in the time of Vespasian.

   H. "'neither will I abhor them': in the time of Trajan.

   I. "'so as to destroy them utterly': in the time of Haman.

   J. "'and break my covenant with them': in the time of the Romans.

   K. "'for I am the Lord their God': in the time of Gog and Magog."

There is no way that the two *davar aher*s can be read apart from one another, because only together do they make the point the compositor wanted to make. The two readings are of course complementary, the one invoking times of trouble in ages past, the other in the perceived present. What we see here is the complementarity of the form; only when we come to Song of Songs Rabbah will the theological uses of the form become evident.

ii. Chapter Three. Esther Rabbah I *Petihta* 3

III:i.

1. A   R. Judah b. R. Simon opened by citing the following verse: "'as if a man fled from a lion and a bear met him; or went into the house and leaned with his hand against the wall, and a serpent bit him' (Amos 5:19)."

2. A   R. Huna and R. Aha in the name of R. Hama bar Hanina: "'as if a man fled from a lion': this refers to Babylonia, called a lion: 'the first was like a lion' (Dan. 7:4).

    B.   "' and a bear met him': this speaks of Media, called a bear: 'And behold, another beast, a second, like a bear' (Dan. 7:5)."

3. A   R. Yohanan said, "The word for a bear is written defectively."

    B.   That is consistent with the position of R. Yohanan, which is as follows: "'Therefore a lion out of the forest slays them' (Jer. 5:6): this speaks of Media.

    C.   "'A leopard watches over their cities: this is Greece.

    D.   "'Everyone who goes out of there is torn into pieces': this is Edom."

4. A   [Reverting to 2.B:] "'or went into the house':

    B.   "This speaks of Greece in the time of the temple.

    C.   "'and leaned with his hand against the wall, and a serpent bit him': this speaks of Edom: 'The sound thereof shall go like the serpent's (Jer. 46:22)."

5. A   Along these same lines: "Open to me, my sister, my love, my dove, my undefiled" (Song 5:2):

    B.   "Open to me, my sister": this is Babylonia.

    C.   "my love": this is Media.

    D.   "my dove": this is Greece.

    E.   "my undefiled": this is Edom.

    F.   "Dove" speaks of the age of Greece, because in the time of the rule of the Greeks the temple was standing, and the Israelites would offer pigeons and doves on the altar.

6. A   R. Phineas and R. Levi in the name of R. Hama b. Hanina interpret the following verse of Scripture: "'In my distress I called upon the Lord, and cried to my God. Out of his temple he heard my voice, [and my cry came before him into his ears]' (Ps. 18:7).

    B.   "'In my distress I called upon the Lord': in Babylonia.

    C.   "'and cried to my God': in Media.

    D.   "'Out of his temple he heard my voice': in Greece.

7. A   Said R. Huna in his own name, "'Open to me, my sister, my love, my dove, my undefiled':

    B.   "'My dove': this is the kingdom of Greece, because in the time of the rule of the Greeks the temple was standing, and the Israelites would offer pigeons and doves on the altar.

    C.   "Therefore: 'Out of his temple he heard my voice.'

    D.   "'and my cry came before him into his ears': this speaks of Edom."

8. A   Another interpretation of the verse, "as if a man fled from a lion and a bear met him; or went into the house and leaned with his hand against the wall, and a serpent bit him" (Amos 5:19).

    B.   "as if a man fled from a lion": this speaks of Nebuchadnezzar.

C.   "and a bear met him": this is Belshazzar.

D.   "or went into the house and leaned with his hand against the wall, and a serpent bit him": this is Haman, who hissed at people like a snake, as it is written, "Rehum the commander and Shimshai the scribe" – the latter is a son of Haman – "wrote a letter to Artaxerxes, the king, in this manner" (Ezra 4:8).

The composition of Nos. 1-8 is somewhat complex, because our intersecting verse, Amos 5:19, competes with Song 5:2, which serves both on its own, at No. 5, and also in conjunction with Ps. 18:7 at No. 6. No. 7 then links the two, which is an odd and rather impressive denouement. No. 8 then reverts to our opening intersecting verse. This is not, strictly speaking, a *davar-aher* composite at all. It shows us that authorships could deliver the messages they wished to set forth by appealing to diverse verses; but we see, too, that when we repeatedly address a single verse of Scripture, the messages that we derive from that verse will prove utterly coherent. Despite the diversity of intersecting verses, the message is repeated and amazingly simple: it is to accomplish the comparison of the several ages through which the Jews had lived, Babylonian, Median, Greek, and Roman.

iii. Chapter Eighteen. Esther Rabbah I Esther 1:9

XVIII:v.

1.   A.   It is written, "From men by your hand, O Lord, from men whose portion in life is of the world. May their belly be filled with what you have stored up for them; may their children have more than enough; may they leave something over to their babes" (Ps. 17:14).

     B.   R. Hanina son of R. Aha went to a certain place. He found the following verse of Scripture at the head of the order [of lections]:

     C.   "But that which is left over of the meal-offering shall belong to Aaron and his sons" (Lev. 2:10).

     D.   [In his presentation in this connection,] he commenced with the following: "'From men by your hand, O Lord, from men whose portion in life is of the world. [May their belly be filled with what you have stored up for them; may their children have more than enough; may they leave something over to their babes]':

     E.   "How heroic are these who 'have received their portion from your hand O Lord!' And who are they? They are the tribe of Levi.

     F.   "'From men from the world': those who received no portion in the land.

     G.   "'from men whose portion in life': this refers to the Holy Things of the sanctuary.

     H.   "'May their belly be filled with what you have stored up for them': this refers to the Holy Things set apart for the priesthood in the provinces.

     I.   "'may their children have more than enough: ' 'Every male among the priests may eat thereof' (Lev. 6:22).

J.   "'may they leave something over to their babes': 'But that which is left over of the meal-offering shall belong to Aaron and his sons.'"

2. A.   Another explanation of the verse, "From men by your hand, O Lord, from men whose portion in life is of the world. May their belly be filled with what you have stored up for them; may their children have more than enough; may they leave something over to their babes" (Ps. 17:14):

B.   How heroic are these who "have received their portion from your hand O Lord!" And who are they? They are the generation of the repression [by Hadrian].

C.   [Since the word translated as 'from men' may be read 'they are put to death,] thus: "they are put to death by your hand."

D.   "from the world": this refers to those on whose flesh sores developed on account of their acts of sanctification of your name.

E.   Who are they?

F.   They are R. Simeon b. Yohai and R. Eleazar, his son.

G.   They spent time hiding in a cave during the thirteen years of the repression, until their flesh was covered with sores. They were eating carobs and figs.

H.   At the end of the thirteen years R. Simeon b. Yohai went out and sat himself down at the entrance of the cave. He saw a hunter spread his net to trap birds. He heard an echo say, "*Demos* [amnesty]," and the bird flew off, and then again he heard the echo say, "*Spiculum* [condemned]," and the bird was trapped.

I.   He said, "Even as to a bird, without the judgment of Heaven it cannot flee, all the more so ourselves! [We have made it only because Heaven protects us. So let us take care of our sores.] Let us go down and heal ourselves in the hot springs of Tiberias."

J.   They went down and found healing in the hot springs of Tiberias.

K.   They said, "We have to do an act of good and pleasure for the people of this place, just as our father, Jacob, did: 'And he conferred benefit upon the city' (Gen. 33:18). He set up a market and sold goods cheaply." So they set up a market and sold goods cheaply.

3. A.   [Another explanation of the verse, "From men by your hand, O Lord, from men] whose portion in life is of the world. [May their belly be filled with what you have stored up for them; may their children have more than enough; may they leave something over to their babes" (Ps. 17:14)]:

B.   Said David before the Holy One, blessed be He, "Lord of the world, Is it possible that I have a portion with them in this world?"

C.   Said to him the Holy One, blessed be He, "David, No! What is written here is not, 'what they have stored up will fill your belly' but rather, 'May their belly be filled with what you have stored up for them.'

D.   "The meaning is, everyone is going to eat of the surplus of your wealth. [Simon, p. 51, n. 2: will enjoy the hereafter for your sake.]"

E.   David was therefore informed that he has a portion in the world to come.

F.   And he further said, "Lord of the world, these come by reason of the power of the Torah, religious obligations, and good deeds, that they have accrued. But as for me: 'I shall behold your face through charity' (Ps. 17:15) forever." [David will merit the world to come by reason of philanthropy.]

4. A.   [Another explanation of the verse, "From men by your hand, O Lord, from men] whose portion in life is of the world. [May their belly be filled with what you have stored up for them; may their children have more than enough; may they leave something over to their babes" (Ps. 17:14)]:

B.   "From men by your hand, O Lord": How heroic are these who "have received their portion from your hand O Lord!" And who are they? They are Nebuchadnezzar.

C.   "from men whose portion in life is of the world": These are the ones who have taken their portion in the earth.

D.   "whose portion is of the world": They who took their portion while they were alive.

E.   "'May their belly be filled with what you have stored up for them': They got rich from the treasures of the Temple.

F.   "may their children have more than enough: " this refers to Evil-merodach and Belshazzar.

G.   "may they leave something over to their babes":

H.   One orphan was left to him [Vashti is daughter of Belshazzar], and you made her queen over a kingdom that did not even belong to her, and who was it? It was Vashti.

I.   [Supply: "Queen Vashti also gave a banquet for the women in the palace which belonged to King Ahasuerus."]

No. 1 deals with the Levites and their reliance upon God; No. 2 turns to the generation of repression and their loyalty to God; No. 3 proceeds to David and how he has suffered the loss of the world to come. No. 4 proceeds to the distinction between those who suffer in this world but enjoy the world to come, and those who get their reward in this world and lose the world to come. Do these messages fit together? They surely do, in that those who rely upon God but in this world pay the price – the generation of repression – are assured that in the world to come, they will get their just reward; those who rely upon God in this world have a good future; those who sin in this world but enjoy this world nonetheless turn out to lose the world to come. The whole then makes a single point, even though each composition, on its own, can be read in an autonomous way. The power of the intersecting verse, supplied by No. 1, derives from its reference to the future: "Their children are satisfied." That allows us once more to refer to the irony that Belshazzar had a single heir, Vashti, and how that act of grace did not produce a good end. No. 1 of course has its own interest, which is the exposition of Lev. 6:22 through Ps. 17:14, now with reference to the priesthood. The requirement of our compilation is far from sight. No. 2 is truncated, since it really does not appeal to our base verse at all, and then No. 3 is truncated in a different way, since it takes up the base verse where No. 2 has left off. That the two sherds do not fit together is self-evident. One might claim that the point in common is the virtue of philanthropy – setting up markets for Simeon b. Yohai's Jacob. But that seems to me farfetched. No. 4 then reverts to the program and form of No. 1, with excellent results.

iv. Chapter Twenty-Three. Esther Rabbah I Esther 1:14

XXIII:i.

1. A.   ["the men next to him being Carshena, Shethar, Admatha, Tarshish, Merses, Marsena, and Memucan, the seven princes of Persia and Media, who saw the king's face and sat first in the kingdom":]

    B.   "The righteous man is rescued from trouble, and the wicked man takes his place. [The impious man destroys his neighbor through speech, but through their knowledge the righteous are rescued. When the righteous prosper the city exults; when the wicked perish there are shouts of joy]" (Prov. 11:8-10):

    C.   "The righteous man is rescued from trouble": this refers to the tribe of Issachar.

    D.   "and the wicked man takes his place": this refers to the seven princes of Persia and Media [Simon, p. 57: for according to the rabbis, Ahasuerus subsequently slew them for their advice to execute Vashti.]

2. A.   Another comment on the verse, "the men next to him being [Carshena, Shethar, Admatha, Tarshish, Merses, Marsena, and Memucan, the seven princes of Persia and Media, who saw the king's face and sat first in the kingdom":]

    B.   It is written, "The impious man destroys his neighbor through speech, but through their knowledge the righteous are rescued":

    C.   "The impious man destroys his neighbor through speech": this refers to the seven princes of Persia and Media.

    D.   "but through their knowledge the righteous are rescued": this refers to the portion of Issachar.

3. A.   Another comment on the verse, "the men next to him being [Carshena, Shethar, Admatha, Tarshish, Merses, Marsena, and Memucan, the seven princes of Persia and Media, who saw the king's face and sat first in the kingdom":]

    B.   It is written, "A wise man is diffident and shuns evil, but a dullard rushes in confidently" (Prov. 14:16):

    C.   "A wise man is diffident and shuns evil": this is the tribe of Issachar.

    D.   "but a dullard rushes in confidently": this refers to the seven princes of Persia and Media.

4. A.   Another comment on the verse, "the men next to him being [Carshena, Shethar, Admatha, Tarshish, Merses, Marsena, and Memucan, the seven princes of Persia and Media, who saw the king's face and sat first in the kingdom":]

    B.   It is written, "The shrewd man saw trouble and took cover; the simple kept going and paid the penalty" (Prov. 22:3):

C.   "The shrewd man saw trouble and took cover": this is the tribe of Issachar.

D.   "the simple kept going and paid the penalty": this refers to the seven princes of Persia and Media.

The form is now pristine: our base verse, followed by an intersecting verse that contrasts the wise and the fools, and that underlines the reading of the base verse, which is that the reference to the "wise men" is to Israelites, and the fools then are the seven-named princes of Persia and Media. The variety of possibilities of intersecting verses recurrently makes the same point in the same way, and the form is perfectly achieved time and again. I cannot point to more persuasive evidence that, in the intersecting-verse/base-verse form, the several *davar ahers* are ordinarily meant to make a single point in a variety of ways; there is no unlimited repertoire. But were we to ask theological questions of the results before us, we should find no sustaining answers that I can discern. So far we have only a literary point concerning the hermeneutical principle attaching to the use of *davar aher.* To be sure, Green's initial assertion rests on a considerable foundation of evidence, and that result, for the moment suffices.

We shall now see that, without a *davar aher* at the head, the principle of agglutination of multiple meanings of the same verse remains constant: the same verse yields the same meaning, but the meaning may be imputed to a variety of discrete explanations of the verse. So we must make provision for the simple fact that, where one verse is interpreted in a number of ways, all of the interpretations are meant to say the same thing. In literary-exegetical terms, we therefore replicate the philosophical position implicit in the Mishnah, as spelled out in the opening Part of this book.

XXIII:ii.

1.   A   ["the men next to him being Carshena, Shethar, Admatha, Tarshish, Merses, Marsena, and Memucan, the seven princes of Persia and Media, who saw the king's face and sat first in the kingdom":]

       B.   "the men next to him":

       C.   they drew the punishment near to themselves.

2.   A   "being Carshena":

       B.   He was in charge of the vetches [*karshinim*].

3.   A.   "Shethar":

       B.   he was in charge of the wine.

4.   A.   "Admatha":

       B.   he was in charge of surveying the land [Simon: land measurements].

5.   A.   "Tarshish:

       B.   He was first in command of the household.

6.   A.   "Merses":

	B.	he would make chicken hash [Simon: he used to make a hash of (nenares) the poultry].
7.	A.	"Marsena":
	B.	he would beat the flour [with oil].
8.	A.	"and Memucan":
	B.	he was the one who provided food for all of them, for his wife would prepare for them everything they needed.
9.	A.	["Carshena, Shethar, Admatha, Tarshish, Merses, Marsena, and Memucan"]:
	B.	Said the ministering angels before the Holy One, blessed be He, "If the counsel of that wicked man [Haman] is carried out, who will offer you offerings?" [So the names of the counsellors refer to offerings in the temple, thus:]
	C.	"Carshena":
	D.	"Who will offer you an ox of the first year?" [*par ben shanah*].
10.	A.	"Shethar":
	B.	"Who will offer you two pigeons" [*shete torim*].
11.	A.	"Admatha":
	B.	"Who will build you an altar of earth: 'An altar of earth you shall make to me' (Ex. 20:21)?"
12.	A.	"Tarshish":
	B.	"Who will wear the priestly garments and minister before you: 'A beryl [*tarshish*] and an onyx and a jasper' (Ex. 28:20)?"
13.	A.	"Merses":
	B.	"Who will stir [*memeres*] the blood of the birds that are sacrificed before you?"
14.	A.	"Marsena":
	B.	"Who will mix the flour and oil before you?"
15.	A.	"and Memucan":
	B.	"Who will set up the altar before you: 'And they set up the altar upon its bases' (Ezra 3:3).
16.	A.	Thereupon said the Holy One, blessed be He, to them, "The Israelites are my children, my companions, my nearest, my loving ones, the sons of my beloved, Abraham: 'The seed of Abraham that loved me' (Isa. 41:8).
	B.	"I will exalt their horn: 'And he has lifted up a horn for his people' (Ps. 148:14)."
17.	A.	Another explanation for the verse, "Carshena, [Shethar, Admatha, Tarshish, Merses, Marsena, and Memucan]":
	B.	[As to Carshena,] said the Holy One, blessed be He, "I will scatter vetches before them and clear them out of the world [Simon, p. 58, n. 4: as one feeds an animal before killing it]."
	C.	"Shethar": "I shall make them drink a cup of reeling."
	D.	"Admatha, Tarshish": "I shall treat their blood as free as water."
	E.	"Merses, Marsena, and Memucan": "[Simon, p. 58:] I will stir, twist, and crush [*memares, mesares, mema'ek*] their souls within their bellies."
	F.	And where was the doom of all of them made ready?
	G.	Said R. Josiah, "It is in line with that which Isaiah, the prophet, said, 'Prepare slaughter for his children for the iniquity of their

fathers, that they may not rise up and possess the earth' (Isa. 14:21)."

We have three sets of explanations for the seven names, all of them working with the letters of the respective names and imputing to them other meanings sustained by the same consonants. The first set of explanations deals with the tasks each of the princes carried out in the palace, feeding the king. The next deals with the rites of the temple that each name stands for; here the princes are given a good task, which is to thwart the advice of Haman. But the upshot is to match feeding the wicked (or stupid) king, Ahasuerus, as against tending the King of kings of kings, God. And the third set of explanations then assigns to the seven the punishment that is owing to the wicked government that has endangered the lives of the Jews. So three distinct, and yet complementary, hermeneutical interests coincide: pagan government and the feeding of pagan kings, divine government and the counterpart, which is the temple cult, and, finally, God's punishment for the pagan government. While, it goes without saying, each set of seven names can stand on its own, it seems to me clear that the compositor has appealed to a single cogent program in order to accomplish what I see as a beautiful piece of sustained and coherent exposition, one that makes a variety of distinct components of a single important proposition. I cannot imagine a finer execution of the exposition of details aimed at registering a major conception.

v. Chapter Thirty-Two. Esther Rabbah I Esther 2:1

What is interesting in the rather sizable composition of Leviticus Rabbah XII:I.1 Esther Rabbah XXXII:i.1ff. is the multiple meanings assigned to one particular clause, so we shall turn directly to that part of the whole. What we see is that the framers take a single word, PRS, and work through the many meanings that those letters yield; at the same time, however, the multiple senses associated with those letters turn out in many ways to mean one thing.

XXXII:i.

9. A.   "In the end it bites like a snake and stings (PRS, also: separates) like an adder" (Prov. 23:32):

    B.   Just as a viper distinguishes (PRS) between life and death, so wine caused a separation between Adam and Eve.

    C.   For said R. Judah b. R. Ilai, "The tree from which Adam ate was a grape vine.

    D.   "That is in line with the following verse of Scripture: 'For their grapes are grapes of poison, their clusters are bitter, their wine is the poison of serpents, and the cruel venom of asps' (Dt. 32:32).

    E.   "It follows that grapevines brought bitterness into the world."

10. A.   Another interpretation of the verse, "In the end it bites like a
         snake and stings (PRS, also: separates) like an adder" (Prov. 23:32):

    B.   Just as a viper distinguishes (PRS) between life and death, so wine
         caused a separation between Noah and his sons in the matter of
         slavery.

    C.   That is in line with the following verse of Scripture: "Noah was the
         first tiller of the soil. He planted a vineyard and drank of the wine,
         became drunk, and lay uncovered in his tent. And Ham, the
         father of Canaan, saw the nakedness of his father and told his two
         brothers outside. Then Shem and Japheth took a garment, laid it
         upon both their shoulders, and walked backward, and covered the
         nakedness of their father; their faces were turned away, and they
         did not see their father's nakedness. When Noah awoke from his
         wine and knew what his youngest son had done to him..."

    D.   On that account: "He said, Cursed be Canaan, a slave of slaves
         shall he be to his brothers" (Gen. 9:20-25).

11. A.   Another interpretation of the verse, "In the end it bites like a
         snake and stings (PRS, also: separates) like an adder" (Prov. 23:32):

    B.   Just as a viper distinguishes (PRS) between life and death, so wine
         caused a separation between Lot and his daughters in the matter
         of bastardy.   ·

    C.   That is in line with the following verse of Scripture: "Come, let us
         make our father drink wine, and we will lie with him, that we may
         preserve offspring through our father. So they made their father
         drink wine that night, and the firstborn went in and lay with her
         father; he did not know when she lay down or when she arose.
         And on the next day the firstborn said to the younger, Behold, I
         lay last night with my father; let us make him drink wine tonight
         also; then you go in and lie with him, that we may preserve
         offspring through our father. So they made their father drink wine
         that night also; and the younger arose and lay with him, and he
         did not know when she lay down or when she arose. Thus both the
         daughters of Lot were with child by their father" (Gen. 19:32-36).

    D.   On that account: "No Ammonite or Moabite shall enter the
         assembly of the Lord" (Dt. 23:3).

12. A.   Another interpretation of the verse, "In the end it bites like a
         snake and stings (PRS, also: separates) like an adder" (Prov. 23:32):

    B.   Just as a viper distinguishes (PRS) between life and death, so wine
         caused a separation between Aaron and his sons as to death.

    C.   For it has been taught on Tannaite authority: R. Ishmael said,
         "The two sons of Aaron died only because they entered the tent of
         meeting when they were drunk."

    D.   R. Phineas in the name of R. Levi in regard to this statement of R.
         Ishmael said, "The matter may be compared to a king who had a
         reliable steward. He observed the man standing at the doorway
         of a wine shop. He cut off his head without revealing the reason,
         and appointed someone else as steward in place of the first.

    E.   "Now we do not know on what account he killed the first. But from
         his instructions to the second, we may draw the proper conclusion,
         for he said, 'Do not go into that wine shop.' So we know on what
         account he killed the first.

F.   "Now here it is written, 'And fire came forth from the presence of the Lord and devoured them and they died before the Lord' (Lev. 10:2).

G.   "Now we do not know on what account they were put to death. But from what the Holy One, blessed be He, instructed Aaron, saying to him, 'Drink no wine nor strong drink, you nor your sons with you, when you go into the tent of meeting, lest you die' (Lev. 10:8), we may draw the conclusion that they were put to death only on account of wine."

13. A   Another interpretation of the verse, "In the end it bites like a snake and stings (PRS, also: separates) like an adder" (Prov. 23:32):

B.   Just as a viper distinguishes (PRS) between life and death, so wine caused a separation between the ten tribes in the matter of the exile.

C.   That is in line with what is written: "Woe to those who rise early in the morning, that they may run after strong drink, who tarry late in the evening till wine inflames them" (Isa. 5:11).

D.   "Who drink wine in bowls" (Amos 6:6).

E.   On this account: "Therefore they shall now be the first of those who go into exile" (Amos 6:7).

14. A   Another interpretation of the verse, "In the end it bites like a snake and stings (PRS, also: separates) like an adder" (Prov. 23:32):

B.   Just as a viper distinguishes (PRS) between life and death, so wine caused a separation between the tribes of Judah and Benjamin in the matter of the exile.

C.   For it is written, "These also reel with wine and stagger with strong drink; the priest and the prophet reel with strong drink, they are confused with wine, they stagger with strong drink" (Isa. 28:7).

D.   These and also those are subject to judgment.

15. A   Another interpretation of the verse, "In the end it bites like a snake and stings (PRS, also: separates) like an adder" (Prov. 23:32):

B.   Just as a viper distinguishes (PRS) between life and death, so wine caused a separation between one reign and another in the matter of the death of a reigning monarch.

C.   For it is written: "King Belshazzar made a great feast for a thousand of his lords and drank wine in front of the thousand. Belshazzar, when he tasted the wine, commanded that the vessels of gold and of silver which Nebuchadnezzar his father had taken out of the temple in Jerusalem be brought, that the king and his lords, his wives and his concubines, might drink from them. Then they brought in the golden and silver vessels which had been taken out of the temple, the house of God in Jerusalem, and the king and his lords, his wives and his concubines drank from them. They drank wine and praised the gods of gold and silver, bronze, iron, wood, and stone" (Dan. 5:1-4).

D.   On this account: "That very night Belshazzar the Chaldean king was slain, and Darius the Mede received the kingdom" (Dan. 5:30).

16. A   Another interpretation of the verse, "In the end it bites like a snake and stings (PRS, also: separates) like an adder" (Prov. 23:32):

B.   Just as a viper distinguishes (PRS) between life and death, so wine caused a separation between Ahasuerus and Vashti, the queen, in the matter of the death penalty.

C.   For it is said, "On the seventh day, when the heart of the king was merry with wine, he commanded Mehuman, Biztha, Harbona, Bigtha, and Abagtha, Zethar and Carkas, the seven eunuches who served King Ahasuerus as chamberlains, to bring Queen Vashti before the king with her royal crown, in order to show the peoples and the princes her beauty; for she was fair to behold. But Queen Vashti refused to come at the king's command conveyed by the eunuches. At this the king was enraged, and his anger burned within him" (Est. 1:10-12).

D.   He wanted to bring her in naked, but she did not accept his commandment. Therefore he became angry with her and killed her. After he had killed her, he began to wonder at what he had done.

E.   [Supply, as at Lev. R. XII:I.14.E: That is in line with the following verse of Scripture: "After these things, when the anger of King Ahasuerus had abated, he remembered Vashti and what she had done, and what had been decreed against her."]

What meanings are imputed to PRS? The distinction between life and death, Adam and Eve; Noah and his sons; Lot and his daughters; Aaron and his sons; Ten Tribes in the matter of the exile; Judah and Benjamin in the matter of the exile; one reign and another in the matters of Belshazzar; and Ahasuerus and Vashti. If now we see these entries in sequence, we have a catalogue of all of the principal events that the Judaism of the Dual Torah identified as history. Here is (at last) a case in which the sustained interest in saying many things in one way has yielded not merely literary, but theological results: wine is the source of all evil events in both humanity's and Israel's history. But we stand at a considerable distance from our goal of finding in the many meanings that add up to one meaning a theological repertoire of recurrent symbols; when we do, it will look much like this.

6

Cases of *Davar Aher* in Ruth Rabbah

i. Chapter Two. Ruth Rabbah *Petihta* 2

II:i.

1. A. "And it came to pass in the days when the judges ruled":

   B. "Slothfulness casts into a deep sleep, and an idle person will suffer hunger. [He who keeps the commandment keeps his life; he who despises the word will die]" (Prov. 19:15-16):

   C. ["Slothfulness casts into a deep sleep"] because the Israelites were slothful about burying Joshua:

   D. "And they buried him in the border of his inheritance...on the north of the mountain of Gaash" (Josh. 24:30).

   E. Said R. Berekhiah, "We have reviewed the entire Scripture and have found no place called Gaash.

   F. "What is the meaning of 'the mountain of Gaash'?'

   G. "It is that the Israelites were preoccupied [a word that uses the same consonants as the word Gaash] so that they were slothful about burying Joshua.

   H. "[Why was that the case? Because] at that time the land of Israel was being divided up, and the parcelling out was too important to them.

   I. "The Israelites were occupied with their own work. This one was occupied with his field, and that one was occupied with his vineyard, and the other with his olives, and the other with his stone quarry. Thus: 'and an idle person will suffer hunger.'

   J. "So the Israelites were slothful about burying Joshua.

   K. "The Holy One, blessed be He, wanted to cause an earthquake to come upon the inhabitants of the world: 'Then the earth did shake [a word that uses the same consonants as the word for mount Gaash] and quake' (Ps. 18:8).

2. A. "and an idle person will suffer hunger":

   B. It is because they were deceiving the Holy One, blessed be He.

	C.	Some of them were worshipping idols.
	D.	Therefore he starved them of the Holy Spirit [as in the continuation of the intersecting verse, "He who keeps the commandment keeps his life; he who despises the word will die"]:
	E.	"And the word of the Lord was precious in those days."
3.	A.	Another interpretation of the verse, "Slothfulness casts into a deep sleep, and an idle person will suffer hunger. [He who keeps the commandment keeps his life; he who despises the word will die]" (Prov. 19:15-16):
	B.	["Slothfulness casts into a deep sleep"] because the Israelites were slothful about repenting in the time of Elijah.
	C.	"casts into a deep sleep": — prophecy increased.
	D.	But the verse says, "causes to fall," [meaning, prophecy decreased] and you say that it increased?
	E.	It is in line with the saying, "the market for fruit has fallen" [because a lot of fruit has come to the market for sale, the price of fruit has gone down].
	F.	Said R. Simon, "It is like someone who says to his fellow, 'Here is the bag, the money, the measure; go eat."
4.	A.	For R. Derusa said, "Sixty myriads of prophets arose for the Israelites in the time of Elijah."
	B.	R. Jacob said, "One hundred twenty myriads."
	C.	Said R. Yohanan, "Between Gabbath and Antipatris there were sixty myriads of townships. Among them none was more corrupt than Jericho and Beth El, Jericho because of the curse of Joshua, Beth El because of the Golden calf of Jeroboam's having been set up there. And yet it is written, 'And the sons of the prophets who were at Beth El came forth to Elishah' (2 Kgs. 2:3). ['And the sons of the prophets who were at Jericho came near to Elisha (2 Kgs. 2:5).]
	D.	"And the reference to 'prophets' in the plural means a minimum of two. [Rabinowitz, p. 5, n. 3: If in the most corrupt towns there was a minimum of two prophets, the sixty myriad townships had a minimum of 120 myriads of prophets.]"
5.	A.	How come their prophecy was not publicized?
	B.	For there was no need for it in the coming generations.
	C.	It follows that any prophecy that is not needed for coming generations is not publicized.
	D.	But in the age to come the Holy One, blessed be He, will come and bring them with him, and their prophecy will be publicized: "And the Lord my God will come and all the holy ones with you" (Zech. 14:5).
6.	A.	"and an idle person will suffer hunger":
	B.	It is because they were deceiving the Holy One, blessed be He.
	C.	Some of them were worshipping idols, and some of them were worshipping the Holy One, blessed be He.
	D.	That is in line with what Elijah said to them, "How long will you halt between two opinions" (1 Kgs. 18:21).
7.	A.	"...will suffer hunger":
	B.	a famine in the days of Elijah: "As the Lord of hosts lives, before whom I stand" (1 Kgs. 18:15).

8.   A   Another interpretation of the verse, "Slothfulness casts into a
            deep sleep, [and an idle person will suffer hunger]":
     B.   ["Slothfulness casts into a deep sleep"] because the Israelites were
            slothful about repentance in the time of the judges,
     C.   they were "cast into a deep sleep."
9.   A   "and an idle person will suffer hunger":
     B.   Because they were deceiving the Holy One, blessed be He: some
            of them were worshipping idols, and some of them were
            worshipping the Holy One, blessed be He,
     C.   the Holy One, blessed be He, brought a famine in the days of
            their judges:
     D.   [Supply: "And it came to pass in the days when the judges ruled,
            there was a famine in the land."]

The sequence of "other matters" begins with Joshua; the Israelites'
sloth is indicated by their not promptly burying him. Their sloth then
led to hunger, which means, hunger of the Holy Spirit. Thus the first
pair is completed. The second pair involves Elijah and prophecy.
Because they deceived God, they were deprived of prophecy. The
third pair involves the time of the judges, and the famine now is not of
the Holy Spirit or of prophecy but real. The message then is that if
people deceive God, they will lose the access to him through the Holy
Spirit and through prophecy, and this, moreover, yields quite this-
worldly consequences. I take that to be a coherent message, delivered
through three well-articulated readings of the same verse in three
different ways. As before, what we do not find is a fixed theologumen,
that is to say, a sequence of constantly joined verbal symbols that will
recur and indicate a substrate of fixed thought.

This is an enormously successful *petihta*, because it moves us on to a
second component of our base verse, stays close to the theme of the base
verse, which is the cause of famine, and, yet, draws upon an intersecting
verse with its own rich repertoire of meanings. The only thing lacking,
as in *Petihta* 1, is the reversion to the base verse, but that seems to me
no serious problem at all; there is no sense to be made without that
reversion, such as I have supplied. The intersecting verse bears three
interpretations: slothfulness in the time of Joshua, because of excess
commitment to one's own affairs (Nos. 1, 2), slothfulness in the time of
Elijah, now about repentance (Nos. 3, 6-7, with the interpolated
materials of Nos. 4, 5), and, finally, slothfulness about repentance in
the time of the judges, Nos. 8-9. I cannot imagine a more perfect
execution of the *petihta* program than the one before us; it is genuinely
affecting, and its points are coherent with one another.

ii. Chapter Three. Ruth Rabbah *Petihta* 3

III:i.

1. A. "And it came to pass in the days when the judges ruled, there was a famine in the land":
   B. "The way of the guilty man is crooked and strange, but the conduct of the pure is right" (Prov. 21:8):
   C. This speaks of Esau, who comes crookedly against Israel with harsh decrees:
   D. "You have stolen!" "We have not stolen."
   E. "You have murdered!" "We have not murdered."
   F. "You have not stolen? Then who stole with you?"
   G. "You have not murdered? Then who was your accomplice?"
   H. He fines them on false charges: "Produce your share of the crop, produce your poll tax, produce your state tax."

2. A. "man":
   B. this speaks of Esau: "And Esau was a man, a cunning hunter" (Gen. 25:27).
   C. "strange":
   D. for he estranged himself from circumcision and from the obligations of religious duties.
   E. "the pure":
   F. this refers to the Holy One, blessed be He,
   G. who behaves toward him in a fair measure and gives him his reward in this world, like a worker who in good faith carries out work for a householder.

3. A. Another interpretation of the verse, "The way of the guilty man is crooked and strange, but the conduct of the pure is right" (Prov. 21:8):
   B. "The way of the guilty man is crooked": this speaks of the nations of the world, who come crookedly against Israel with harsh decrees.
   C. "man": for they derive from Noah, who is called a man.
   D. "strange":
   E. for they worship alien gods.
   F. "the pure":
   G. this refers to the to the Holy One, blessed be He,
   H. who behaves toward him in a fair measure [supply: and gives him his reward in this world, like a worker who in good faith carries out work for a householder].

4. A. R. Aha said, "'the way...is crooked' refers to the Israelites: 'For they are a crooked generation' (Dt. 32:20).
   B. "'man': 'Now the men of Israel had sworn' (Judges 21:1).
   C. "'strange': they alienated themselves from the Holy One, blessed be He: 'They have dealt treacherously against the Lord for they have produced strange children' (Hos. 5:7).
   D. "'but the conduct of the pure is right': this speaks of the Holy One, blessed be He, who behaves toward him in a fair measure in this world, but gives them the full reward that is coming to them in the world to come,

E.   "like a worker who in good faith carries out work for a householder.

F.   "At that time said the Holy One, blessed be He, 'My children are in rebellion. But as to exterminating them, that is not possible, and to bring them back to Egypt is not possible, and to trade them for some other nation is something I cannot do. But this shall I do for them: lo, I shall torment them with suffering and afflict them with famine in the days when the judges judge.'

G.   "That is in line with this verse: 'And it came to pass in the days when the judges ruled, there was a famine in the land.'"

The interpretations of Prov. 21:8 lead us to Esau/Rome, with his false charges against the Jews; with his estrangement from God; then the nations of the world, with harsh decrees and their estrangement from God. But, finally, we have also Israel, with its rebellion against God, even though, in God's case, the rule is not harsh but just and merciful. I cannot imagine a more coherent message, beginning with the specific, Rome, then the general, the nations of the world, and, finally, the contrast and complement of Israel and God. No part of the whole can have been removed without losing the sense that the compositor wished to express, even though, obviously, the individual units make solid points each in its own right.

We have yet another absolutely perfect execution of the intersecting-verse/base-verse form. The intersecting verse draws us immediately to Esau, who of course stands for Rome. No. 1 then invites us to lament Israel's condition; No. 2, which is continuous, underlines the message. It further explains Rome's present prosperity; they get their reward in this world. No. 3 then broadens the matter to encompass all of the nations of the world. Then No. 4 brings us back to Israel, matching Nos. 1-2 with precision; Israel gets its reward in the world to come, because, through suffering in this world, Israel repents. The picture is then complete, and the famine in the time of the rule of the judges falls into place within the larger program of God for Israel. I cannot imagine a more fully realized and wholly unitary exposition, and the whole surely has been made up for the purpose of the compilers of the document in which the composition now occurs.

iii. Chapter Twenty. Ruth Rabbah to Ruth 1:16

XX:i.

2   A.   "to leave you or to return from following you, for where you go I will go, and where you lodge I will lodge; your people shall be my people, and your God my God":

    B.   "Under all circumstances I intend to convert, but it is better that it be through your action and not through that of another."

3.   A.   When Naomi heard her say this, she began laying out for her the
            laws that govern proselytes.
     B.   She said to her, "My daughter, it is not the way of Israelite women
            to go to theaters and circuses put on by idolators."
     C.   She said to her, "Where you go I will go."
     D.   She said to her, "My daughter, it is not the way of Israelite women
            to live in a house that lacks a mezuzah."
     E.   She said to her, "Where you lodge I will lodge."
     F.   "your people shall be my people":
     G.   This refers to the penalties and admonitions against sinning.
     H.   "and your God my God":
     I.   This refers to the other religious duties.
4.   A.   Another interpretation of the statement, "for where you go I will
            go":
     B.   to the tent of meeting, Gilgal, Shiloh, Nob, Gibeon, and the
            eternal house.
     C.   "and where you lodge I will lodge":
     D.   "I shall spend the night concerned about the offerings."
     E.   "your people shall be my people":
     F.   "so nullifying my idol."
     G.   "and your God my God":
     H.   "to pay a full recompense for my action."

What is of interest to us is the collection of amplifications of
"where you go, I will go...," since we see that through "another matter"
we have a number of versions of one matter. Nos. 2-3 begin with the
duties of the convert. No. 3 then explains the relevance of each of
Ruth's statements to the duties of the Israelite, and No. 4 restates
matters in terms of the holy life of the cult. This is how theology comes
to expression in exegesis, since the point of the doublet is that the holy
way of life of the individual corresponds to the sacrifices of the
Temple.

iv. Chapter Fifty-Six. Ruth Rabbah to Ruth 3:7

LVI:i.
1.   A.   "And when Boaz had eaten and drunk and his heart was merry":
     B.   Why was "his heart merry"?
     C.   For he had said a blessing for his food.
2.   A.   Another explanation of the phrase, "And when Boaz had eaten
            and drunk and his heart was merry":
     B.   for he had eaten various sorts of sweets after the meal, since they
            make the tongue used to Torah.
3.   A.   Another explanation of the phrase, "And when Boaz had eaten
            and drunk and his heart was merry":
     B.   For he had occupied himself with teachings of the Torah: "The
            Torah of your mouth is good to me" (Ps. 119:72).
4.   A.   Another explanation of the phrase, "And when Boaz had eaten
            and drunk and his heart was merry":

B.   He was seeking a wife: "Who finds a wife finds a good thing"
            (Prov. 18:22).

The other matters cover conduct in accord with the Torah: saying a
blessing for food; studying Torah, seeking a wife: the good life in flesh
and spirit.

7

Cases of *Davar Aher* in Lamentations Rabbah

i. *Petihta* 17

We start with a very simple case, in which two readings of the same verse prove necessary to make a single point.

XVII.i.

1. A. R. Abbahu commenced [by citing the following verse of Scripture]: "'They who sit in the gate gossip about me [and I am the song of drunkards]' (Ps. 69:13).

   B. "This refers to the nations of the world, who take their seats in theaters and circuses.'

   C. "'and I am the song of drunkards':

   D. "After they take their seats and eat and drink and get drunk, they sit and gossip about me and make fun of me,

   E. "saying, 'We don't have to eat cheap food such as carobs, like the Jews.'

   F. "And they say to one another, 'How long do you want to live?'

   G. "And one replies, 'Like the shirt of a Jew that he keeps for the Sabbath.'

   H. "And they bring a camel into their theaters, and put their shirts on it, and ask, 'Why is the camel in mourning?'

   I. "And one replies, 'These Jews are observing the Seventh Year, so they don't have greens, and they are eating the thorns that belong to such as this, so he is in mourning on their account.'

   J. "And they bring a clown [following Cohen, p. 23] into the theater, with his head shaved, and they say to one another, 'How come this one's head is shaved?'

   K. "And one replies, 'These Jews keep the Sabbath, so whatever they earn all week long, they eat upon on the Sabbath. They don't have wood to cook with, so they break up their beds and use the wood for cooking and then they sleep on the dirt and get covered with the dust, and therefore they have to cover themselves with oil, which gets very costly on that account.'" [Cohen, p. 23, n. 3: 'Therefore, after a time they cannot afford it at all, and so shave their heads so as not to need it.")

2. A.   Another interpretation of the verse: "They who sit in the gate gossip about me": this refers to Israel, who take seats in synagogues and schoolhouses.

    B.   "and I am the song of drunkards": after they have sat and eaten and drunk and gotten drunk at the banquet prior to the ninth of Ab,

    C.   they sit down and recite lamentations and dirges:

    D.   "Alas! Lonely sits the city once great with people!"

That Nos. 1, 2 form a unity cannot be doubted, and the contrast is powerful. Not only so, but the public ridicule of Jews' religious rites contrasts with the Jews' own perception of their condition. The exposition of Ps. 69:13 in terms of gentiles' ridicule of Jews' practices – the Jews' poverty, their Sabbath and Seventh Year observance – is followed by a reexposition of the Jews' practices, now with respect to the ninth of Ab. The one odd note is the admission that, prior to the ninth of Ab, Jews get drunk at their banquets. But clearly that does not trouble the author of the whole, and it is not possible to imagine that the composition is other than unitary and totally cogent. Here then is a standard for a harmonious and wholly crafted composition, numerous other of the *petihtaot* appear jerry-built and in no way unitary, so we cannot ascribe the success merely to the literary form at hand.

ii. *Petihta* 20

XX.i.

1. A.   R. Alexandri commenced [by citing the following verse of Scripture]: "'I watch and become like a sparrow that is alone on the roof' (Ps. 102:8).

    B.   "Said the Holy One, blessed be He, 'I watched to bring my children into the Land of Israel.

    C.   "Forthwith: 'I watch and become like a sparrow that is alone on the roof.'

    D.   "Just as a sparrow is driven from roof to roof and fence to fence and tree to tree and bush to bush, [Cohen, p. 24, n. 5 adds: *so I had to wander with Israel from place to place for forty years. I was eager to give the Torah to Israel immediately on their departure from Egypt but:*]

    E.   "when the Israelites came forth from Egypt, they were journeying in contention and encamping in contention: 'And they journeyed...and they encamped...' (Num. 33:3).

    F.   "When they came to Mount Sinai, they all formed a harmonious community. 'And they encamped' is not what is written here, but rather, 'Israel encamped there' (Ex. 19:2).

	G.	"At that moment, said the Holy One, blessed be He, 'Lo, the time has come for me to give the Torah to my children.'"
2.	A.	Another interpretation of the verse, "I watch [and become like a sparrow that is alone on the roof]" (Ps. 102:8):
	B.	Said the Holy One, blessed be He, "I watched so as to bring my Presence to rest upon the house of the sanctuary forever."
	C.	"and become like a sparrow":
	D.	Just as in the case of a sparrow, when you take its young, it is left alone, so, said the Holy One, blessed be He, "I have burned my house, destroyed my city, exiled my people among the nations of the world, and now I sit alone."
	E.	"Alas! Lonely sits the city once great with people!" (Lam. 1:1).

The contrast is the same as drawn in the immediately prior *petihta*, between redemption and disaster; there we dealt with Passover and the ninth of Ab, here, the giving of the Torah and the destruction of the Temple. This is drawn with great force, first at No. 1, then at No. 2. No 1 without No. 2 then is not only incomplete but also misleading. In fact the "another interpretation" is not "other," but complementary and necessary. I do not see the necessity for Cohen's additional language, since D without that language yields E. The sense is clear as E, followed by F with its contrasting formulations of "encamp," makes the point full well. Then No. 2 completes the exposition, and the whole moves naturally to the base verse. Here is a fine instance in which the intersecting verse opens up new perspectives upon the base verse. I cannot imagine a more perfect exposition of an intersecting verse, in which all elements lead to a single point, the one at which the intersecting verse contributes: God like a sparrow, with two distinct yet interdependent expositions of the metaphor!

iii. *Petihta* 25

Here again the *davar aher*s coalesce to make a single point, which concerns the nature of Israel's relationship to God, which is ambiguous: divorced and yet not divorced, widow yet not fully free to remarry.

XXV:vi.

1.	A.	"How like a widow has she become":
	B.	Said R. Aibu, "They did not fully explore the limits of the measure of justice, so the measure of justice did not go to extremes against them.
	C.	"They did not fully explore the limits of the measure of justice: 'And the people were like murmurers' (Num. 11:1).
	D.	"What is written is not 'murmurers,' but only, 'like murmurers.'"
	E.	"'The princes of Judah are like those who remove the landmark' (Num. 5:10).
	F.	"What is written is not 'remove,' but 'like those who remove.'
	G.	"'For Israel is like a stubborn heifer' (Hos. 4:16).

	H.	"What is written is not 'a stubborn heifer,' but 'like a stubborn heifer.'
	I.	"What is written here is not 'a widow' but 'like a widow.'
	J.	"She is like a woman waiting for her husband, who has left her and gone on a distant journey.
	K.	"'He has bent his bow like an enemy' (Lam. 2:4).
	L.	"What is written here is not 'an enemy' but 'like an enemy.'"
2.	A.	Another interpretation of the clause, "How like a widow has she become":
	B.	R. Hama b. Uqba and rabbis:
	C.	R. Hama bar Uqba said, "To what may the Israelites be likened? To a widow who has laid claim for living expenditures but has not laid claim for the payout of her marriage-settlement [upon the death of her husband. By doing so, she has forfeited the latter claim. So Israel has refused to be parted from the Temple (Cohen, p. 72, n. 1).]"
	D.	Rabbis say, "The matter may be compared to the case of a king who grew angry with his wife and wrote out her writ of divorce and handed it over to her, but then went and snatched it back.
	E.	"Whenever she wishes to be married to a third party, he says to her, 'Where is your writ of divorce, proving that I have divorced you?'
	F.	"And whenever she lays claim for her living expenditure, he says to her, 'I've already divorced you.'
	G.	"Thus whenever the Israelites seek to worship an idol, the Holy One, blessed be He, says to them, 'Where is the writ of your mother's divorce from me' (Isa. 50:1).
	H.	"And whenever they want him to do a miracle for them, he says to them, 'I have already divorced you.'
	I.	"That is in line with this verse: 'I had put her away and given her a writ of divorce' (Jer. 3:8)."
3.	A.	Another interpretation of the clause, "How like a widow has she become":
	B.	R. Aqiba and rabbis:
	C.	R. Aqiba says, "She is a widow, but you say, 'like a widow'?
	D.	"But she is widowed as to the ten tribes but not as to the tribes of Judah and Benjamin."
	E.	And rabbis say, "She is a widow from these and those, but not from the Holy One, blessed be He:
	F.	"'For Israel is not widowed, not Judah of his God' (Isa. 51:5)."

No. 1 does not fully work out its announced proposition, since the second clause, "so the measure of justice did not go to extremes against them," is not developed. What we have is a quite separate set of prooftexts for the proposition that the prophetic critique of Israel is mitigated by mercy. There is no proof that just as the Israelites did not go to extremes in sinning, so the measure of justice did not do so. But that is the announced proposition. Buber's printed text revises to meet that need by using H-L to prove the counterpart point. No. 2 is well worked out, a successful demonstration that Israel stands in an ambiguous relationship with God, both divorced and not divorced. The clause that is explicated serves only the first of the two positions, however, and that means the passage was made up in its own terms and then inserted here because of its usefulness to the compilers of our document or this passage therein. No. 3 seems to me more apropos, since it does focus upon our base clause and both parties deal with the same issue in the same way.

iv. Chapter Thirty-Nine. Parashah I. Lamentations 1:5

XXXIX.i.
1. A. "Her foes have become the head":
   B. Said R. Hillel b. Berekhiah, "Whoever comes to torment Jerusalem is made head,
   C. "for it is written, 'Her foes have become the head.'
   D. "[Following the order of Cohen's text, p. 100:] You find that before Jerusalem was destroyed, no city was regarded as important. Afterward, Caesarea became a metropolis, Antipatris, a city, and Neapolis a colony."
2. A. Another reading of "Her foes have become the head":
   B. this refers to Nebuchadnezzar.
3. A. "Her foes have become the head":
   B. this refers to Nebuzaradan.
4. A. Another interpretation of the phrase "Her foes have become the head":
   B. this refers to Vespasian.
   C. "her enemies prosper":
   D. this refers to Titus.

The single point is made three times: whoever torments Jerusalem is made head. This does not comprise three "other matters" but the same matter three times.

v. Chapter Sixty. Parashah II. Lamentations 2:4

LX.i.
1. A. "He has bent his bow like an enemy, with his right hand set like a foe":
   B. Said R. Aibu, "They did not fully explore the limits of the measure of justice, so the measure of justice did not go to extremes against them.
   C. "They did not fully explore the limits of the measure of justice: 'And the people were like murmurers' (Num. 11:1).
   D. "What is written is not 'murmurers,' but only, 'like murmurers.'"
   E. "'The princes of Judah are like those who remove the landmark' (Num. 5:10).
   F. "What is written is not 'remove,' but 'like those who remove.'
   G. "'For Israel is like a stubborn heifer' (Hos. 4:16).

H.   "What is written is not 'a stubborn heifer,' but 'like a stubborn heifer.'

I.   And the Attribute of Justice did not go to extremes against them.

J.   "What is written here is not 'an enemy' but 'like an enemy.'"

2 A. Another interpretation of the verse, "He has bent his bow like an enemy, [with his right hand set like a foe]":

B.   This is Pharaoh: "The enemy said..." (Ex. 15:9).

3. A. "with his right hand set like a foe":

B.   This is Haman: "An adversary and an enemy, even wicked Haman" (Est. 7:6).

4. A. Another interpretation of the verse, "He has bent his bow like an enemy, with his right hand set like a foe":

B.   This alludes to Esau: "Because the enemy has said against you, Aha" (Ezek. 36:2).

We deal with "another matter" pertaining to the phrase, "He has bent his bow like an enemy...." The first item sets up the Attribute of Justice as the enemy; the Attribute is merciful and does not go to extremes. Then we contrast God's treatment of Israel with [2] Pharaoh, [3] Haman, [4] Esau.

vi. Chapter Sixty-Nine. Parashah II. Lamentations 2:13

LXIX.i.

1. A. "What can I say for you [call to witness against you], to what compare you, O daughter of Jerusalem":

B.   Said the Holy One, blessed be He, to Israel, "How many prophets did I call to witness against you?"

C.   Rabbi [Judah the Patriarch] and R. Nathan:

D.   Rabbi said, "One in the morning, one at twilight: 'Yet the Lord forewarned Israel and Judah by the hand of every prophet and of every seer' (2 Kgs. 17:13)."

E.   R. Nathan said, "Two in the morning and two at night: 'And though I have sent to you all my servants the prophets, sending them betimes and often' (Jer. 7:25).

F.   "'betimes': in the morning.

G.   "'often': at night."

2 A. Another interpretation of the verse, "What can I say for you [call to witness against you], to what compare you, O daughter of Jerusalem":

B.   "In how many places did I meet with you! In the tent of meeting, at Gilgal, Shiloh, Nob, Gibeon, and the two temples."

3. A. Another interpretation of the verse, "What can I say for you [call to witness against you], to what compare you, O daughter of Jerusalem":

B.   Rabbi said, "With how many ornaments did I adorn you!"

C.   R. Yohanan said, "Sixty myriads of ministering angels came down with the Holy One, blessed be He, at Sinai, each with a crown in his hand, to crown every Israelite."

D.   R. Abba b. Kahana said in the name of R. Yohanan, "A hundred and twenty myriads came down, one to adorn each, another to crown him."

E.   R. Huna of Sepphoris said, "They girdled them: 'He looses the bonds of kings and binds their loins with a girdle' (Job 12:18)."

The three other-matters have, first, God's sending the prophets; second, God's meeting with Israel himself; third, God's sending angels. In all these three ways, the same point is made, which is that God has favored and been wholly accessible to Israel.

vii. Chapter One Hundred and One. Parashah IV. Lamentations 4:1

CI.

1.   A.   "How the gold has grown dim, how the pure gold is changed":

    B.   R. Samuel said, "How has the gold been covered over, in line with the meaning of the word in this verse: 'There is no secret that they can hide from you' (Ezek. 28:3). [Cohen, p. 215, n. 1: "The gold has become covered over, so that it is not recognizable as gold while it yet remains gold. Similarly, in spite of their sins, occasioned to some extent by misery and exile, the nation in its heart of hearts remained faithful to God."]

    C.   R. Hama b. Hanina said, "'How has the gold become dim,' [having lost its sheen (Cohen, p. 215, n. 3), as it is said, 'How is the gold grown dim.'"

2.   A.   R. Hiyya taught, "When the verse [Lev. 16:12, 'And he shall take a censer full of coals of fire'] speaks of coals, might one suppose that they are dully burning?

    B.   "Scripture says, 'coals of fire.'

    C.   "If the intent were only 'fire,' it would have been possible to suppose that the intent were the flame.

    D.   "Thus Scripture says, 'coals.'

    E.   "How so? He is to take glowing coals."

3.   A.   "The holy stones lie scattered at the head of every street":

    B.   This refers to the disciples of sages who had to go out to make a living.

    C.   Of them Scripture says, "The holy stones lie scattered at the head of every street."

4.   A.   Another interpretation [of the verse, "How the gold has grown dim, how the pure gold is changed, the holy stones lie scattered at the head of every street":]

    B.   This speaks of Josiah.

    C.   "How the gold has grown dim":

    D.   He was like a golden ornament.

    E.   "how the pure gold is changed":

    F.   His body was like precious stones and pearls.

    G.   "the Holy stones lie scattered at the head of every street":

    H.   this refers to the quarter-logs of his blood that Jeremiah collected and buried [when he was killed].

I.   For it is written, "And he was buried in the sepulchres of his fathers" (2 Chr. 35:24).

J.   How many sepulchres did he require?

K.   Since Scripture speaks of "the sepulchres of his fathers," it refers to the two quarter-logs of his blood that Jeremiah collected and buried.

5. A. Another interpretation of the verse: "How the gold has grown dim, how the pure gold is changed, the Holy stones lie scattered at the head of every street":

B.   This speaks of the men of Jerusalem, who were like a golden ornament.

C.   Their bodies were like precious stones and pearls.

D.   If anyone maintains that the verse does not speak of them, then note the following one: "The precious sons of Zion, worth their weight in fine gold, how they are reckoned as earthen pots, the work of a potter's hands."

Our sequence is now [1] disciples of sages; [2] Josiah; [3] the men of Jerusalem. These form the subject of the lament. I cannot say I know what the three have in common, but if Josiah represents the Messiah, the disciples of the sages stand for the Torah, and then the men of Jerusalem should represent the Temple and its cult, a common composition indeed.

viii. Chapter One Hundred and Two.
Parashah IV. Lamentations 4:2

CII:i.

1. A. "The precious sons of Zion, [worth their weight in fine gold, how they are reckoned as earthen pots, the work of a potter's hands!]:

B.   What made them precious?

C.   When a villager made a woman of Jerusalem, he would give to her her weight in gold.

D.   When a Jerusalemite married a village-woman, she would give him his weight in gold.

2. A. Another matter concerning "The precious sons of Zion, [worth their weight in fine gold, how they are reckoned as earthen pots, the work of a potter's hands!]:

B.   What made them precious?

C.   When a Jerusalemite married up, he spent more on the wedding feast than on furniture.

D.   When he married down, he spent more on furniture than on the wedding feast.

3. A. Another matter concerning "The precious sons of Zion, [worth their weight in fine gold, how they are reckoned as earthen pots, the work of a potter's hands!]:

B.   What made them precious?

C.   When one of them was invited to a banquet, he would not go unless he was invited twice.

4. A. There was the case of a man who was in Jerusalem and made a banquet. He said to his messenger, "Go and bring my friend, Qamsa."

B. He went and brought to him his enemy, Bar Qamsa.

C. The latter came in and sat himself among the invited guests.

D. He said to him, "How is it that you are my enemy and you sit in my house? Get out of here."

E. He said to him, "Since I have come, don't humiliate me. I'll pay you back for the cost of whatever I eat."

F. He said to him, "You are not to recline at this banquet."

G. He said to him, "Get out of here."

H. R. Zechariah b. Eucolus, who was there, could have stopped it, but he did not intervene.

I. Bar Qamsa then left. He said to himself, "Since these are feasting in luxury, I am going to go and inform against them at court."

J. What did he do? He went to the ruler and said to him, "These sacrifices that you contribute [to the temple] they eat, and they offer others in their place [which are inferior]."

K. He put him off [rejecting the charge].

L. He went back to him again and said, "These sacrifices that you contribute [to the temple] they eat, and they offer others in their place [which are inferior]. If you don't believe me, send an hyparch and some animals for sacrifice back with me, and you will know that I am not a liar."

M. He sent with him a third-grown calf.

N. While they were on the way, the hyparch dozed off, and the other got up by night and secretly blemished the beasts [so that they could not be offered on the altar and had to be replaced].

O. When the priest saw it, he substituted others for them.

P. The king's agent said to him, "Why don't you offer the animals I brought?"

Q. He said to him, "I'll do it tomorrow."

R. He came on the third day, but the priest had not offered them up.

S. He sent word to the king, "That matter involving the Jews is true."

T. The king immediately came forth against the temple and destroyed it.

U. That is the source of the saying, "Because of the difference between Qamsa and Bar Qamsa, the temple was destroyed."

V. R. Yosé said, "It was the self-effacing character of Zechariah b. Eucolus that burned the temple."

5. A. Another matter concerning "The precious sons of Zion, [worth their weight in fine gold, how they are reckoned as earthen pots, the work of a potter's hands!]:

B. What made them precious?

C. None of them produced a defective child in limb or a child blemished in body.

6. A. There was the case of Joshua b. Hananiah, who went to Rome.

B. He was told that there was a boy in prison, kept there for pederasty.

C. He went and saw there a youngster of beautiful eyes, a lovely face, curly locks, who was used for pederasty.

D.   He stood by the door to find out his character, reciting to him this verse, "Who gave Jacob for a spoil, and Israel to the robbers" (Isa. 42:24).

E.   The boy responded, "Did not the Lord? He against whom we have sinned, and in whose ways they would not walk, neither did they obey his Torah" (Isa. 42:24).

F.   When he heard this, he wept and recited the verse, "The precious sons of Zion, [worth their weight in fine gold, how they are reckoned as earthen pots, the work of a potter's hands!]"

G.   He said, "I call heaven and earth to witness against me, that I will not budge without ransoming him at any price they demand."

H.   They say that he did not budge without ransoming him at any price they demanded.

I.   And not much time went by before he became a teacher in Israel.

J.   And what was his name? R. Ishmael b. Elisha.

7. A.   Another matter concerning "The precious sons of Zion, [worth their weight in fine gold, how they are reckoned as earthen pots, the work of a potter's hands!]:

B.   What made them precious?

C.   They would not attend a dinner unless they knew who else was invited,

D.   or sign a document unless they knew who else was a signatory.

E.   This carries out the verse: "Put not your hand with the wicked to be an unrighteous witness" (Ex. 23:1).

8. A.   Another matter concerning "The precious sons of Zion, [worth their weight in fine gold, how they are reckoned as earthen pots, the work of a potter's hands!]:

B.   What made them precious?

C.   When one of them was invited to attend a dinner, he would change his buckle [from the right to the left shoulder, indicating that he had accepted an invitation to a banquet].

D.   Why so?

E.   So that if someone else should come to invite him to a banquet, he should not burden him needlessly.

9. A.   Another matter concerning "The precious sons of Zion, [worth their weight in fine gold, how they are reckoned as earthen pots, the work of a potter's hands!]:

B.   What made them precious?

C.   None of them made a claim he could not justify.

D.   R. Simeon b. Gamaliel taught, "There was a superb custom in Jerusalem.

E.   "When one of them came to a meal, a cloth was spread over the door [showing that the meal was underway].

F.   "So long as the cloth was spread, the guests would come in.

G.   "When it was taken away, guests could take only three steps into the house."

10. A.   Another matter concerning "The precious sons of Zion, [worth their weight in fine gold, how they are reckoned as earthen pots, the work of a potter's hands!]:

B.   What made them precious?

C. When one of them was making a banquet, he would hand over the meal to a caterer, so that if something went wrong with the meal, they would penalize the caterer.

D. And this was done in accord with the standing of the host and guests.

11. A. Another matter concerning "The precious sons of Zion, [worth their weight in fine gold, how they are reckoned as earthen pots, the work of a potter's hands!]:

B. What made them precious?

C. When one of them gave a banquet, he would [Cohen, p. 219:] indicate all the courses on a menu.

D. Why so?

E. So that those who were meticulous about their food would have to eat what was distasteful to them.

12. A. R. Hiyya, the Scripture teacher, in the name of R. Samuel b. Nahman said, "From the day that the temple was destroyed, wine turned into jelly, white glass was no longer used."

B. What is white glass?

C. [Cohen, p. 219:] "Such as can be folded up."

13. A. ["The precious sons of Zion, worth their weight in fine gold, how they are reckoned as earthen pots, the work of a potter's hands":]

B. There was the case of a man who said to his house servant, "Go and bring me water," and he watched him go from the top of the roof.

C. The servant came back and said, "I couldn't find any."

D. The master said to him, "Throw your pitcher down in front of me."

E. He did so.

F. The master threw himself down from the rooftop and fell and died, and his limbs were mixed with the pieces of earthenware.

G. In his regard Scripture says, "The precious sons of Zion, worth their weight in fine gold, how they are reckoned as earthen pots, the work of a potter's hands."

The shared point of the many *davar aher*s is self-evident. The passage shows us what it means to claim that "another thing" is simply the same thing twice. The long series of examples of the refinement of Jerusalemites – Nos. 1-3, 5, 7-11 – hardly seems demanded by the program of our compilation. No. 4 is added because it involves the customs as to hospitality to which reference is made. The item at No. 6 is inserted for a more substantial reason, since it uses the base verse for its own purposes. No. 12 does not seem to me pertinent, though perhaps it was originally joined to No. 11 before insertion here, and No. 13 concludes with a fine example of the Jerusalemites being "reckoned as earthen pots." My sense is that the materials are richer than required for the base verse.

ix. Chapter One Hundred and Twenty-Three.
Parashah V. Lamentations 5:1

CXXIII:i.

1. A.   "Remember, O Lord, what has befallen us; [behold and see our disgrace]":

   B.   R. Isaac opened [discourse by citing the following verse of Scripture]: "'[There are three that are stately of stride, four that carry themselves well: the lion is mightiest among the beasts, and recoils before none;] the greyhound, the he-goat, [the king whom none dares resist]' (Prov. 30:31).

   C.   "[Since the word for greyhound and the word for gladiator use the same letters, we interpret the verse to speak of gladiators, as follows:] ordinarily if a person trains two gladiators in his household, one stronger than the other, he puts down the stronger, rather than the weaker, [Buber adds: so that he will not go and kill him], so as to protect his property.

   D.   "[Buber (cf. Cohen, p. 236, n. 2):] You, however, do not protect your people but leave them among the nations. [Cohen: God's punishment had fallen upon the weaker and not on the strong nations which had devastated them.]"

2. A.   ["Remember, O Lord, what has befallen us; behold and see our disgrace]":

   B.   Said R. Berekhiah, "Said the Community of Israel before the Holy One, blessed be He:

   C.   "'Lord of all worlds, you have said to us, 'Remember what Amalek did to you by the way' (Dt. 25:17).

   D.   "'Do you think that he did it to us and that to you he did nothing?

   E.   "'Did he not destroy your holy house?'"

3. A.   ["Remember, O Lord, what has befallen us; behold and see our disgrace]":

   B.   Rabbis say, "Said the Community of Israel before the Holy One, blessed be He: 'We are yours and the nations are yours.

   C.   "'Why don't you have pity on your people Israel?

   D.   "'the king whom none dares resist'!"

4. A.   ["Remember, O Lord, what has befallen us; behold and see our disgrace]":

   B.   Said R. Isaac, "Said the Community of Israel before the Holy One, blessed be He:

   C.   "'As to us, we can forget, but as to you, there is no such thing as forgetting. Therefore you do the remembering: 'Remember, O Lord, against the children of Edom the day of Jerusalem; who said, 'Raze it, raze it, even to the foundations thereof' (Ps. 137:7)."

I am inclined to see the three *davar ahers* as an illustration of the "three that are stately of stride" of the intersecting verse; but that is only a guess. Clearly, the point of Nos. 2, 3, and 4 is this: when the nations of the world afflict Israel, they are attacking God too. No. 2

has that statement for Amalek, No. 3 for Israel before God, No. 4 for Edom/Rome.

x. Chapter One Hundred and Thirty.
Parashah V. Lamentations 5:8

CXXX:i.
1. A. "Slaves rule over us":
   B. This refers to the Egyptians.
2. A. "there is none to deliver us from their hand":
   B. Were it not for Moses.
3. A. Another interpretation of the matter: "Slaves rule over us":
   B. This refers to the four kingdoms.
4. A. "there is none to deliver us from their hand":
   B. Were it not for the Holy One, blessed be He.

The redemption of past and future are joined together in this beautifully crafted statement. There is no possibility of reading the "another matters" as other than the same matter; and both are necessary to make the point at hand.

xi. Chapter One Hundred and Forty-Two.
Parashah V. Lamentations 5:20

CXLII:i.
1. A. "Why do you forget us for ever, why do you so long forsake us":
   B. Said R. Joshua b. Abin, "Four expressions were used by Jeremiah: rejecting, loathing, forgetting, forsaking.
   C. "Rejecting and loathing: 'Have you utterly rejected Judah? Has your soul loathed Zion' (Jer. 14:19). And Moses answered, "I will not reject them, nor will I abhor them' (Lev. 26:44).
   D. "Forgetting and forsaking: 'Why do you forget us for ever, why do you so long forsake us.' And Isaiah answered, 'Yes, these may forget, but I will not forget you' (Isa. 49:15)."
2. A. [Another comment on "Why do you forget us for ever, why do you so long forsake us":]
   B. Said R. Joshua b. Levi, "Four expressions were used by Jeremiah: rejecting, anger, forsaking, and forgetting.
   C. "Rejection was answered by Jeremiah himself: 'Thus says the Lord, If heaven above can be measured and the foundation of the earth searched out beneath, then I will also cast off all the seed of Israel for all that they have done, says the Lord' (Jer. 31:37).
   D. "Anger was answered by Isaiah: 'I will not contend for ever, neither will I always be angry' (Isa. 57:16).

The message of the composition of two "other matters" of course is essentially the same. It is that punishment and rejection will be followed by forgiveness and reconciliation. The authorities differ on detail, so as to underline the main point on which they concur.

8

Cases of *Davar Aher* in Song of Songs Rabbah

i. From Literature to Theology?

Our probe has yielded only one of our two points of interest, the literary-hermeneutical one. "Another matter" signals "another way of saying the same thing;" or the formula bears the sense, "these two distinct things add up to one thing," with the further proviso that both are necessary to make one point that transcends each one. But that essentially hermeneutical point, confirming Green's initial observation, has no bearing upon theology and yields no method for the inquiry into the substrate theological system that sustains the whole. What we now need to ask is whether the fixed formula of the *davar-aher* compilation points toward fixed formulas of theological thought: sets of coherent verbal symbols that work together (e.g., David, Solomon, Messiah at the end of time; this age, the age to come; the Exodus from Egypt, Sinai, the age to come) to point toward a theological structure that undergirds the episodic expressions in hand. In Song of Songs Rabbah we find some evidence that sustains that hypothesis, or, at least, renders it plausible. This seems to me one starting point in resuming the quest begun by Kadushin: how language yields logic. But I emphasize, it is only a starting point; and immediately upon concluding this examination of a repertoire of language usages, I forthwith revert to our literary analysis, in Part Three only by implication making some suggestions bearing use in theological description.

ii. Chapter One. Song of Songs Rabbah to Song 1:1

I:i.

1. A.   "The song of songs":
    B.   This is in line with that which Scripture said through Solomon: "Do you see a man who is diligent in his business? He will stand before kings, he will not stand before mean men" (Prov. 22:29).
    C.   "Do you see a man who is diligent in his business":
    D.   This refers to Joseph: "But one day, when he went into the house to do his work [and none of the men of the house was there in the house, she caught him by his garment, saying, 'Lie with me.' But he left his garment in her hand and fled and got out of the house]" (Gen. 39:10-13).
    E.   R. Judah and R. Nehemiah:
    F.   R. Judah said, "[Following Gen. R; LXXXVII:VII:] It was a festival day for the Nile. [Everybody went to see it, but he went to the household to take up his master's account-books]."
    G.   R. Nehemiah said, "It was a day of theater. Everybody went to see it, but he went to the household to take up his master's account-books."

2. A.   R. Phineas says in the name of R. Samuel bar Abba, "Whoever serves his master properly goes forth to freedom.
    B.   "Whence do we learn that fact? From the case of Joseph.
    C.   "It was because he served his master properly that he went forth to freedom."

3. A.   "He will stand before kings":
    B.   this refers to Pharaoh: "Then Pharaoh sent and called Joseph and they brought him hastily from the dungeon" (Gen. 41:14).

4. A.   "he will not stand before mean men":
    B.   this refers to Potiphar, whose eyes the Holy One, blessed be He, darkened [the word for 'darkened' and 'mean men' share the same consonants], and whom he castrated.

5. A.   Another interpretation of the verse, "Do you see a man who is diligent in his business" (Prov. 22:29):
    B.   this refers to our lord, Moses, in the making of the work of the tabernacle.
    C.   Therefore: "He will stand before kings."
    D.   this refers to Pharaoh: "Rise up early in the morning and stand before Pharaoh" (Ex. 8:16).
    E.   "he will not stand before mean men":
    F.   this refers to Jethro.
    G.   Said R. Nehemiah, "[In identifying the king with Pharaoh,] you have made the holy profane.
    H.   "Rather, 'He will stand before kings': this refers to the King of kings, the Holy One, blessed be He: 'And he was there with the Lord forty days' (Ex. 34:28).
    I.   "'he will not stand before mean men': this refers to Pharaoh: 'And there was thick darkness' (Ex. 10:22)."

6. A.   Another interpretation of the verse, "Do you see a man who is diligent in his business" (Prov. 22:29):

	B.	this refers to those righteous persons who are occupied with the work of the Holy One, blessed be He.
	C.	Therefore: "He will stand before kings."
	D.	this refers to for they stand firm in the Torah: "By me kings rule" (Prov. 8:15).
	E.	"he will not stand before mean men":
	F.	this refers to the wicked: "And their works are in the dark" Isa. 29:15); "Let their way be dark and slippery" (Ps. 35:6).
7.	A.	Another interpretation of the verse, "Do you see a man who is diligent in his business" (Prov. 22:29):
	B.	this refers to this is R. Hanina.
8.	A.	They say:
	B.	One time he saw people of his village bringing whole-offerings and peace-offerings up [on a pilgrimage to the Temple].
	C.	He said, "All of them are bringing peace-offerings to Jerusalem, but I am not bringing up a thing! What shall I do?"
	D.	Forthwith he went out to the open fields of his town, the unoccupied area of his town, and there he found a stone. He went and plastered it and polished it and painted it and said, "Lo, I accept upon myself the vow to bring it up to Jerusalem."
	E.	He sought to hire day workers, saying to them, "Will you bring this stone up to Jerusalem for me?"
	F.	They said to him, "Pay us our wage, a hundred gold pieces, and we'll be glad to carry your stone up to Jerusalem for you."
	G.	He said to them, "Where in the world will I get a hundred gold pieces, or even fifty, to give you?"
	H.	Since at the time he could not find the funds, they immediately went their way.
	I.	Immediately the Holy One, blessed be He, arranged for him for fifty angels in the form of men [to meet him]. They said to him, "My lord, give us five *selas*, and we shall bring your stone to Jerusalem, on condition that you help us with the work."
	J.	So he put his hand to the work with them, and they found themselves standing in Jerusalem. He wanted to pay them their wage, but he could not find them.
	K.	The case came to the Chamber of the Hewn Stone [where the high court was in session]. They said to him, "It appears that in the case of our lord, ministering angels have brought the stone up to Jerusalem."
	L.	Immediately he gave sages that wage for which he had hired the angels.
9.	A.	Another interpretation of the verse, "Do you see a man who is diligent in his business" (Prov. 22:29):
	B.	this refers to Solomon son of David.
	C.	"He will stand before kings."
	D.	for he was diligent in building the house of the sanctuary: "So he spent seven years in building it" (1 Kgs. 6:38).
10.	A.	[Supply: "So he spent seven years in building it" (1 Kgs. 6:38),] but a different verse says, "And Solomon was building his own house for thirteen years" (1 Kgs. 7:1).

B.   so the building of the house of Solomon was lovelier and more elaborate than the building of the house of the sanctuary.

C.   But this is what they said:

D.   In the building of his house he was slothful, in the building of the house of the sanctuary he was diligent and not slothful.

11. A. Huna in the name of R. Joseph: "All help the king, all the more so do all help out on account of the glory of the King of kings of kings, the Holy One, blessed be He,

B.   "even spirits, demons, ministering angels."

12. A. Isaac b. R. Judah b. Ezekiel said, "'I have surely built you a house of habitation' (1 Kgs. 8:13): 'I have built what is already built.'"

13. A. R. Berekiah said, "'The house that they were building' is not what is said,

B.   "but rather, 'the house in its being built' (1 Kgs. 6:7), which is to say, it was built of itself.

C.   "'It was built of stone made ready at the quarry' (1 Kgs. 6:7):

D.   "that it says is not 'built' but 'it was built,' which is to say, the stones carried themselves and set themselves on the row."

14. A. Said Rab, "Do not find this astonishing. What is written elsewhere? 'And a stone was brought and laid upon the mouth of the den' (Dan. 6:18).

B.   "Now are there any stones in Babylonia? [Of course not.] But from the land of Israel it flew in a brief moment and came and rested on the mouth of the pit."

15. A. R. Huna in the name of R. Joseph said [concerning the verse, "And a stone was brought and laid upon the mouth of the den" (Dan. 6:18)], "An angel came down in the form of a lion made of stone and put itself at the mouth of the pit.

B.   "That is in line with this verse: 'My God has sent his angel and has shut the lions' mouths' (Dan. 6:23).

C.   "Now do not find it astonishing. If for the honor owing to that righteous man, it is written, 'a certain stone was brought' (Dan. 6:18), for the honoring of the Holy One, blessed be He, how much the more so [will stones be provided in a magical manner]."

16. A. [Resuming where the discussion of 8.D:] "He will stand before kings."

B.   before the kings of the Torah he will stand.

C.   "he will not stand before mean men":

D.   this refers to a conspiracy of wicked men.

17. A. Said R. Joshua b. Levi, "When they took a vote and decided, **Three kings and four ordinary folk have no share in the world to come [M. San. 10:1],**

B.   "they wanted to include Solomon with them.

C.   "But an echo came forth and said, 'Do not lay hands on my anointed ones' (Ps. 105:15)."

D.   Said R. Judah b. R. Simon, "And not only so, but he was given the place of honor at the head of three genealogical tables: 'And Rehoboam, son of Solomon, reigned in Judah' (1 Kgs. 14:21). [Simon, p. 4: "He was placed at the head of a genealogical tree...." Simon, p. 4, n. 11: "The mention of his name here being superfluous implies that he was a founder of a royal line.]

E.   Said R., Yudan b. R. Simon, "Not only so, but the Holy Spirit rested on him, and he said the following three books: Proverbs, the Song of Songs, and Qohelet."

While this somewhat overburdened composition hardly conforms to the required form, its basic outlines are not difficult to discern. We have an intersecting verse, Prov. 22:29, aimed at reaching the goal of Solomon, who is author of the Song of Songs, and showing him in the context of Joseph, the righteous, and Moses, four in all. The reason in both cases is the same: each one of them "stood before kings, not before mean men." Our proposed fixed formula then involves examples of the righteous, who are judged by those worthy of judging them.

The invocation of the figure of Joseph ought to carry in its wake the contrast between the impure lust of Potiphar's wife and the pure heart of Joseph, and, by extension, Solomon in the Song. But I do not see that motif present. The form is scarcely established – clause by clause exegesis in light of the principal's life – before it is broken with the insertion of 1.E-G, lifted whole from Gen. R. LXXXVII:VII, where it belongs. No. 2 is then parachuted down as part of the Joseph sequence; but it does not occur in the parallel. No. 3 then resumes the broken form, and No. 4 completes it. So the first statement of the formal program is not difficult to follow. The confluence of the consonants for "mean" and "dark" accounts for the sequence of applications of the third clause to the theme of darkness.

The second exercise, with Moses, is laid out with little blemish in No. 5. No. 6 goes on to the righteous, and here too the sages' passage is worked out with no interpolations. No. 7, by contrast, provides an excuse to insert No. 8. Without No. 7, No. 8 of course would prove incomprehensible in this context (though entirely clear standing on its own). Finally, at No. 9, we come to Solomon. Perhaps the coming theme of the magical works performed through stones, those used in the Temple, with Daniel, and so on, persuaded the person who inserted Nos. 7-8 of the relevance of those passages; but even if they prove thematically in place, the sequence is disruptive and hardly respects the formal program that clearly has guided the framer. One may theorize, to be sure, that the break-up of the initial form – three cases, disruptive insertion, then the goal and purpose of the whole – signals the advent of the central figure in the exegesis. But that would prove a viable thesis only if we should find a fair number of other instances. It is the simple fact that the Mishnah's rhetoric allows for signals of that kind, and we cannot rule out the possibility. But in the present case it seems to me we have nothing more than a rude interpolation. But that is not the only disruptive component of Solomon's passage.

No. 10 introduces the contrast of the two verses, our prooftext at No. 9 plus a contradictory one. This yields a suitable harmonization, which sustains the supplements at Nos. 11, 12, and 13. Nos. 11 and 12 are simply free-standing sentences. No. 13, with Nos. 14, 15, in its wake, by contrast is a full-scale composition, again about miracles done with stones. Hanina's passage would have found a more comfortable home here (if anywhere). Only at No. 16 are we permitted to resume our progress through the established form. No. 17 is tacked on because of the reference of 16.D to a conspiracy of wicked men; the issue then is whether Solomon belongs with them, in line with 17.A-B. 17.E forms a bridge to the sustained discussion of Ps. 45:17. But since the exposition of that verse makes no reference to the foregoing, we should regard the rather run-on sequence before us as winding down at No. 17, and, despite the rhetorical joining language of "therefore," I treat the discussion of Ps. 45:17 as autonomous. It assuredly has no formal ties to the intersecting verse on which we have been working. The whole is surely coherent in that the several components complement one another.

iii. Chapter Two. Song of Songs Rabbah to Song 1:2

II:I.
1.   A.   "O that you would kiss me with the kisses of your mouth! [For your love is better than wine]":
     B.   In what connection was this statement made?
     C.   R. Hinena b. R. Pappa said, "It was stated at the sea: '[I compare you, my love,] to a mare of Pharaoh's chariots' (Song 1:9)."
     D.   R. Yuda b. R. Simon said, "It was stated at Sinai: 'The song of songs' (Song 1:1) – the song that was sung by the singers: 'The singers go before, the minstrels follow after' (Ps. 68:26)."
2.   A.   It was taught on Tannaite authority in the name of R. Nathan, "The Holy One, blessed be He, in the glory of his greatness said it: 'The song of songs that is Solomon's' (Song 1:1),
     B.   "[meaning,] that belongs to the King to whom peace belongs."
3.   A.   Rabban Gamaliel says, "The ministering angels said it: 'the song of songs' (Song 1:1) –
     B.   "the song that the princes on high said."
4.   A.   R. Yohanan said, "It was said at Sinai: 'O that you would kiss me with the kisses of your mouth!' (Song 1:2)."
5.   A.   R. Meir says, "It was said in connection with the tent of meeting."
     B.   And he brings evidence from the following verse: "Awake, O north wind, and come, O south wind! Blow upon my garden, let its fragrance be wafted abroad. Let my beloved come to his garden, and eat its choicest fruits" (Song 4:16).
     C.   "Awake, O north wind": this refers to the burnt-offerings, which is slaughtered at the north side of the altar.
     D.   "and come, O south wind": this refers to the peace-offerings, which were slaughtered at the south side of the altar.

E. "Blow upon my garden": this refers to the tent of meeting.

F. "let its fragrance be wafted abroad": this refers to the incense-offering.

G. "Let my beloved come to his garden": this refers to the Presence of God.

H. "and eat its choicest fruits": this refers to the offerings.

6. A. Rabbis say, "It was said in connection with the house of the ages [the Temple itself]."

B. And they bring evidence from the same verse: "Awake, O north wind, and come, O south wind! Blow upon my garden, let its fragrance be wafted abroad. Let my beloved come to his garden, and eat its choicest fruits" (Song 4:16).

C. "Awake, O north wind": this refers to the burnt-offerings, which is slaughtered at the north side of the altar.

D. "and come, O south wind": this refers to the peace-offerings, which were slaughtered at the south side of the altar.

E. "Blow upon my garden": this refers to the house of the ages.

F. "let its fragrance be wafted abroad": this refers to the incense-offering.

G. "Let my beloved come to his garden": this refers to the Presence of God.

H. "and eat its choicest fruits": this refers to the offerings.

I. The rabbis furthermore maintain that all the other verses also refer to the house of the ages.

J. Said R. Aha, "The verse that refers to the Temple is the following: 'King Solomon made himself a palanquin, from the wood of Lebanon. He made its posts of silver, its back of gold, its seat of purple; it was lovingly wrought within by the daughters of Jerusalem'(Song 3:9-10)."

K. Rabbis treat these as the intersecting verses for the verse, 'And it came to pass on the day that Moses had made an end of setting up the tabernacle' (Num. 7:1)."

7. A. In the opinion of R. Hinena [1.C], who said that the verse was stated on the occasion of the Sea, [the sense of the verse, "O that you would kiss me with the kisses of your mouth"] is, "may he bring to rest upon us the Holy Spirit, so that we may say before him many songs."

B. In the opinion of Rabban Gamaliel, who said that the verse was stated by the ministering angels, [the sense of the verse, "O that you would kiss me with the kisses of your mouth"] is, "may he give us the kisses that he gave to his sons."

C. In the opinion of R. Meir, who said that the verse was stated in connection with the tent of meeting, [the sense of the verse, "O that you would kiss me with the kisses of your mouth"] is, "May he send fire down to us and so accept his offerings."

D. In the opinion of R. Yohanan, who said that the verse was stated in connection with Sinai, [the sense of the verse, "O that you would kiss me with the kisses of your mouth"] is, "May he cause kisses to issue for us from his mouth.

E. "That is why it is written, 'O that you would kiss me with the kisses of your mouth.'"

Our fixed list encompasses [1] Israel at the sea; [2] the ministering angels; [3] the tent of meeting; [4] the eternal house [the Temple]; [5] Sinai. This is somewhat curious, mixing as it does occasions in time, locations, the place of the cult, and the Torah. But if we hold them together, we are given the theological repertoire of suitable verbal symbols or reference points: the redemption from Egypt, the Temple and its cult, and the revealed Torah of Sinai. This composite then is not only complementary in a general sense, it also is explicit in a very particular sense, specifying as it does the range of suitable assignees for the authorship and occasion of the poem, and that range then encompasses the acceptable theological vocabulary of – shall we say, Judaism? the Torah? the Midrash exegesis of our verse? I am not sure of what, but it is clear to me that we may now expect a variety of such lists, a repertoire of those topics or points that all together add up to the relationship between God and Israel that the document, the Song of Songs, portrays. Indeed, even now we may wish to propose that when we seek the theology of the Judaism of the Dual Torah, we may do worse than to look in the way in which the Song of Songs is made into a metaphor for everything evocative of the relationship of God and Israel – that is to say, the subject and problematic of the theology of Judaism.

Let us attend to the specifics of the passage, if briefly. No. 7 once again shows us that our compilers are first-class editors, since they have assembled quite disparate materials and drawn them together into a cogent statement. But the subject is not our base verse, and hence the compilers cannot have had in mind the need of a commentary of a verse-by-verse principle of conglomeration and organization. The passage as a whole refers in much more general terms to the Song of Songs, and hardly to Song 1:2 in particular. That is shown by the simple fact that various opinions invoke other verses than the one to which the whole is ultimately assigned. No. 1 serves Song 1:1, and so does No. 2. Indeed, No. 2 could have been placed in the prior assembly without any damage to its use and meaning. The same is to be said for No. 3. In fact, only Yohanan requires the verse to stand where it now does. No. 5 and No. 6 of course invoke Song 4:16 and do a fine job of reading that verse in light of the tent of meeting in the wilderness or the Temple in Jerusalem. Song 3:9-10 serves as an appropriate locus as well. Then the conclusion draws a variety of senses for Song 1:2 alone, and that conclusion points to the compilers of the whole for its authorship. This is once more highly sophisticated work of compilation, involving rich editorial intervention indeed.

iv. Chapter Five. Song of Songs Rabbah to Song 1:5

V:i.

1. A. "I am very dark, but comely, [O daughters of Jerusalem, like the tents of Kedar, like the curtains of Solomon]" (Song 1:5):
    B. "I am dark" in my deeds.
    C. "But comely" in the deeds of my forebears.
2. A. "I am very dark, but comely":
    B. Said the Community of Israel, "'I am dark' in my view, 'but comely' before my Creator."
    C. For it is written, "Are you not as the children of the Ethiopians to Me, O children of Israel, says the Lord" (Amos 9:7):
    D. "as the children of the Ethiopians" – in your sight.
    E. But "to Me, O children of Israel, says the Lord."
3. A. Another interpretation of the verse, ""I am very dark": in Egypt.
    B. "but comely": in Egypt.
    C. "I am very dark" in Egypt: "But they rebelled against me and would not hearken to me" (Ezek. 20:8).
    D. "but comely" in Egypt: with the blood of the Passover-offering and circumcision, "And when I passed by you and saw you wallowing in your blood, I said to you, In your blood live" (Ezek. 16:6) – in the blood of the Passover.
    E. "I said to you, In your blood live" (Ezek. 16:6) – in the blood of the circumcision.
4. A. Another interpretation of the verse, "I am very dark": at the sea, "They were rebellious at the sea, even the Red Sea" (Ps. 106:7).
    B. "but comely": at the sea, "This is my God and I will be comely for him" (Ex. 15:2) [following Simon's rendering of the verse].
5. A. "I am very dark": at Marah, "And the people murmured against Moses, saying, What shall we drink" (Ex. 15:24).
    B. "but comely": at Marah, "And he cried to the Lord and the Lord showed him a tree, and he cast it into the waters and the waters were made sweet" (Ex. 15:25).
6. A. "I am very dark": at Rephidim, "And the name of the place was called Massah and Meribah" (Ex. 17:7).
    B. "but comely": at Rephidim, "And Moses built an altar and called it by the name 'the Lord is my banner' (Ex. 17:15).
7. A. "I am very dark": at Horeb, "And they made a calf at Horeb" (Ps. 106:19).
    B. "but comely": at Horeb, "And they said, All that the Lord has spoken we will do and obey" (Ex. 24:7).
8. A. "I am very dark": in the wilderness, ""How often did they rebel against him in the wilderness" (Ps. 78:40).
    B. "but comely": in the wilderness at the setting up of the tabernacle, "And on the day that the tabernacle was set up" (Num. 9:15).
9. A. "I am very dark": in the deed of the spies, "And they spread an evil report of the land" (Num. 13:32).
    B. "but comely": in the deed of Joshua and Caleb, ""Save for Caleb, the son of Jephunneh the Kenizzite" (Num. 32:12).

10. A.   "I am very dark": at Shittim, "And Israel abode at Shittim and the people began to commit harlotry with the daughters of Moab" (Num. 25:1).

    B.   "but comely": at Shittim, "Then arose Phinehas and wrought judgment" (Ps. 106:30).

11. A.   "I am very dark": through Achan, "But the children of Israel committed a trespass concerning the devoted thing" (Josh. 7:1).

    B.   "but comely": through Joshua, "And Joshua said to Achan, My son, give I pray you glory" (Josh. 7:19).

12. A.   "I am very dark": through the kings of Israel.

    B.   "but comely": through the kings of Judah.

    C.   If with my dark ones that I had, it was such that "I am comely," all the more so with my prophets.

The contrast of dark and comely yields a variety of applications; in all of them the same situation that is the one also is the other, and the rest follows in a wonderfully well-crafted composition. What is the repertoire of items? Dark in deeds but comely in ancestry; dark in my view but comely before God; dark when rebellious, comely when obedient, a point made at Nos. 3, for Egypt, 4, for the sea, and 5 for Marah, 6, for Massah and Meribah, 7 for Horeb, 8 for the wilderness, 9 for the spies in the Land, 10 for Shittim, 11 for Achan/Joshua and the conquest of the Land, 12 for Israel and Judah. We therefore have worked through the repertoire of events that contained the mixture of rebellion and obedience; the theological substrate of this catalogue is hardly difficult to articulate. At VII:ii.5 we have the articulation:

V:ii.

5. A.   [As to the verse, "I am very dark, but comely," R. Levi b. R. Haita gave three interpretations:

    B.   "'I am very dark': all the days of the week.

    C.   "'but comely': on the Sabbath.

    D.   "'I am very dark': all the days of the year.

    E.   "'but comely': on the Day of Atonement.

    F.   "'I am very dark': among the Ten Tribes.

    G.   "'but comely': in the tribe of Judah and Benjamin.

    H.   "'I am very dark': in this world.

    I.   "'but comely': in the world to come."

v. Chapter Twenty-Three. Song of Songs Rabbah to Song 2:6

XXIII:i.

1. A.   "O that his left hand were under my head":

    B.   this refers to the first tablets.

    C.   "and that his right hand embraced me":

    D.   this refers to the second tablets.

2. A.   Another interpretation of the verse, "O that his left hand were under my head":

    B.   this refers to the show-fringes.

C. "and that his right hand embraced me":

D. this refers to the phylacteries.

3. A. Another interpretation of the verse, "O that his left hand were under my head":

B. this refers to the recitation of the *Shema.*

C. "and that his right hand embraced me":

D. this refers to the Prayer.

4. A. Another interpretation of the verse, "O that his left hand were under my head":

B. this refers to the tabernacle.

C. "and that his right hand embraced me":

D. this refers to the cloud of the Presence of God in the world to come: "The sun shall no longer be your light by day nor for brightness will the moon give light to you" (Isa. 60:19). Then what gives light to you? "The Lord shall be your everlasting light" (Isa. 60:20).

Now our repertoire of reference points is [1] the Ten Commandments; [2] the show-fringes and phylacteries; [3] the *Shema* and the Prayer; [4] the tabernacle and the cloud of the Presence of God in the world to come. Why we invoke, as our candidates for the metaphor at hand, the Ten Commandments, show-fringes and phylacteries, recitation of the *Shema* and the Prayer, the tabernacle and the cloud of the Presence of God, and the *mezuzah,* seems to me clear from the very catalogue. These reach their climax in the analogy between the home and the tabernacle, the embrace of God and the Presence of God. So the whole is meant to list those things that draw the Israelite near God and make the Israelite cleave to God, as the base verse says, hence the right hand and the left stand for the most intimate components of the life of the individual and the home with God.

vi. Chapter Twenty-Five. Song of Songs Rabbah to Song 3:8

XXV:i.

1. A. "The voice of my beloved! Behold he comes [leaping upon the mountains, bounding over the hills]":

B. R. Judah and R. Nehemiah and Rabbis:

C. R. Judah says, "'The voice of my beloved! Behold he comes': this refers to Moses.

D. "When he came and said to the Israelites, 'In this month you will be redeemed,' they said to him, 'Our lord, Moses, how are we going to be redeemed? And did not the Holy One, blessed be He, say to Abraham, "And they shall work them and torment them for four hundred years" (Gen. 15:13), and now we have in hand only two hundred and ten years!'

E. "He said to them, 'Since he wants to redeem you, he is not going to pay attention to these reckonings of yours.

F. "'But: "leaping upon the mountains, bounding over the hills." The reference here to mountains and hills in fact alludes to calculations and specified times. "He leaps" over reckonings, calculations, and specified times.

G. "'And in this month you are to be redeemed: "This month is the beginning of months" (Ex. 12:1).'"

2. A. R. Nehemiah says, "'The voice of my beloved! Behold he comes': this refers to Moses.

B. "When he came and said to the Israelites, 'In this month you will be redeemed,' they said to him, 'Our lord, Moses, how are we going to be redeemed? We have no good deeds to our credit.'

C. "He said to them, 'Since he wants to redeem you, he is not going to pay attention to bad deeds.'

D. "'And to what does he pay attention? To the righteous people among you and to their deeds,

E. "'for example, Amram and his court.

F. "''leaping upon the mountains, bounding over the hills": mountains refers only to courts, in line with this usage: "I will depart and go down upon the mountains" (Judges 11:37).

G. "'And in this month you are to be redeemed: "This month is the beginning of months" (Ex. 12:1).'"

3. A. Rabbis say, "'The voice of my beloved! Behold he comes': this refers to Moses.

B. "When he came and said to the Israelites, 'In this month you will be redeemed,' they said to him, 'Our lord, Moses, how are we going to be redeemed? And the whole of Egypt is made filthy by our own worship of idols!'

C. "He said to them, 'Since he wants to redeem you, he is not going to pay attention to your worship of idols.

D. "'Rather, "leaping upon the mountains, bounding over the hills": mountains and hills refer only to idolatry, in line with this usage: "They sacrifice on the tops of the mountains and offer upon the hills" (Hos. 4:13).

E. "'And in this month you are to be redeemed: "This month is the beginning of months" (Ex. 12:1).'"

4. A. R. Yudan and R. Hunia:

B. R. Yudan in the name of R. Eliezer son of R. José the Galilean, and R. Hunia in the name of R. Eliezer b. Jacob say, "'The voice of my beloved! Behold he comes': this refers to the royal messiah.

C. "When he says to the Israelites, 'In this month you are to be redeemed, they will say to him, 'How are we going to be redeemed? And has not the Holy One, blessed be He, taken an oath that he would subjugate us among the seventy nations.'

D. "Now he will reply to them in two ways.

E. "He will say to them, 'If one of you is taken into exile to Barbary and one to Sarmatia, it is as though all of you had gone into exile.

F. "'And not only so, but this state conscripts troops from all of the world and from every nation, so that if one Samaritan or one Barbarian comes and subjugates you, it is as though his entire nation had ruled over you and as if you were subjugated by all the seventy nations.

G.   "'In this month you are to be redeemed: "This month is the beginning of months" (Ex. 12:1).'"

Nos. 1-3 form a perfectly matched set; remove one and you lose the whole. A fixed catalogue emerges, which can be used in any number of ways to exploit available metaphors. The items go over the trilogy of the timing of redemption, the moral condition of those to be redeemed, and the past religious misdeeds of those to be redeemed. Against these three arguments Moses argues that God will redeem at God's own time, as an act of grace and forgiveness. The theological message emerges with enormous power through invoking the love of God for Israel, God "leaping upon the mountains." I cannot point to a better or more telling example of the rewards accruing to the framers of the document from their decision to work on just this part of Scripture. The obvious necessity of No. 4 to complete the message requires no comment. Any conception that first comes from the individual units, then the completed composition, seems to me to take second place before the notion that the plan of the whole – as a theological statement, I mean – came prior to the formation of the parts. Then it hardly matters whose names are tacked on to the formally matched and perfect components.

vii. Chapter Twenty-Six. Song of Songs Rabbah to Song 2:9

In this unit we move out from the another-matters to explore a sustained repertoire of exegetical possibilities, which, all together, comprise a complete theological program. Here therefore I show how we may move beyond the restrictions of a literary form to the broader possibilities of a fixed set of reference points, which hold together rather diffuse and not-well-disciplined materials.

XXVI:i.

1. A.   "My beloved is like a gazelle":

     B.   Said R. Isaac, "Said the Congregation of Israel before the Holy One, blessed be He, 'Lord of the world, you have said to us, [Simon:] "My love, my love." You are the one who says, "My love, my love" to us first.' [Simon, p. 118: *Dew* is an exclamation of affection. Jastrow: Thou art sighing for us first, instead of our aspiring for Thee.]

2. A.   "My beloved is like a gazelle":

     B.   Just as a gazelle leaps from mountain to mountain, hill to hill, tree to tree, thicket to thicket, fence to fence,

     C.   so the Holy One, blessed be He, lept from Egypt to the sea, from the sea to Sinai, from Sinai to the age to come.

     D.   In Egypt they saw him: "For I will go through the land of Egypt" (Ex. 12:12).

     E.   At the sea they saw him: "And Israel saw the great hand" (Ex. 14:31); "This is my God and I will glorify him" (Ex. 15:2).

F.   At Sinai they saw him: "The Lord spoke with you face to face in the mountain" (Dt. 5:4); "The Lord comes from Sinai" (Dt. 33:2).

3. A.   "or a young stag":

    B.   R. Yosé b. R. Hanina said, "Meaning, like young deer."

4. A.   "Behold, there he stands behind our wall":

    B.   behind our wall at Sinai: "For on the third day the Lord will come down" (Ex. 19:11).

5. A.   "gazing in at the windows":

    B.   "And the Lord came down upon mount Sinai, at the top of the mountain" (Ex. 19:11).

6. A.   "looking through the lattice":

    B.   "And God spoke all these words" (Ex. 20:1).

7. A.   "My beloved speaks and says to me, ['Arise, my love, my fair one, and come away] (Song 2:10)'":

    B.   What did he say to me?

    C.   "I am the Lord your God" (Ex. 20:2).

No. 1 appears to be free-standing and narrowly exegetical. But in the rerun that follows, it is shown to be integral to the whole. Nos. 2-7 form a sustained and coherent unit, reading the clauses of the verse as an allusion to Israel at Sinai and God's expression of his love. So now it is God who is talking.

XXVI:ii.

1. A.   Another explanation of the verses, "My beloved is like a gazelle":

    B.   Said the Community of Israel before the Holy One, blessed be He, "Lord of the world, you have said to us, [Simon:] "My love, my love." You are the one who says, "My love, my love" to us first.' [Simon, p. 118: *Dew* is an exclamation of affection. Jastrow: Thou art sighing for us first, instead of our aspiring for Thee.]

2. A.   "My beloved is like a gazelle":

    B.   Just as a gazelle leaps from mountain to mountain, hill to hill, tree to tree, thicket to thicket, fence to fence,

    C.   so the Holy One, blessed be He, leaps from synagogue to synagogue, school house to school house.

    D.   All this why? So as to bestow blessing upon Israel.

    E.   And on account of what merit?

    F.   It is for the merit accruing to Abraham: "And the Lord appeared to him by the terebinths of Mamre and he was sitting" (Gen. 18:1).

3. A.   R. Berekhiah in the name of R. Simeon b. Laqish: "While read as 'sitting,' the word is written as, 'sat.'

    B.   "Abraham intended to stand up. Said to him the Holy One, blessed be He, 'Remain seated, Abraham. You provide a model for your children. Just as you sit while I stand, so your children will be when they enter the synagogue and the school house and recite the Shema: they will sit, while my Glory will stand among them.

    C.   "What verse of Scripture indicates it? 'God stands in the congregation of God' (Ps. 82:1)."

4. A.   [Supply: "God stands in the congregation of God" (Ps. 82:1):]

	B.	R. Haggai in the name of R. Isaac said, "What is written here is not, 'God is standing,' but rather, 'God stands.'
	C.	"What is the meaning of 'God stands'?
	D.	"It is, [Simon:] 'ready to attention,' as it says: 'And present yourself there to me on the top of the mount' (Ex. 34:2); 'And it shall come to pass that before they call, I will answer' (Isa. 65:24)."
5.	A.	Rabbi in the name of R. Hanina: "Upon the occasion of every expression of praise with which the Israelites praise the Holy One, blessed be He, the Holy One, blessed be He, sits among them:
	B.	"'You are holy, enthroned upon the praises of Israel' (Ps. 22;4)."
6.	A.	"or a young stag":
	B.	R. Yosé b. R. Hanina said, "Meaning, like young deer."
7.	A.	"Behold, there he stands behind our wall":
	B.	behind the walls of the synagogues and school houses.
8.	A.	"gazing in at the windows":
	B.	from between the shoulders of the priests.
9.	A.	"looking through the lattice":
	B.	from between the fingers of the priests.
10.	A.	"My beloved speaks and says to me":
	B.	What did he say to me?
	C.	"The Lord bless you and keep you" (Num. 6:24).

We go over the same matter as before, moving on from the redemption at Sinai to the union of synagogue, school house, and Temple, with the priestly blessing at the climax.

XXVI:iii.

1.	A.	Another explanation of the verse, "My beloved is like a gazelle":
	B.	Said the Community of Israel before the Holy One, blessed be He, "Lord of the world, you have said to us, [Simon:] "My love, my love." You are the one who says, "My love, my love" to us first.' [Simon, p. 118: *Dew* is an exclamation of affection. Jastrow: Thou art sighing for us first, instead of our aspiring for Thee.]
2.	A.	"or a young stag":
	B.	Just as a stag appears and then disappears, appears and then disappears,
	C.	so the first redeemer [Moses] came but then disappeared and then reappeared.
3.	A.	How long did he disappear?
	B.	R. Tanhuma said, "Three months: 'And they met Moses and Aaron' (Ex. 5:20)."
	C.	Judah b. Rabbi said, "Intermittently."
	D.	So the final redeemer will appear to them and then disappear from sight.
	E.	And how long will he disappear from them?
	F.	Forty-five days: "And from the time that the continual burnt-offering shall be taken away and the detestable thing that causes abomination be set up, there shall be a thousand and two hundred ninety days" (Dan. 12:11); "Happy is he who waits and comes to the thousand three hundred and thirty-five days" (Dan. 12:13).

	G.	What are the additional days?
	H.	R. Yohanan, the laundry woman's son, said in the name of R. Jonah, "These are the forty-five days on which he will disappear from them."
	I.	In those days the Israelites will pick salt-wort and juniper-roots for food: "They pluck salt-wort with wormwood and the roots of the broom are their food" (Job 30:3).
	J.	Where will he led them?
	K.	Some say, "To the wilderness of Judah."
	L.	Some say, "To the wilderness of Sihon and Og."
	M.	Those who say, "To the wilderness of Judah," cite the following: "I will yet again make you dwell in tents as in the days of the appointed season" (Hos. 12:10).
	N.	Those who say, "To the wilderness of Sihon and Og cite the following: "Therefore behold I will allure her and bring her into the wilderness and speak tenderly to her. And I will give her vineyards from there" (Hos. 2:16-17).
	O.	And whoever believes in him and follows him and waits for him will live.
	P.	But whoever does not believe in him and follow him and wait for him but goes over to the nations of the world in the end will be killed by them.
	Q.	Said R. Isaac b. R. Merion, "In the end of the forty-five days [H-I above], he will reappear to them and bring down manna for them.
	R.	"For 'there is nothing new under the sun.'"
4.	A.	"or a young stag":
	B.	meaning, like young deer.
5.	A.	"Behold, there he stands behind our wall":
	B.	behind the Western Wall of the house of the sanctuary.
	C.	Why so?
	D.	Because the Holy One, blessed be He, took an oath to him that it would never be destroyed.
	E.	And the Priests' Gate and the Huldah Gate will never be destroyed before the Holy One, blessed be He, will restore them.
6.	A.	"gazing in at the windows":
	B.	through the merit of the matriarchs.
7.	A.	"My beloved speaks and says to me":
	B.	What did he say to me?
	C.	"This month shall be for you the beginning of the months" (Ex. 12:2).

Obviously overwhelmed by interpolations, this next reading of our base verses introduces the messianic theme, the third in line as we have now come to expect. The secondary accretions of No. 3 do not spoil the exegetical program, which resumes and is completed at Nos. 4ff., despite the erroneous, "another interpretation". The opening of the next unit repeats that error.

viii. Chapter Thirty. Song of Songs Rabbah to Song 2:13

What follows is a fine exemplification of the literary-theological phenomenon I have proposed to identify. We have a series of interpretations of the same matter, in fact bearing the desired formula. We proceed to examine these matters: Israel's redemption from Sinai (XXX:i); the forty years in the wilderness and the conquest of the Land and presentation of its fruits in the cult (XXX:ii); the governance of Daniel, Ezra, and the return to Zion and restoration to the Land, the destruction of the gentile oppressors and the rebuilding of the Temple (XXX:iii); Elijah and the Messiah, the end of gentile rule and the destruction of the pagan kingdoms (XXX:iv). When I propose to identify the literary evidences of a theological structure, this is the kind of composition that seems to me to provide those evidences. The theology before us, of course, is familiar. It is the way in which we impute that theology to our authorships that I claim to be the contribution potentially present in the approach taken here.

XXX:i.

1. A.   "The fig tree puts forth its figs":
   B.   this refers to the Israelite sinners who perished during the three days of darkness: "And there was thick darkness...they did not see one another" (Ex. 10:22-23).
   C.   "and the vines are in blossom; they give forth fragrance":
   D.   this refers to the survivors, who repented and were redeemed.
   E.   Moses came along to them and said to them, "All this good fragrance is wafted about you, and yet you sit here!
   F.   "'Arise, my love, my fair one, and come away.'"

The Exodus supplies the conclusion of the treatment of the successive verses. We now rework the entire set in several fresh ways.

XXX:ii.

1. A.   Another comment on the verses, "My beloved speaks and says to me, ['Arise, my love, my fair one, and come away, for lo, the winter is past, the rain is over and gone. The flowers appear on the earth, the time of singing has come, and the voice of the turtledove is heard in our land. The fig tree puts forth its figs, and the vines are in blossom; they give forth fragrance. Arise, my love, my fair one, and come away']" (Song 2:10-13):
   B.   "My beloved speaks and says to me":
   C.   R. Azariah said, "Are not 'speaking' and 'saying' the same thing?
   D.   "But 'he spoke to me' through Moses, and 'said to me' through Aaron."
2. A.   What did he say to me? "Arise, my love, my fair one, and come away, for lo, the winter is past":
   B.   This refers to the forty years that the Israelites spent in the wilderness.

3. A. "the rain is over and gone":

    B. This refers to the thirty-eight years that the Israelites were as though excommunicated in the wilderness.

    C. For the Word did not speak with Moses until that entire generation had perished: "And the days in which we came from Kadesh-barnea...moreover the hand of the Lord was against them...so it came to pass that when all the men of war were consumed...the Lord spoke to me saying" (Dt. 2:14-17).

4. A. "The flowers appear on the earth":

    B. the conquerors appear on the earth,

    C. that is, the princes: "Each prince on his day" (Num. 7:11).

5. A. "the time of singing has come":

    B. the time of the foreskin to be removed.

    C. the time for the Canaanites to be cut off.

    D. the time for the land of Israel to be split up: "Unto these the land shall be divided" (Num. 26:53).

6. A. "and the voice of the turtledove is heard in our land":

    B. Said R. Yohanan, "'The voice of the good pioneer is heard in our land' [the words for turtledove and pioneer or explorer using the same consonants].

    C. "This refers to Joshua when he said, 'Pass in the midst of the camp.'"

7. A. "The fig tree puts forth its figs":

    B. this refers to the baskets of first fruits.

8. A. "and the vines are in blossom; they give forth fragrance":

    B. this refers to drink-offerings.

The form is now established and will be followed quite carefully. The first set of applications deals with the Exodus and the conquest of the land.

XXX:iii.

1. A. Another reading of the verse, "My beloved speaks and says to me":

    B. He "spoke to me" through Daniel,

    C. and "said to me" through Ezra.

    D. And what did he say to me?

2. A. "Arise, my love, my fair one, and come away, for lo, the winter is past":

    B. this refers to the seventy years that the Israelites spent in Exile.

3. A. "the rain is over and gone":

    B. this is the fifty-two years between the time that the first Temple was destroyed and the kingdom of the Chaldeans was uprooted.

    C. But were they not seventy years?

    D. Said R. Levi, "Subtract from them the eighteen years that an echo was circulated and saying to Nebuchadnezzar, 'Bad servant! Go up and destroy the house of your Master, for the children of your Master have not obeyed him.'"

4. A. "The flowers appear on the earth":

    B. For example, Mordecai and his colleagues, Ezra and his colleagues.

5. A.   "the time of singing has come":
    B.   the time of the foreskin to be removed.
    C.   the time for the wicked to be broken: "The Lord has broken off the staff of the wicked" (Isa. 14:5),
    D.   the time for the Babylonians to be destroyed,
    E.   the time for the Temple to be rebuilt: "And saviors shall come up on Mount Zion" (Obad. 1:21); "The glory of this latter house shall be greater than that of the former" (Hag. 2:9).
6. A.   "and the voice of the turtledove is heard in our land":
    B.   Said R. Yohanan, "'The voice of the good pioneer is heard in our land' [the words for turtledove and pioneer or explorer using the same consonants].
    C.   "This refers to Cyrus: 'Thus says Cyrus, king of Persia...all the kingdoms of the earth...whoever there is among you of all his people...let him go up...and build the house of the Lord' (Ezra 1:2-3)."
7. A.   "The fig tree puts forth its figs":
    B.   this refers to the baskets of first fruits.
8. A.   "and the vines are in blossom; they give forth fragrance":
    B.   this refers to drink-offerings.

The second reading carries us to the second redemption, with the restoration of Israel to Zion. The decision to create the entire composition comes prior to the inquiry into what materials may serve, since the repetitions fill obvious gaps. These are not then mistakes (*pace* Simon, p. 124, n. 2, on my No. 5: "This is really out of place here and is repeated from above").

XXX:iv.
1. A.   Another explanation of the verse, "My beloved speaks and says to me":
    B.   He "spoke" through Elijah,
    C.   and "said to me" through the Messiah.
    D.   What did he say to me?
2. A.   "Arise, my love, my fair one, and come away, for lo, the winter is past":
    B.   Said R. Azariah, "'for lo, the winter is past': this refers to the kingdom of the Cutheans [Samaritans], which deceives [the words for winter and deceive use some of the same consonants] the world and misleads it through its lies: 'If your brother, son of your mother...entices you' (Dt. 13:7)."
3. A.   "the rain is over and gone":
    B.   this refers to the subjugation.
4. A.   "The flowers appear on the earth":
    B.   the conquerors appear on the earth.
    C.   Who are they?
    D.   R. Berekhiah in the name of R. Isaac: "It is written, 'And the Lord showed me four craftsmen' (Zech. 2:3),
    E.   "and who are they? Elijah, the royal Messiah, the Melchizedek, and the military Messiah."
5. A.   "the time of singing has come":

B.   the time for the Israelites to be redeemed has come,
C.   the time of the foreskin to be removed.
D.   the time for kingdom of the Cutheans to perish,
E.   the time for the kingdom of Heaven to be revealed: "and the Lord shall be king over all the earth" (Zech. 14:9).

6. A.   "and the voice of the turtledove is heard in our land":
    B.   What is this? It is the voice of the royal Messiah,
    C.   proclaiming, "How beautiful upon the mountains are the feet of the messenger of good tidings" (Isa. 52:7).

7. A.   "The fig tree puts forth its figs":
    B.   Said R. Hiyya b. R. Abba, "Close to the days of the Messiah a great pestilence will come to the world, and the wicked will perish."

8. A.   "and the vines are in blossom; they give forth fragrance":
    B.   this speaks of those who will remain, concerning whom it is said, "And it shall come to pass that he who is left in Zion and he who remains in Jerusalem" (Isa. 4:3).

The trilogy now comes to its climax with the third and final redemption, the Exodus and conquest, the return to Zion, and the ultimate salvation then forming the entire corpus for which the language of the Song serves as metaphor. Seeing the whole together, we easily discern the components of a straightforward theological program, holding together all elements of Israel's life at home and in the world at large.

ix. Chapter Eighty-Seven. Song of Songs Rabbah to Song 6:11

Let me give yet another example of the same phenomenon, lest readers suppose that I have chosen what is not necessarily exemplary but merely adventitious – a series of one. To the contrary, what follows is perfectly routine for Song of Songs Rabbah.

LXXXVII:i.

1. A.   Another explanation of the phrase, "I went down to the nut orchard":
    B.   Said R. Joshua b. Levi, "The Israelites are compared to a nut-tree:
    C.   "just as a nut-tree is pruned and improved thereby, for, like hair that is trimmed and grows more abundantly, and like nails that are trimmed and grow more abundantly,
    D.   "so is the case with Israel, for they are pruned of the return on their work, which they gave to those who labor in the Torah in this world, and it is for their good that they are so pruned, for that increases their wealth in this world and the reward that is coming to them in the world to come."

2. A.   R. Joshua of Sikhnin in the name of R. Levi said, "Just as, while in the case of other plantings, if you cover their roots when they are planted, they prosper, and if not, they do not prosper,
    B.   "in the case of a nut-tree, if you cover its roots when it is planted it does not do well,

    C.   "so as to Israel: 'He who covers his transgressions will not prosper' (Prov. 28:13)."

3. A.   [Supply: "the nut orchard":]
    B.   Said R. Elasa, "Scripture ought to have said, 'to a vegetable patch.
    C.   "Why then 'nut orchard'?
    D.   "This serves to teach that he gave them the staying power of trees and the sheen of a vegetable patch."

4. A.   [Supply: "the nut orchard":]
    B.   R. Azariah made two statements:
    C.   "Just as in the case of a nut, the husk guards the fruit, so the unlettered people in Israel strengthen [those who are engaged in] study of the Torah: 'It is a tree of life to those who strengthen her' (Prov. 83:18)."
    D.   He made another statement: "Just as if a nut falls into the mud, you take it and wipe it and rinse it and wash it and it is perfectly fine for eating, so in the case of Israel, however they are made filthy in transgressions throughout the days of the year, the Day of Atonement comes along and covers over their sins: 'For on this day shall atonement be made for you, to cleanse you' (Lev. 16:30)."

5. A.   [Supply: "the nut orchard":]
    B.   R. Judah b. R. Simon says, "Just as a nut has two shells, so the Israelites have two religious duties, the act of circumcision and the act of cutting away the flesh of the penis."

6. A.   Another explanation of the phrase, "I went down to the nut orchard":
    B.   Said R. Simeon b. Laqish, "Just as a nut-tree is unwrinkled – "
    C.   **For we have learned in the Mishnah, Also on the smooth trunk of nut-trees" [M. Peah 4:1]** –
    D.   "so whoever climbs to the top of it and does not pay attention to how he is climbing will fall down and die and get his from the nut-tree,
    E.   "so whoever exercises authority over the community in Israel and does not pay a mind to how he governs Israel in the end will fall and get his on their account:
    F.   "'Israel is the Lord's holy portion, his first fruits of the increase, all who consume him will be held guilty' (Jer. 2:3)."

7. A.   Another explanation of the phrase, "I went down to the nut orchard":
    B.   Just as a nut is a toy for children and a treat for kings,
    C.   so are the Israelites in this world on account of transgression: "I am become a joke to all my people" (Lam. 3:14),
    D.   but in the world to come: "kings will be your foster-fathers" (Isa. 49:23).

8. A.   Another explanation of the phrase, "I went down to the nut orchard":
    B.   Just as in the case of a nut-tree, there are soft ones, medium ones, and hard ones,
    C.   so in the case of Israel, there are those who carry out acts of righteousness [through charity] on their own volition, there are those whom you ask and will give, and there are those whom you ask and who do nothing.

    D.   Said R. Levi, "There is the saying: 'the door that you don't open for a religious duty you will open for the doctor.'"

9. A.   Another explanation of the phrase, "I went down to the nut orchard":

    B.   just as in the case of a nut, a stone breaks it,

    C.   so the Torah is called a stone, [and] the impulse to do evil is called a stone.

    D.   The Torah is called a stone: "And I will give you the tables of stone" (Ex. 24:12).

    E.   The impulse to do evil is called a stone: "And I will take away the stony heart out of your flesh" (Ez. 36:26).

    F.   Said R. Levi, "[The matter may be compared to the case of] a lonely spot, which is infested with terrorists. What does the king do? He assigns there brigades to guard the place so that the terrorists will not attack travellers on the way.

    G.   "So said the Holy One, blessed be He, 'The Torah is called a stone, and the impulse to do evil is called a stone.

    H.   "'Let stone guard stone.'"

10. A.   Another explanation of the phrase, "I went down to the nut orchard":

    B.   Just as a stone cannot deceive the customs collector because it is betrayed by its rattle,

    C.   so with the Israelites, in any place to which one of them goes, he cannot say, "I'm not a Jew."

    D.   Why not?

    E.   Because he is a marked man: "All who see them will recognize them, that they are the seed which the Lord has blessed" (Isa. 61:9).

11. A.   Another explanation of the phrase, "I went down to the nut orchard":

    B.   Just as in the case of a nut, if you have a full bag of nuts in hand, you can still put in any amount of sesame seeds and mustard seeds and there will be room for them,

    C.   so how many proselytes have come and been attached to Israel: "Who has counted the dust of Jacob" (Num. 23:10).

12. A.   Another explanation of the phrase, "I went down to the nut orchard":

    B.   Just as in the case of a nut, if you take one out of the pile, all the rest fall down on one another,

    C.   so in the case of Israel, if one of them is smitten, all of them feel it:

    D.   "Shall one man sin and you will be angry with all the congregation" (Num. 16:22).

13. A.   [Supply: Another explanation of the phrase, "I went down to the nut orchard":]

    B.   Said R. Berekhiah, "Just as a nut is divided into four chambers with a hole in the middle,

    C.   "so the Israelites were ensconced in the wilderness by four standards, into four camps, with the tent of meeting in the middle:

    D.   "'Then the tent of meeting...shall set forward in the midst of the camps' (Num. 2:17)."

14. A.   Another explanation: "I went down to the nut orchard":

B.   this is the world.

C.   "to look at the blossoms of the valley":

D.   this is Israel.

E.   "to see whether the vines had budded": this refers to synagogues and houses of study.

F.   "whether the pomegranates were in bloom":

G.   this refers to children who are in session, occupied with the Torah, sitting row by row like pomegranate seeds."

I do not think our compilers and authors of the individual compositions can be better represented than by this fully realized exercise, in which the base verse yields a large variety of metaphorizations for Israel – all of which make the same rather limited number of points. What do the compilers say through their readings of the metaphor of the nut-tree for Israel? First, Israel prospers when it gives scarce resources for the study of the Torah or for carrying out religious duties (Nos. 1, 4, and, I assume, No. 8 and for different reasons No. 13 fall into this group); second, Israel sins but atones, and Torah is the medium of atonement (Nos. 2, 3, 4, 9); third, Israel is identified through carrying out its religious duties, e.g., circumcision (Nos. 5, 10); fourth, Israel's leaders had best watch their step (No. 6); fifth, Israel may be nothing now but will be in glory in the coming age (No. 7); sixth, Israel has plenty of room for outsiders but cannot afford to lose a single member (Nos. 11, 12). Only No. 13 is anomalous, and not really so: Israel forms Israel by reason of the tent of meeting that is in the middle of the whole. These several propositions rework the basic word symbols: Israel, Torah, religious duty, saying the same thing in a variety of ways.

Part Three
FROM UNITY TO DIVERSITY

9

The Three Stages in the Formation of Rabbinic Writings

Each of the score of documents that make up the canon of Judaism in late antiquity exhibits distinctive traits in logic, rhetoric, and topic, so that we may identify the purposes and traits of form and intellect of the authorship of that document. It follows that documents possess integrity and are not merely scrapbooks, compilations made with no clear purpose or aesthetic plan. But, as is well known, some completed units of thought – propositional arguments, sayings, and stories, for instance – travel from one document to another. It follows that the several documents intersect through shared materials. Furthermore, writings that peregrinate by definition do not carry out the rhetorical, logical, and topical program of a particular document. In framing a theory to accommodate the fact that documents are autonomous but also connected through such shared materials, therefore, we must account for the history of not only the documents in hand but also the completed pieces of writing that move from here to there. We have at present no theory of the formation of the various documents of the rabbinic literature that derives from an inductive sifting of the evidence. Nor do we have even a theory as to the correct method for the framing of a hypothesis for testing against the evidence.

My theory on the literary history of the rabbinic canon posits three stages in the formation of writing. Moving from the latest to the earliest, one stage is marked by the definition of a document, its topical program, its rhetorical medium, its logical message. The document as we know it in its basic structure and main lines therefore comes at the end. It follows that writings that clearly serve the program of that document and carry the purposes of its authorship were made up in connection with the formation of *that* document. Another, and I think, prior stage is marked by the preparation of writings that do not serve the needs of a particular document now in our hands, but can have carried out the purposes of an authorship working on a document of a *type* we now have. The existing documents then form a model for defining other kinds of writings worked out to meet the program of a documentary authorship.

But there are other types of writings that in no way serve the needs or plans of any document we now have, and that, furthermore, also cannot find a place in any document of a type that we now have. These writings, as a matter of fact, very commonly prove peripatetic, traveling from one writing to another, equally at home in, or alien to, the program of the documents in which they end up. These writings therefore were carried out without regard to a documentary program of any kind exemplified by the canonical books of the Judaism of the Dual Torah. They form what I conceive to be the earliest in the three stages of the writing of the units of completed thought that in the aggregate form the canonical literature of the Judaism of the Dual Torah of late antiquity.

As a matter of fact, therefore, a given canonical document of the Judaism of the Dual Torah draws upon three classes of materials, and these were framed in temporal order. Last comes the final class, the one that the redactors themselves defined and wrote; prior is the penultimate class that can have served other redactors but did not serve these in particular; and earliest of all in the order of composition (at least, from the perspective of the ultimate redaction of the documents we now have) is the writing that circulated autonomously and served no redactional purpose we can now identify within the canonical documents.

i. The Correct Starting Point

In beginning the inquiry with the traits of documents seen whole, I reject the assumption that the building block of documents is the smallest whole unit of thought, the lemma, nor can we proceed in the premise that a lemma traverses the boundaries of various documents and is unaffected by the journey.[1] The opposite premise is that we start our work with the traits of documents as a whole, rather than with the traits of the lemmas of which documents are (supposedly) composed. In

---

[1]As a matter of fact, the identification of the lemma as the primary unit of inquiry rests upon the premise that the person to whom a saying is assigned really said that saying. That premise is untenable. But for the sake of argument, I bypass that still more fundamental flaw in the methodology at hand.

a variety of books[2] I have set forth the documentary hypothesis for the analysis of the rabbinic literature of late antiquity. But how shall we proceed, if we take as our point of entry the character and conditions of the document, seen whole? And what are the results of doing so?

Having demonstrated beyond any doubt that a rabbinic text is a document, that is to say, a well-crafted text and not merely a compilation of this and that, and further specified in acute detail precisely the aesthetic, formal, and logical program followed by each of those texts, accordingly, I am able to move to the logical next step. That is to show that in the background of the documents that we have is writing that is *not* shaped by documentary requirements, writing that is not shaped by the documentary requirements of the compilations we now have, and also writing that is entirely formed within the rules of the documents that now present that writing. These then are the three kinds of writing that form, also, the three stages in the formation of the classics of Judaism.

ii. Redaction and Writing: The Extreme Case of the Mishnah

My example of a document that is written down essentially in its penultimate and ultimate stages, that is, a document that takes shape within the redactional process and principally there, is, of course, the Mishnah. In that writing, the patterns of language, e.g., syntactic structures, of the apodosis and protasis of the Mishnah's smallest whole units of discourse are framed in formal, mnemonic patterns. They follow a few simple rules. These rules, once known, apply nearly everywhere and form stunning evidence for the document's cogency. They permit anyone to reconstruct, out of a few key phrases, an entire cognitive unit, and even complete intermediate units of discourse. Working downward from the surface, therefore, anyone can penetrate into the deeper layers of meaning of the Mishnah. Then and at the same time, while discovering the principle behind the cases, one can easily memorize the whole by mastering the recurrent rhetorical pattern dictating the expression of the cogent set of cases. For it is easy to note the shift from one rhetorical pattern to another and to follow the repeated cases, articulated in the new pattern downward to its logical substrate. So syllogistic propositions, in the Mishnah's authors'

---

[2]Particularly see *From Tradition to Imitation. The Plan and Program of Pesiqta deRab Kahana and Pesiqta Rabbati, Canon and Connection: Intertextuality in Judaism, Midrash as Literature: The Primacy of Documentary Discourse,* and *The Bavli and its Sources: The Question of Tradition in the Case of Tractate Sukkah,* as well as *The Talmud of the Land of Israel. 35. Introduction. Taxonomy,* and *Judaism. The Classic Statement. The Evidence of the Bavli.*

hands, come to full expression not only in *what* people wish to state but also in *how* they choose to say it. The limits of rhetoric define the arena of topical articulation.

Now to state my main point in heavy emphasis: *the Mishnah's formal traits of rhetoric indicate that the document has been formulated all at once, and not in an incremental, linear process extending into a remote (mythic) past, (e.g., to Sinai).* These traits, common to a series of distinct cognitive units, are redactional, because they are imposed at that point at which someone intended to join together discrete (finished) units on a given theme. The varieties of traits particular to the discrete units and the diversity of authorities cited therein, including masters of two or three or even four strata from the turn of the first century to the end of the second, make it highly improbable that the several units were formulated in a common pattern and then preserved, until, later on, still further units, on the same theme and in the same pattern, were worked out and added. The entire indifference, moreover, to historical order of authorities and concentration on the logical unfolding of a given theme or problem without reference to the sequence of authorities, confirm the supposition that the work of formulation and that of redaction go forward together.

The principal framework of formulation and formalization in the Mishnah is the intermediate division rather than the cognitive unit. The least-formalized formulary pattern, the simple declarative sentence, turns out to yield many examples of acute formalization, in which a single distinctive pattern is imposed upon two or more (very commonly, groups of three or groups of five) cognitive units. While an intermediate division of a tractate may be composed of several such conglomerates of cognitive units, it is rare indeed for cognitive units formally to stand wholly by themselves. Normally, cognitive units share formal or formulary traits with others to which they are juxtaposed and the theme of which they share. It follows that the principal unit of formulary formalization is the intermediate division and not the cognitive unit. And what that means for our inquiry, is simple: we can tell when it is that the ultimate or penultimate redactors of a document do the writing. Now let us see that vast collection of writings that exhibit precisely the opposite trait: a literature in which, while doing some writing of their own, the redactors collected and arranged available materials.

iii. When the Document Does Not Define the Literary Protocol: Stories Told But Not Compiled

Now to the other extreme. Can I point to a kind of writing that in no way defines a document now in our hands or even a type of document we can now imagine, that is, one that in its particulars we do not have but that conforms in its definitive traits to those that we do have? Indeed I can, and it is the writing of stories about sages and other exemplary figures. To show what might have been, I point to the simple fact that the final organizers of the Bavli, the Talmud of Babylonia had in hand a tripartite corpus of inherited materials awaiting composition into a final, closed document. First, the first type of material, in various states and stages of completion, addressed the Mishnah or took up the principles of laws that the Mishnah had originally brought to articulation. These the framers of the Bavli organized in accord with the order of those Mishnah-tractates that they selected for sustained attention. Second, they had in hand received materials, again in various conditions, pertinent to Scripture, both as Scripture related to the Mishnah and also as Scripture laid forth its own narratives. These they set forth as Scripture commentary. In this way, the penultimate and ultimate redactors of the Bavli laid out a systematic presentation of the two Torahs, the oral, represented by the Mishnah, and the written, represented by Scripture.

And, third, the framers of the Bavli also had in hand materials focused on sages. These in the received form, attested in the Bavli's pages, were framed around twin biographical principles, either as strings of stories about great sages of the past or as collections of sayings and comments drawn together solely because the same name stands behind all the collected sayings. These can easily have been composed into biographies. In the context of Christianity and of Judaism, it is appropriate to call the biography of a holy man or woman, meant to convey the divine message, a gospel.[3] This is writing that is utterly

---

[3] I use the word "gospel" with a small G as equivalent to "didactic life of a holy man, portraying the faith." Obviously, the Christian usage, with a capital G, must maintain that there can be a Gospel only about Jesus Christ. Claims of uniqueness are, of course, not subject to public discourse. In the present context, I could as well have referred to lives of saints, since Judaism of the Dual Torah produced neither a gospel about a central figure nor lives of saints. Given the centrality of Moses "our rabbi," for example, we should have anticipated a "Gospel of Moses" parallel to the Gospels of Jesus Christ, and, lacking that, at least a "life of Aqiba," scholar, saint, martyr, parallel to the lives of various saints. We also have no autobiographies of any kind, beyond some "I"-stories, which themselves seem to me uncommon.

outside of the documentary framework in which it is now preserved; nearly all narratives in the rabbinic literature, not only the biographical ones, indeed prove remote from any documentary program exhibited by the canonical documents in which they now occur.

The Bavli as a whole lays itself out as a commentary to the Mishnah. So the framers wished us to think that whatever they wanted to tell us would take the form of Mishnah commentary. But a second glance indicates that the Bavli is made up of enormous composites, themselves closed prior to inclusion in the Bavli. Some of these composites – around 35% to 40% of Bavli's, if my sample is indicative[4] – were selected and arranged along lines dictated by a logic other than that deriving from the requirements of Mishnah commentary. The components of the canon of the Judaism of the Dual Torah prior to the Bavli had encompassed amplifications of the Mishnah, in the Tosefta and in the Yerushalmi, as well as the same for Scripture, in such documents as Sifra to Leviticus, Sifré to Numbers, another Sifré, to Deuteronomy, Genesis Rabbah, Leviticus Rabbah, and the like. But there was no entire document, now extant, organized around the life and teachings of a particular sage. Even The Fathers According to Rabbi Nathan, which contains a good sample of stories about sages, is not so organized as to yield a life of a sage, or even a systematic biography of any kind. Where events in the lives of sages do occur, they are thematic and not biographical in organization, e.g., stories about the origins, as to Torah study, of diverse sages; death scenes of various sages. The sage as such, whether Aqiba or Yohanan ben Zakkai or Eliezer b. Hyrcanus, never in that document defines the appropriate organizing principle for sequences of stories or sayings. And there is no other in which the sage forms an organizing category for any material purpose.[5]

---

[4]I compared Bavli and Yerushalmi tractates Sukkah, Sanhedrin, and Sotah, showing the proportion of what I call Scripture-units of thought to Mishnah-units of thought. See my *Judaism. The Classic Statement. The Evidence of the Bavli* (Chicago, 1986: University of Chicago Press).

[5]The occasion, in the history of Judaism, at which biography defines a generative category of literature, therefore also of thought, will therefore prove noteworthy. The model of biography surely existed from the formation of the Pentateuch, with its lines of structure, from Exodus through Deuteronomy, set forth around the biography of Moses, birth, call, career, death. And other biographies did flourish prior to the Judaism of the Dual Torah. Not only so, but the wall of the Dura synagogue highlights not the holy people so much as saints, such as Aaron and Moses. Accordingly, we must regard as noteworthy and requiring explanation the omission of biography from the literary genres of the canon of the Judaism of the Dual Torah. One obvious shift is marked by

Accordingly, the decision that the framers of the Bavli reached was to adopt the two redactional principles inherited from the antecedent century or so and to reject the one already rejected by their predecessors, even while honoring it. [1] They organized the Bavli around the Mishnah. But [2] they adapted and included vast tracts of antecedent materials organized as scriptural commentary. These they inserted whole and complete, not at all in response to the Mishnah's program. But, finally, [3] while making provision for small-scale compositions built upon biographical principles, preserving both strings of sayings from a given master (and often a given tradent of a given master) as well as tales about authorities of the preceding half millennium, they *never* created redactional compositions, of a sizable order, that focused upon given authorities. But sufficient materials certainly lay at hand to allow doing so.

We have now seen that some writings carry out a redactional purpose. The Mishnah was our prime example. Some writings ignore all redactional considerations we can identify. The stories about sages in The Fathers According to Rabbi Nathan for instance show us kinds of writing that are wholly out of phase with the program of the document that collects and compiles them. We may therefore turn to midrash compilations and find the traits of writing that clearly are imposed by the requirements of compilation. We further identify writings that clearly respond to a redactional program, but not the program of any compilation we now have in hand. There is little speculation about the identification of such writings. They will conform to the redactional patterns we discern in the known compilations, but presuppose a collection other than one now known to us. Finally, we turn to pieces of writing that respond to no redactional program known to us or susceptible to invention in accord with the principles of defining compilation known to us.

iv. Pericopes Framed for the Purposes of the Particular Document in Which They Occur

My analytical taxonomy of the writings now collected in various midrash compilations point to not only three stages in the formation of the classics of Judaism. It also suggests that writing went on outside of the framework of the editing of documents, and also within the limits of the formation and framing of documents. Writing of the former kind then constituted a kind of literary work to which redactional planning proved irrelevant. But the second and the third kinds of writing

---

Hasidism, with its special interest in stories about saints and in compiling those stories.

respond to redactional considerations. So in the end we shall wish to distinguish between writing intended for the making of books – compositions of the first three kinds listed just now – and writing not responsive to the requirements of the making of compilations.

The distinctions upon which these analytical taxonomies rest are objective and no no way subjective, since they depend upon the fixed and factual relationship between a piece of writing and a larger redactional context.

[1] We know the requirements of redactors of the several documents of the rabbinic canon, because I have already shown what they are in the case of a large variety of documents. When, therefore, we judge a piece of writing to serve the program of the document in which that writing occurs, it is not because of a personal impulse or a private and incommunicable insight, but because the traits of that writing self-evidently respond to the documentary program of the book in which the writing is located.

[2] When, further, we conclude that a piece of writing belongs in some other document than the one in which it is found, that too forms a factual judgment.

My example is a very simple one: writing that can serve only as a component of a commentary on a given scriptural book has been made up for the book in which it appears (or one very like it, if one wants to quibble). My example may derive from any of the ten midrash compilations of late antiquity. Here is one among innumerable possibilities.

Sifré to Numbers

I:VII.

1. A.   "[The Lord said to Moses, 'Command the people of Israel that they put out of the camp every leper and every one having a discharge, and every one that is unclean through contact with the dead.] You shall put out both male and female, putting them outside the camp, that they may not defile their camp, in the midst of which I dwell'" (Gen. 5:1-4)

    B.   I know, on the basis of the stated verse, that the law applies only to male and female [persons who are suffering from the specified forms of cultic uncleanness]. How do I know that the law pertains also to one lacking clearly defined sexual traits or to one possessed of the sexual traits of both genders?

    C.   Scripture states, "...putting *them* outside the camp." [This is taken to constitute an encompassing formulation, extending beyond the male and female of the prior clause.]

    D.   I know, on the basis of the stated verse, that the law applies only to those who can be sent forth. How do I know that the law pertains also to those who cannot be sent forth?

E.	Scripture states, "...putting them outside the camp." [This is taken to constitute an encompassing formulation, as before.]
F.	I know on the basis of the stated verse that the law applies only to persons. How do I know that the law pertains also to utensils?
G.	Scripture states, "...putting *them* outside the camp." [This is taken to constitute an encompassing formulation.]

I:VII.
2. A.   [Dealing with the same question as at 1.F,] R. Aqiba says, "'You shall put out both male and female, putting them outside the camp.' Both persons and utensils are implied."

B.   R. Ishmael says, "You may construct a logical argument, as follows:

C.   "Since man is subject to uncleanness on account of *negaim* ["plagues"], and clothing [thus: utensils] are subject to uncleanness on the same count, just as man is subject to being sent forth [ostracism], likewise utensils are subject to being sent forth."

D.   No, such an argument is not valid [and hence exegesis of the actual language of Scripture, as at A, is the sole correct route]. If you have stated the rule in the case of man, who imparts uncleanness when he exerts pressure on an object used for either sitting or lying, and, on which account, he is subject to ostracism, will you say the same rule of utensils, which do not impart uncleanness when they exert pressure on an object used for sitting and lying? [Clearly there is a difference between the uncleanness brought about by a human being from that brought about by an inanimate object, and therefore the rule that applies to the one will not necessarily apply to the other. Logic by itself will not suffice, and, it must follow, the proof of a verse of Scripture alone will suffice to prove the point.]

E.   [No, that objection is not valid, because we can show that the same rule does apply to both an inanimate object and to man, namely] lo, there is the case of the stone affected with a *nega*, which will prove the point. For it does not impart uncleanness when it exerts pressure on an object used for sitting or lying, but it does require ostracism [being sent forth from the camp, a rule that Scripture itself makes explicit].

F.   Therefore do not find it surprising that utensils, even though they in general do not impart uncleanness when they exert pressure on an object used for sitting or lying, are to be sent forth from the camp." [Ishmael's logical proof stands.]

I:VII.
3. A.   R. Yosé the Galilean says, "'You shall put out both male and female, putting them outside the camp, that they may not defile their camp, in the midst of which I dwell.'

B.   "What marks as singular male and female is that they can be turned into a generative source of uncleanness [when they die and are corpses], and, it follows, they are to be sent forth from the camp when they become unclean [even while alive], so anything which can become a generative source of uncleanness will be subject to being sent forth from the camp.

C.   "What is excluded is a piece of cloth less than three by three fingerbreadths, which in the entire Torah is never subject to becoming a generative source of uncleanness."

I:VII.

4. A.   R. Isaac says, "Lo, Scripture states, '[And every person that eats what dies of itself or what is to torn by beasts, whether he is a native or a sojourner, shall wash his clothes and bathe himself in water and be unclean until the evening; they he shall be clean.] But if he does not wash them or bathe his flesh, he shall bear his iniquity' (Lev. 17:15-16).

    B.   "It is on account of failure to wash one's body that Scripture has imposed the penalty of extirpation.

    C.   "You maintain that it is on account of failure to wash one's body that Scripture has imposed the penalty of extirpation. But perhaps Scripture has imposed a penalty of extirpation only on account of the failure to launder one's garments.

    D.   "Thus you may construct the argument to the contrary [*su eipas*]: if in the case of one who has become unclean on account of corpse-uncleanness, which is a severe source of uncleanness, Scripture has not imposed a penalty merely because of failure to launder one's garments, as to one who eats meat of a beast that has died of itself, which is a minor source of uncleanness, it is a matter of reason that Scripture should not impose a penalty on the account of having failed to launder the garments."

Why do I maintain that the composition can serve only the document in which it occurs? The reason is that we read the verse in a narrow framework: what rule do we derive from the *actual* language at hand. No. 1 answers the question on the basis of an exegesis of the verse. No. 2 then provides an alternative proof. Aqiba provides yet another reading of the language at hand. Ishmael goes over the possibility of a logical demonstration. I find it difficult to see how Yosé's pericope fits in. It does not seem to me to address the problem at hand. He wants to deal with a separate issue entirely, as specified at C. No. 4 pursues yet another independent question. So Nos. 3, 4 look to be parachuted down. On what basis? No. 3 deals with our base verse. But No. 4 does not. Then what guided the compositors to introduce Nos. 1, 2, 3, and 4? Nos. 1, 2 deal with the exegesis of the limited rule at hand: how do I know to what classifications of persons and objects ostracism applies? No. 1 answers to questions, first, the classifications, then the basis for the rule. No. 2 introduces the second question: on what basis do we make our rule? The answer, as is clear, is Scripture, not unaided reason. Now at that point the issue of utensils emerges. So Yosé the Galilean's interest in the rule governing a utensil – a piece of cloth – leads to the intrusion of his item. And the same theme – the rule governing utensils, garments – accounts for the introduction of I:VII.4 as well. In sum, the redactional principle looks to be clear: treat the verse, then the theme generated by the verse. Then this piece of writing can have been formed only for the purpose of a commentary to the book of Numbers: Sifré to Numbers is the only one we have. Q.E.D.

v. Pericopes Framed for the Purposes of a Particular Document, But Not of a Type We Now Possess

A piece of writing that serves nowhere we now know may nonetheless conform to the rules of writing that we can readily imagine and describe in theory. For instance, a propositional composition, that runs through a wide variety of texts to make a point autonomous of all of the texts that are invoked, clearly is intended for a propositional document, one that (like the Mishnah) makes points autonomous of a given prior writing, e.g., a biblical book, but that makes points that for one reason or another cohere quite nicely on their own. Authors of propositional compilations self-evidently can imagine that kind of redaction. We have their writings, but not the books that they intended to be made up of those writings. In all instances, the reason that we can readily imagine a compilation for that will have dictated the indicative traits of a piece of writing will prove self-evident: we have compilations of such a type, if not specific compilations called for by a given composition. A single example suffices. It derives from Sifra.

If the canon of Judaism included a major treatise or compilation on applied logic and practical reason, then a principal tractate, or set of tractates, would be devoted to proving that reason by itself cannot produce reliable results. And in that treatise would be a vast and various collection of sustained discussions, which spread themselves across Sifra and Sifré to Numbers and Sifré to Deuteronomy, the Yerushalmi and the Bavli, as well as other collections. Here is a sample of how that polemic has imposed itself on the amplification of Lev. 1:2 and transformed treatment of that verse from an exegesis to an example of an overriding proposition. It goes without saying that where we have this type of proof of the priority of Scripture over logic, or of the necessity of Scripture in the defining of generative taxa, the discussion serves a purpose that transcends the case, and on that basis I maintain the proposition proposed here. It is that there were types of collections that we can readily imagine but that were not made up. In this case, it is, as is clear, a treatise on applied logic, and the general proposition of that treatise is that reliable taxonomy derives only from Scripture.

Sifra Parashat Vayyiqra Dibura Denedabah Parashah 2

III.I.

1. A.   "Speak to the Israelite people [and say to them, 'When any [Hebrew: Adam] of you presents an offering of cattle to the Lord, he shall choose his offering from the herd or from the flock. If his offering is a burnt-offering from the herd, he shall offer a male without blemish; he shall offer it at the door of the tent of meeting, that he may be accepted before the Lord;] he shall lay [his hand upon the head of the burnt-offering, and it shall be accepted for him to make atonement for him]'" (Lev. 1:2):

    B.   "He shall lay his hand": Israelites lay on hands, gentiles do not lay on hands.

    C.   [But is it necessary to prove that proposition on the basis of the cited verse? Is it not to be proven merely by an argument of a logical order, which is now presented?] Now which measure [covering the applicability of a rite] is more abundant, the measure of wavings or the measure of laying on of hands?

    D.   The measure of waving [the beast] is greater than the measure of laying on of hands.

    E.   For waving [the sacrifice] is done to both something that is animate and something that is not animate, while the laying on of hands applies only to something that is animate.

    F.   If gentiles are excluded from the rite of waving the sacrifice, which applies to a variety of sacrifices, should they not be excluded from the rite of laying on of hands, which pertains to fewer sacrifices? [Accordingly, I prove on the basis of reason the rule that is derived at A-B from the verse of Scripture.]

    G.   [I shall now show that the premise of the foregoing argument is false:] [You have constructed your argument] from the angle that yields waving as more common and laying on of hands as less common.

    H.   But take the other angle, which yields laying on of hands as the more common and waving as the less common.

    I.   For the laying on of hands applies to all partners in the ownership of a beast [each one of whom is required to lay hands on the beast before it is slaughtered in behalf of the partnership in ownership of the beast as a whole],

    J.   but the waving of a sacrifice is not a requirement that applies to all partners in the ownership of a beast.

    K.   Now if I eliminate [gentiles' laying on of hands] in the case of the waving of a beast, which is a requirement applying to fewer cases, should I eliminate them from the requirement of laying on of hands, which applies to a larger number of cases?

    L.   Lo, since a rule pertains to the waving of the sacrifice that does not apply to the laying on of hands, and a rule pertains to the laying on of hands that does not apply to the waving of the sacrifice, it is necessary for Scripture to make the statement that it does, specifically:

    M.   "He shall lay his hand": Israelites lay on hands, gentiles do not lay on hands.

The basic premise is that when two comparable actions differ, then the more commonly performed one imposes its rule upon further actions, the rule governing which is unknown. If then we show that action A is more commonly performed than action B, other actions of the same classification will follow the rule governing A, not the rule governing B. Then the correct route to overturn such an argument is to show that each of the actions, the rule governing which is known, differs from the other in such a way that neither the one nor the other can be shown to be the more commonly performed. Then the rule governing the further actions is not to be derived from the one governing the two known actions. The powerful instrument of analytical and comparative reasoning proves that diverse traits pertain to the two stages of the rite of sacrifice, the waving, the laying on of hands, which means that a rule pertaining to the one does not necessarily apply to the other. On account of that difference we must evoke the specific ruling of Scripture. The polemic in favor of Scripture, uniting all of the components into a single coherent argument, then insists that there really is no such thing as a genus at all, and Scripture's rules and regulations serve a long list of items, each of them *sui generis,* for discovering rules by the logic of analogy and contrast is simply not possible.

vi. Pericopes Framed for Purposes Not Particular to a Type of Document Now in Our Hands

Some writings stand autonomous of any redactional program we have in an existing compilation or of any we can even imagine on the foundations of said writings. Compositions of this kind, as a matter of hypothesis, are to be assigned to a stage in the formation of classics prior to the framing of all available documents. For, as a matter of fact, all of our now extant writings adhere to a single program of conglomeration and agglutination, and all are served by composites of one sort, rather than some other. Hence we may suppose that at some point prior to the decision to make writings in the model that we now have but in some other model people also made up completed units of thought to serve these other kinds of writings. These persist, now, in documents that they do not serve at all well. And we can fairly easily identify the kinds of documents that they can and should have served quite nicely indeed. These then are the three stages of literary formation in the making of the classics of Judaism.

Of the relative temporal or ordinal position of writings that stand autonomous of any redactional program we have in an existing compilation or of any we can even imagine on the foundations of said writings we can say nothing. These writings prove episodic; they are commonly singletons. They serve equally well everywhere, because they demand no traits of form and redaction in order to endow them with sense and meaning. Why not? Because they are essentially free-standing and episodic, not referential and allusive. They are stories that contain their own point and do not invoke, in the making of that point, a given verse of Scripture. They are sayings that are utterly ad hoc. A variety of materials fall into this – from a redactional perspective – unassigned, and unassignable, type of writing. They do not belong in books at all. By that I mean, whoever made up these pieces of writing did not imagine that what he was forming required a setting beyond the limits of his own piece of writing; the story is not only complete in itself but could stand entirely on its own; the saying spoke for itself and required no nurturing context; the proposition and its associated proofs in no way was meant to draw nourishment from roots penetrating nutriments outside of its own literary limits.

Where we have utterly hermetic writing, able to define its own limits and sustain its point without regard to anything outside itself, we know that here we are in the presence of authorships that had no larger redactional plan in mind, no intent on the making of books out of their little pieces of writing. We may note that, among the "unimaginable" compilations is not a collection of parables, since parables rarely[6] stand free and never are inserted for their own sake. Whenever in the rabbinic canon we find a parable, it is meant to serve the purpose of an authorship engaged in making its own point; and the point of a parable is rarely, if ever, left unarticulated. Normally it is put into words, but occasionally the point is made simply by redactional setting. It must follow that, in this canon, the parable cannot have constituted the generative or agglutinative principle of a large-scale compilation. It further follows, so it seems to me, that the parable always takes shape within the framework of a work of composition for the purpose of either a large-scale exposition or, more commonly still, of compilation of a set of expositions into what we should now call the chapter of a book; that is to say, parables link to purposes that transcend the tale that they tell (or even the point that the tale makes). Let me now give one example of what I classify as a free-standing piece of writing, one with no place for itself in accord with the purposes of compilers either of documents we now have in hand or of documents we can readily envisage or imagine. My example again derives from Sifra, although, as a matter of fact, every document of the canon yields illustrative materials for all three types of writing.

---

[6]I should prefer to say "never," but it is easier to say what is in the rabbinic literature than what is never there.

The issue of the relationship between the Mishnah and Scripture deeply engaged a variety of writers and compilers of documents. Time and again we have evidence of an interest in the scriptural sources of laws, or of greater consequence in the priority of Scripture in taxonomic inquiry. We can show large-scale compositions that will readily have served treatises on these matters. But if I had to point to a single type of writing that is quite commonplace in the compilations we do have, but *wholly* outside of the repertoire of redactional possibilities we have or can imagine, it must be a sustained piece of writing on the relationship of the Mishnah to Scripture. Such a treatise can have been enormous, not only because, in theory, every line of the Mishnah required attention. It is also because, in practice, a variety of documents, particularly Sifra, the two Sifrés, and the Talmuds, contain writing of a single kind, meant to amplify the Mishnah by appeal to Scripture (but never to amplify Scripture by appeal to the Mishnah!). It is perfectly clear that no one imagined compiling a commentary to the Mishnah that would consist principally of proofs, of a sustained and well-crafted sort, that the Mishnah in general depends upon Scripture (even though specific and sustained proofs that the principles of taxonomy derive from Scripture are, as I said, susceptible of compilation in such treatises). How do we know that fact? It is because, when people did compile writings in the form of sustained commentaries to the Mishnah, that is to say, the two Talmuds, they did not focus principally upon the scriptural exegesis of the Mishnah; that formed only one interest, and, while an important one, it did not predominate; it certainly did not define the plan and program of the whole; and it certainly did not form a center of redactional labor. It was simply one item on a list of items that would be brought into relationship, where appropriate, with sentences of the Mishnah. And even then, it always was the intersection at the level of sentences, not sustained discourses, let alone with the Mishnah viewed whole and complete.

And yet – and yet if we look into compilations we do have, we find sizable sets of materials that can have been joined together with the Mishnah, paragraph by paragraph, in such a way that Scripture might have been shaped into a commentary to the Mishnah. Let me now give a sustained example of what might have emerged, but never did emerge, in the canonical compilations of Judaism. I draw my case from Sifra, but equivalent materials in other midrash compilations as well as in the two Talmuds in fact are abundant. In bold face type are direct citations of Mishnah passages. I skip Nos. 2-12, because these are not germane to this part of my argument.

Sifra Parashat Behuqotai Parashah 3
CCLXX:I.
1. A.   ["The Lord said to Moses, Say to the people of Israel, When a man makes a special vow of persons to the Lord at your Valuation, then your Valuation of a male from twenty years old up to sixty years old shall be fifty shekels of silver according to the shekel of the sanctuary. If the person is a female, your Valuation shall be thirty shekels. If the person is from five years old up to twenty years old, your Valuation shall be for a male twenty shekels and for a female ten shekels. If the person is from a month old up to five years old, your Valuation shall be for a male five shekels of silver and for a female your Valuation shall be three shekels of silver. And if the person is sixty years old and upward, then your Valuation for a male shall be fifteen shekels and for a female ten shekels. And if a man is too poor to pay your Valuation, then he shall bring the person before the priest, and the priest shall value him; according to the ability of him who vowed the priest shall value him" (Lev. 27:1-8).]

   B.   **"Israelites take vows of Valuation, but gentiles do not take vows of Valuation [M. Ar. 1:2B].**

   C.   "Might one suppose they are not subject to vows of Valuation?

   D.   "Scripture says, 'a man,'" the words of R. Meir.

   E.   Said R. Meir, "After one verse of Scripture makes an inclusionary statement, another makes an exclusionary statement.

   F.   "On what account do I say that gentiles are subject to vows of Valuation but may not take vows of Valuation?

   G.   **"It is because greater is the applicability of the rule of subject to the pledge of Valuation by others than the applicability of making the pledge of Valuation of others [T. Ar. 1:1A].**

   H.   **"For lo, a deaf-mute, idiot, and minor may be subjected to vows of Valuation, but they are not able to take vows of Valuation [M. Ar. 1:1F]."**

   I.   **R. Judah says, "Israelites are subject to vows of Valuation, but gentiles are not subject to vows of Valuation [M. Ar. 1:2C].**

   J.   "Might one suppose that they may not take vows of Valuation of third parties?

   K.   "Scripture says, 'a man.'"

   L.   Said R. Judah, "After one verse of Scripture makes an inclusionary statement, another makes an exclusionary statement.

   M.   "On what account do I say that gentiles are not subject to vows of Valuation but may take vows of Valuation?

   N.   **"It is because greater is the applicability of the rule of pledging the Valuation of others than the applicability of being subject to the pledge of Valuation by others [T. Ar. 1:1C].**

   O.   **"For a person of doubtful sexual traits and a person who exhibits traits of both sexes pledge the Valuation of others** but are not subjected to the pledge of Valuation to be paid by others" [M. Ar. 1:1D].

13. A. And how do we know that the sixtieth year is treated as part of the period prior to that year?

B. Scripture says, "from twenty years old up to sixty years old" –

C. this teaches that the sixtieth year is treated as part of the period prior to that year.

D. I know only that that is the rule governing the status of the sixtieth year. How do I know the rule as to assigning the fifth year, the twentieth year?

E. It is a matter of logic:

F. Liability is incurred when one is in the sixtieth year, the fifth year, and the twentieth year.

G. Just as the sixtieth year is treated as part of the period prior to that year,

H. so the fifth and the twentieth years are treated as part of the period prior to that year.

I. But if you treat the sixtieth year as part of the prior period, imposing a more stringent law [the Valuation requiring a higher fee before than after sixty],

J. shall we treat the fifth year and the twentieth year as part of the period prior to that year, so imposing a more lenient law in such cases [the Valuation being less expensive]?

K. Accordingly, Scripture is required to settle the question when it refers repeatedly to "year,"

L. thus establishing a single classification for all such cases:

M. just as the sixtieth year is treated as part of the prior period, so the fifth and the twentieth years are treated as part of the prior period.

N. And that is the rule, whether it produces a more lenient or a more stringent ruling [M. Ar. 4:4M-Q, with somewhat different wording].

14. A. R. Eliezer says, "How do we know that a month and a day after a month are treated as part of the sixtieth year?

B. "Scripture says, 'up...':

C. "Here we find reference to 'up...,' and elsewhere we find the same. Just as 'up' used elsewhere means that a month and a day after the month [are included in the prior span of time], so the meaning is the same when used here. [M. Ar. 4:4R: R. Eleazar says, "The foregoing applies so long as they are a month and a day more than the years which are prescribed."]

15. A. I know only that this rule applies after sixty. How do I know that the same rule applies after five or twenty?

B. It is a matter of logic:

C. One is liable to pay a pledge of Valuation if the person to be evalued is older than sixty, and one is liable if such a one is older than five or older than twenty.

D. Just as, if one is older than sixty by a month and a day, , the person is as though he were sixty years of age, so if the one is after five years or twenty years by a month and a day, lo, these are deemed to be the equivalent of five or twenty years of age.

16. A.   "And if a man is too poor to pay your Valuation":
     B.   this means, if he is too impoverished to come up with your Valuation.
17. A.   "then he shall bring the person before the priest":
     B.   this then excludes a dead person.
     C.   I shall then exclude a corpse but not a dying person?
     D.   Scripture says, "then he shall bring the person before the priest, and the priest shall value him" –
     E.   one who is subject to being brought is subject to being valuated, and one who is not subject to being brought before the priest [such as a dying man] also is not subject to the pledge of Valuation.
18. A.   Might one suppose that even if someone said, "The Valuation of Mr. So-and-so is incumbent on me," and he died, the man should be exempt?
     B.   Scripture says, "and the priest shall value him."
     C.   That is so even if he is dead.
19. A.   "and the priest shall value him":
     B.   This means that one pays only in accord with the conditions prevailing at the time of the Valuation.
20. A.   "according to the ability of him who vowed the priest shall value him":
     B.   It is in accord with the means of the one who takes the vow, not the one concerning whom the vow is taken,
     C.   whether that is a man, woman or child.
     D.   In this connection sages have said:
     E.   **The estimate of ability to pay is made in accord with the status of the one who vows;**
     F.   **and the estimate of the years of age is made in accord with the status of the one whose Valuation is vowed.**
     G.   **And when this is according to the Valuations spelled out in the Torah, it is in accord with the status, as to age and sex, of the one whose Valuation is pledged.**
     H.   **And the Valuation is paid in accordance with the rate prescribed at the time of the pledge of Valuation [M. Ar. 4:1A-D].**
21. A.   "the priest shall value him":
     B.   This serves as the generative analogy covering all cases of Valuations, indicating that the priest should be in charge.

The program of the Mishnah and the Tosefta predominates throughout, e.g., Nos. 1, 12, 13, 14-15. The second methodical inquiry characteristic of our authorship, involving exclusion and inclusion, accounts for pretty much the rest of this well-crafted discussion. Now we see a coherent and cogent discussion of a topic in accord with a program applicable to all topics, that trait of our document which so won our admiration. Thus Nos. 2-11, 17-20, involve inclusion, exclusion, or extension by analogy. I should offer this excellent composition as an example of the best our authorship has to give us, and a very impressive intellectual gift at that. The point throughout is simple.

We know how the compilers of canonical writings produced treatments of the Mishnah. The one thing that they did not do was to create a scriptural commentary to the Mishnah. That is not the only type of writing lacking all correspondence to documents we have or can imagine, but it is a striking example.

vii. The Three Stages of Literary Formation

Now to return to my starting point, namely, those sizable selections of materials that circulated from one document to another and why I tend to think they were formed earlier than the writings particular to documents. The documentary hypothesis affects our reading of the itinerant compositions, for it identifies what writings are extra-documentary and non-documentary and imposes upon the hermeneutics and history of these writings a set of distinctive considerations. The reason is that these writings serve the purposes not of compilers (or authors or authorships) of distinct compilations, but the interests of a another type of authorship entirely: one that thought making up stories (whether or not for collections) itself an important activity; or making up exercises on Mishnah-Scripture relationships; or other such writings as lie beyond the imagination of the compilers of the score of documents that comprise the canon. When writings work well for two or more documents therefore they must be assumed to have a literary history different from those that serve only one writing or one type of writing, and, also, demand a different hermeneutic.

My "three stages" in ordinal sequence correspond, as a matter of fact, to a taxic structure, that is, three types of writing. The first – and last in assumed temporal order – is writing carried out in the context of the making, or compilation, of a classic. That writing responds to the redactional program and plan of the authorship of a classic. The second, penultimate in order, is writing that can appear in a given document but better serves a document other than the one in which it (singularly) occurs. This kind of writing seems to me not to fall within the same period of redaction as the first. For while it is a type of writing under the identical conditions, it also is writing that presupposes redactional programs in no way in play in the ultimate, and definitive, period of the formation of the canon: when people did things this way, and not in some other. That is why I think it is a kind of writing that was done prior to the period in which people limited their redactional work and associated labor of composition to the program that yielded the books we now have.

The upshot is simple: whether the classification of writing be given a temporal or merely taxonomic valence, the issue is the same:

have these writers done their work with documentary considerations in mind? I believe I have shown that they have not. Then where did they expect their work to make its way? Anywhere it might, because, so they assumed, fitting in nowhere in particular, it found a suitable locus everywhere it turned up. But I think temporal, not merely taxonomic, considerations pertain.

The third kind of writing seems to me to originate in a period prior to the other two. It is carried on in a manner independent of all redactional considerations such as are known to us. Then it should derive from a time when redactional considerations played no paramount role in the making of compositions. A brief essay, rather than a sustained composition, was then the dominant mode of writing. My hypothesis is that people can have written both long and short compositions – compositions and composites, in my language – at one and the same time. But writing that does not presuppose a secondary labor of redaction, e.g., in a composite, probably originated when authors or authorships did not anticipate any fate for their writing beyond their labor of composition itself.

Along these same lines of argument, this writing may or may not travel from one document to another. What that means is that the author or authorship does not imagine a future for his writing. What fits anywhere is composed to go nowhere in particular. Accordingly, what matters is not whether a writing fits one document or another, but whether, as the author or authorship has composed a piece of writing, that writing meets the requirements of any document we now have or can even imagine. If it does not, then we deal with a literary period in which the main kind of writing was ad hoc and episodic, not sustained and documentary.

Now extra- and non-documentary kinds of writing seem to me to derive from either [1] a period prior to the work of the making of midrash compilations and the two Talmuds alike; or [2] a labor of composition not subject to the rules and considerations that operated in the work of the making of midrash compilations and the two Talmuds. As a matter of hypothesis, I should guess that non-documentary writing comes prior to making any kind of documents of consequence, and extra-documentary writing comes prior to the period in which the specificities of the documents we now have were defined. That is to say, writing that can fit anywhere or nowhere is prior to writing that can fit somewhere but does not fit anywhere now accessible to us, and both kinds of writing are prior to the kind that fits only in what documents in which it is now located.

And given the documentary propositions and theses that we can locate in all of our compilations, we can only assume that the non-documentary writings enjoyed, and were assumed to enjoy, ecumenical acceptance. That means, very simply, when we wish to know the consensus of the entire textual (or canonical) community[7] – I mean simply the people, anywhere and any time, responsible for everything we now have – we turn not to the distinctive perspective of documents, but the (apparently universally acceptable) perspective of the extra-documentary compositions. That is the point at which we should look for the propositions everywhere accepted but nowhere advanced in a distinctive way, the "Judaism beyond the texts" – or behind them.

Do I place a priority, in the framing of a hypothesis, over taxonomy or temporal order? Indeed I do. I am inclined to suppose that non-documentary compositions took shape not only separated from, but in time before, the documentary ones did. My reason for thinking so is worth rehearsing, even though it is not yet compelling. The kinds of non-documentary writing I have identified in general focus on matters of very general interest. These matters may be assembled into two very large rubrics: virtue, on the one side, reason, on the other. Stories about sages fall into the former category; all of them set forth in concrete form the right living that sages exemplify. Essays on right thinking, the role of reason, the taxonomic priority of Scripture, the power of analogy, the exemplary character of cases and precedents in the expression of general and encompassing rules – all of these intellectually coercive writings set forth rules of thought as universally applicable, in their way, as are the rules of conduct contained in stories about sages, in theirs. A great labor of generalization is contained in both kinds of non-documentary and extra-documentary writing. And the results of that labor are then given concrete expression in the documentary writings in hand; for these, after all, do say in the setting of specific passages or problems precisely what, in a highly general way, emerges from the writing that moves hither and yon, never with a home, always finding a suitable resting place.

Now, admittedly, that rather general characterization of the non-documentary writing is subject to considerable qualification and clarification. But it does provide a reason to assign temporal priority, not solely taxonomic distinction, to the non-documentary compositions. We can have had commentaries of a sustained and systematic sort on Chronicles, on the one side, treatises on virtue, on the second, gospels, on the third – to complete the triangle. But we do not have these kinds of books.

---

[7] I prefer Brian Stock's "textual community," see his *Implications of Literacy* (Princeton, 1986: Princeton University Press).

In conclusion, let me confess that I wish our sages had made treatises on right action and right thought, in their own idiom to be sure, because I think these treatises will have shaped the intellect of generations to come in a more effective way than the discrete writings, submerged in collections and composites of other sorts altogether, have been able to do. Compositions on correct behavior made later on filled the gap left open by the redactional decisions made in the period under study; I do not know why no one assembled a Midrash on right action in the way in which, in Leviticus Rabbah and Genesis Rabbah, treatises on the rules of society and the rules of history were compiled. And still more do I miss those intellectually remarkable treatises on right thought that our sages can have produced out of the rich resources in hand: the art of generalization, the craft of comparison and contrast, for example. In this regard the Mishnah, with its union of (some) Aristotelian modes of thought and (some) neo-Platonic propositions forms the model, if a lonely one, for what can have been achieved, even in the odd and unphilosophical idiom of our sages.[8] The compositions needed for both kinds of treatises – and, as a matter of fact, many, many of them – are fully in hand. But no one made the compilations of them.

The books we do have not only preserve the evidences of the possibility of commentaries and biographies. More than that, they also bring to rich expression the messages that such books will have set forth. And most important, they also express in fresh and unanticipated contexts those virtues and values that commentaries and biographies ("gospels") meant to bring to realization, and they do so in accord with the modes of thought that sophisticated reflection on right thinking has exemplified in its way as well. So when people went about the work of making documents, they did something fresh with something familiar. They made cogent compositions, documents, texts enjoying integrity and autonomy. But they did so in such a way as to form of their distinct documents a coherent body of writing, of books, a canon, of documents, a system. And this they did in such a way as to say, in distinctive and specific ways, things that, in former times, people had expressed in general and broadly applicable ways.

---

[8]This is fully explained in my *Philosophical Mishnah* (Atlanta, 1989: Scholars Press for Brown Judaic Studies) I-IV, and in my *The Philosophy of Judaism: The First Principles* (in press).

10

Documentary Hermeneutics and the Interpretation of Narrative in the Classics of Judaism

A common attitude of mind among scholars of the literature of formative Judaism is to examine a story or a fable entirely in its own terms and wholly out of literary (let alone theological) context. That viewpoint treats as null the interests of the compilers of a document, who may not only have selected a story or fable for preservation but also revised its indicative traits – whether of narrative or of proposition – to conform to the larger program for which they make their compilation. Indifference to the imperatives of the documentary setting may or may not represent a valid hermeneutic in the analysis of literary and even folkloristic materials. When should we seek the marks of a documentary framing of a piece of writing, and when are we justified in ignoring the documentary interests in an otherwise-autonomous tale? In point of fact, a systematic account of the matter, in theory with one sustained and I think compelling example, will answer these complementary questions.[1]

i. The Starting Point

We do not now know how the various classics of the Judaism of the Dual Torah that reached closure in late antiquity, by the seventh century, took shape. The reason is that the books all are anonymous. We not only do not know who wrote or compiled them, we also do not know when any one of them reached closure. The sole evidence in hand

---

[1] I present here some of the principal propositions of my *Making the Classics in Judaism: The Three Stages in Documentary Formation* (Atlanta, 1989: Scholars Press for Brown Judaic Studies).

is inductive: the characteristic traits, as to rhetoric, logic of cogent discourse, and topic, of the writings themselves. The manner in which that evidence is to be interpreted has to be carefully considered. But, short of believing that all sayings assigned to named authorities were really said by those to whom said sayings are attributed – and such an act of utter gullibility is inconceivable – we have no clear notion of the history of the canonical writings of Judaism from the Mishnah, ca. 200, through the Bavli, ca. 600. Nor do we even know where to begin the work of framing a hypothesis for rigorous testing.

But two starting points present themselves: the whole or the smallest part. That is to say, do we start from the document as a whole and examine its indicative traits? Then the reading of the parts will be in the light of the program of the whole. We shall define the norm on the base line of the whole and ask where, how, and why the parts diverge from the norm. That is the mode of comparison and contrast that will generate our hypotheses of literary history and purpose – and also, therefore our hermeneutics. The manner of analysis dictated by the entry from the outermost layer is simple.

We commence our analytical inquiry from a completed document and unpeel its layers, from the ultimate one of closure and redaction, to the penultimate, and onward into the innermost formation of the smallest whole units of thought of which a document is comprised. In so doing, we treat the writing as a document that has come to closure at some fixed point and through the intellection of purposeful framers or redactor. We start the analytical process by asking what those framers – that authorship – have wanted their document to accomplish and by pointing to the means by which that authorship achieved its purposes. Issues of prevailing rhetoric and logic, as well as the topical program of the whole, guide us in our definition of the document as a whole. The parts then come under study under the aspect of the whole. Knowing the intent of the framers, we ask whether, and how, materials they have used have been shaped in response to the program of the document's authorship.

The alternative point of entry is to begin with the smallest building block of any and all documents, which is the lemma or irreducible minimum of completed thought, and working upward and outward from the innermost layer of the writing. That point of entry ignores the boundaries of discrete documents and asks what we find common within and among all documents. There is the starting point, and the norm is defined by the traits of the saying or lemma as it moves from here to there. Within this theory of the history of the literature, the boundary lines of documents do not demarcate important classifications of data; all data are uniform, wherever they occur. The stress then lies not on the differentiating traits of documents, but the points shared in common among them; these points are sayings that occur in two or more places. Literary history consists in the inquiry into the fate of sayings as they move from one place to another. The hermeneutics of course will focus upon the saying and its history, rather than on the program and plan of documents that encompass, also, the discrete saying. The advantage of this approach, of course, is that it takes account of what is shared among documents, on the one side, and also of what exhibits none of the characteristic traits definitive of given documents, on the other.

ii. The Hypothesis: The Three Stages of Literary Formation

As to method, I maintain that we begin with the whole and work inward, as we peel an onion. As to the parts, we classify them by their indicative traits of relationship with the plan and program of the whole. That is to say, are writings responsive to the program of the compilation in which they occur? Are they responsive to the program of some other compilation, not the one where they now are? Or are they utterly autonomous of the requirements of any redactional setting we have or can envisage?[2]

It is the simple fact that rabbinic documents – particularly midrash compilations – in some measure draw upon a fund of completed compositions of thought that have taken shape without attention to the needs of the compilers of those documents. The second is that some of these same documents draw upon materials that have been composed with the requirements of the respective documents in mind. Within the distinction between writing that serves a redactional purpose and writing that does not, we shall see four types of completed compositions of thought. Each type may be distinguished from the others by appeal to a single criterion of differentiation, that is to say, to traits of precisely the same sort. The indicative traits concern relationship to the redactional purpose of a piece of writing, viewed overall.

[1] Some writings in a given midrash compilation clearly serve the redactional program of the framers of the document in which those writings occur.

[2] Some writings in a given midrash compilation serve not the redactional program of the document in which they occur, but some other document, now in our hands. There is no material difference, as to the taxonomy of the writing of the classics in Judaism, between the first

---

[2]Here we review the results of the preceding chapter; readers may wish to skip this section if they find the review needless or tedious. The papers were written independently of one another.

and second types; it is a problem of transmission of documents, not their formation.

[3] Some writings in a given midrash compilation serve not the purposes of the document in which they occur but rather a redactional program of a document, or of a type of document, that we do not now have, but can readily envision. In this category we find the possibility of imagining compilations that we do not have, but that can have existed but did not survive; or that can have existed and were then recast into the kinds of writings that people clearly preferred (later on) to produce. Numerous examples of writings that clearly have been redacted in accord with a program and plan other than those of any document now in our hands will show precisely what I mean here. Not only so, but the entire appendix is devoted to showing that stories about sages were told and recorded, but not compiled into complete books, e.g., hagiographies about given authorities. In *Why No Gospels in Talmudic Judaism?* I was able to point out one kind of book that we can have received but were not given. The criterion here is not subjective. We can demonstrate that materials of a given type, capable of sustaining a large-scale compilation, were available; but no such compilation was made, so far as extant sources suggest or attest.

[4] Some writings now found in a given midrash compilation stand autonomous of any redactional program we have in an existing compilation or of any we can even imagine on the foundations of said writings.

The first of those four kinds of completed units of thought (pericopes) as matter of hypothesis fall into the final stage of literary formation. That is to say, at the stage at which an authorship has reached the conclusion that it wishes to compile a document of a given character, that authorship will have made up pieces of writing that serve the purposes of the document it wishes to compile. The second through fourth kinds of completed units of thought come earlier than this writing in the process of the formation of the classics of Judaism represented by the compilation in which this writing now finds its place.

The second of the four kinds of completed units of thought served a purpose other than that of the authorship of the compilation in which said kind of writing now occurs. It is therefore, as a matter of hypothesis, to be assigned to a stage in the formation of classics prior to the framing of the document in which the writing now occurs; in the context of a given compilation that now contains that writing, it is in a relative sense earlier than a piece of writing that the framers have worked out to serve their own distinctive and particular purposes. It is then earlier than a writing that has been made up to serve the document in which it now occurs. But it is also later in its formation than what we find in the third kind of writing.

The third of the four kinds of completed units of thought clearly presupposes a location in a document of a kind we do not have. But the characteristics of a set of such writings permits us to identify and define the kind of writing that can readily have contained, and been well served by, pericopes of this kind. Compositions of this kind, as a matter of hypothesis, are to be assigned to a stage in the formation of classics prior to the framing of all available documents. For, as a matter of fact, all of our now-extant writings adhere to a single program of conglomeration and agglutination, and all are served by composites of one sort, rather than some other. Hence we may suppose that at some point prior to the decision to make writings in the model that we now have but in some other model people also made up completed units of thought to serve these other kinds of writings. These persist, now, in documents that they do not serve at all well. And we can fairly easily identify the kinds of documents that they can and should have served quite nicely indeed. These then are the three stages of literary formation in the making of the classics of Judaism.

Type four in the list above stands outside of the three stages of literary formation, because these are kinds of writings that fall outside of any relationship with a redactional program we either have in hand or can even imagine. These free-standing units can have been written any time; the tastes as to redaction of a given set of compilers of documents make no impact upon the writing of such materials. When we find them in existing documents – and they are everywhere – they are parachuted down and bear no clear role in the accomplishment, through the writing, of the redactors' goals for their compilation. They are given, by way of rich example, in my presentation here of the treatment in the compilation, Ruth Rabbah, of Ruth 3:13.

Of the relative temporal or ordinal position of writings that stand autonomous of any redactional program we have in an existing compilation or of any we can even imagine on the foundations of said writings we can say nothing.[3] These writings prove episodic; they are commonly singletons. They serve equally well everywhere, because they demand no traits of form and redaction in order to endow them with sense and meaning. Why not? Because they are essentially free-standing and episodic, not referential and allusive. They are stories that contain their own point and do not invoke, in the making of that point, a given verse of Scripture. They are sayings that are utterly ad hoc. A variety of materials fall into this – from a redactional

---

[3]But I shall qualify this judgment later on.

perspective – unassigned, and unassignable, type of writing. They do not belong in books at all. By that I mean, whoever made up these pieces of writing did not imagine that what he was forming required a setting beyond the limits of his own piece of writing; the story is not only complete in itself but could stand entirely on its own; the saying spoke for itself and required no nurturing context; the proposition and its associated proofs in no way was meant to draw nourishment from roots penetrating nutriments outside of its own literary limits.

My analytical taxonomy of the writings now collected in various midrash compilations points to not only three stages in the formation of the classics of Judaism. It also suggests that writing went on outside of the framework of the editing of documents, and also within the limits of the formation and framing of documents. Writing of the former kind then constituted a kind of literary work on which redactional planning made no impact. But the second and the third kinds of writing responds to redactional considerations. So in the end we shall wish to distinguish between writing intended for the making of books – compositions of the first three kinds listed just now – and writing not responsive to the requirements of the making of compilations – compositions of the fourth kind.

The distinctions upon which these analytical taxonomies rest are objective and no no way subjective, since they depend upon the fixed and factual relationship between a piece of writing and a larger redactional context.

[1] We know the requirements of redactors of the several documents of the rabbinic canon, because I have already shown what they are in the case of a large variety of documents. When, therefore, we judge a piece of writing to serve the program of the document in which that writing occurs, it is not because of a personal impulse or a private and incommunicable insight, but because the traits of that writing self-evidently respond to the documentary program of the book in which the writing is located.

[2] When, further, we conclude that a piece of writing belongs in some other document than the one in which it is found, that too forms a factual judgment.

[3] A piece of writing that serves nowhere we now know may nonetheless conform to the rules of writing that we can readily imagine and describe in theory. For instance, a propositional composition, that runs through a wide variety of texts to make a point autonomous of all of the texts that are invoked, clearly is intended for a propositional document, one that (like the Mishnah) makes points autonomous of a given prior writing, e.g., a biblical book, but that makes points that for one reason or another cohere quite nicely on their own. Authors of

propositional compilations self-evidently can imagine that kind of redaction. We have their writings, but not the books that they intended to be made up of those writings. Another example, as I have already pointed out, is a collection of stories about a given authority, or about a given kind of virtue exemplified by a variety of authorities. These and other types of compilations we can imagine but do not have are dealt with in the present rubric.

[4] And, finally, where we have utterly hermetic writing, sealed off from any broader literary context and able to define its own limits and sustain its point without regard to anything outside itself, we know that here we are in the presence of authorships that had no larger redactional plan in mind, no intent on the making of books out of their little pieces of writing. Here the judgment of what belongs and what does not is not at all subjective, as I shall show in through my concrete examples.

These distinctions form the first step in the analysis of the formation of the rabbinic documents viewed not in isolation from one another but in relationship both to one another and also to shared antecedent writings to which we have access only in the re-presentation of the now-completed documents. I have now completed the bulk of my re-presentation and analysis of the documents of the Judaism of the Dual Torah one by one. Here I begin the analysis of those documents seen not in isolation from one another, but rather in relationship to what may be a common fund of materials framed without. The work of analysis begins with the data *in situ*: as we have them. That is why I give a sizable sample of two of the types I regard as indicative: writing for redactional purposes, writing not at all for redactional purposes, and writing for redactional purposes, but not of the redactors of the document in which that writing appears.

Specifically, in my sample of Ruth Rabbah, the first entry, marked LXII:i, is composed in response to the requirements of a sustained commentary on the verses, read in succession, of the book of Ruth. The second entry, LXII:ii, is made up entirely on its own and organized and set forth in response to an inner-facing interest in narrative. However we divide the bits and pieces that are assembled here, there can be no doubt that the whole hangs together without attention to any broader compilation in which the vast entry may be included. The third entry, LXII:iii, serves to demonstrate a proposition. That proposition is not particular to the book of Ruth, of course. But a treatise of pertinent propositions, e.g., theological-moral virtues, can well have been served by precisely the composition before us. So while we do not have a document the needs of which can have generated the item we shall examine, we can readily imagine such a document and identify the traits of the writing before us as documentary and not free-standing and internally generated.

iii. Our Case: Ruth Rabbah to Ruth 3:13

3:13   "Remain this night and in the morning, if he will do the part of the next
            of kin for you, well; let him do it; but if he is not willing to do the part of
            the next of kin for you, then, as the Lord lives, I will do the part of the
            next of kin for you. Lie down until the morning."

LXII:i.
1.   A   "Remain this night":
     B.   "This night you will spend without a husband, but you will not
            spend another night without a husband."

The opening gloss is trivial. But it clearly serves only the passage at hand, no broader proposition (by contrast to the utilization of our base verse in LXII:iii). This writing conforms to the most limited definition of the redactional requirements of the compilers of a commentary to the book of Ruth. The contrast with what follows is stunning. For what we see is an item parachuted down into this compilation but wholly indifferent to the documentary program of the compilers. It has been made up on its own, not for service in this document.

Let me explain what I mean. Elsewhere[4] I point out some simple facts. The final organizers of the Bavli, the Talmud of Babylonia had in hand a tripartite corpus of inherited materials awaiting composition into a final, closed document. First, the first type of material, in various states and stages of completion, addressed the Mishnah or took up the principles of laws that the Mishnah had originally brought to articulation. These the framers of the Bavli organized in accord with the order of those Mishnah-tractates that they selected for sustained attention. Second, they had in hand received materials, again in various conditions, pertinent to Scripture, both as Scripture related to the Mishnah and also as Scripture laid forth its own narratives. These they set forth as Scripture commentary. In this way, the penultimate and ultimate redactors of the Bavli laid out a systematic presentation of the two Torahs, the oral, represented by the Mishnah, and the written, represented by Scripture. And, third, the framers of the Bavli also had in hand materials focused on sages. These in the received

---

[4]In my *Why No Gospels in Talmudic Judaism?* (Atlanta, 1988: Scholars Press for Brown Judaic Studies) I explain why no other document in the rabbinic canon of late antiquity can have been compiled out of such materials either. In fact there was every possibility of compiling biographies, but it is something that the framers of canonical documents never undertook.

form, attested in the Bavli's pages, were framed around twin biographical principles, either as strings of stories about great sages of the past or as collections of sayings and comments drawn together solely because the same name stands behind all the collected sayings.

These stories, exemplified in what follows, can easily have been composed into biographies. In the context of Christianity and of Judaism, it is appropriate to call the biography of a holy man or woman, meant to convey the divine message, a gospel. Hence the question I raised there: why no gospels in Judaism? The question is an appropriate one, because, as I shall show, there could have been. The final step – assembling available stories into a coherent narrative, with a beginning, middle, and end, for example – was not taken. This suffices for the present to underline that what follows here is simply beyond the framework of compilation – ultimate organization, closure, and redaction – of documents. Hence this writing belongs into the fourth class among those differentiated just now.

LXII:ii.

1. A "and in the morning, if he will do the part of the next of kin for you, well; let him do it; but if he is not willing to do the part of the next of kin for you, then, as the Lord lives, I will do the part of the next of kin for you. [Lie down until the morning]":

    B. On the Sabbath R. Meir was in session and expounding in the school of Tiberias, and Elisha, his master, was passing in the market riding a horse.

    C. They said to R. Meir, "Lo, Elisha your master is passing by in the market."

    D. He went out to him.

    E. He [Elisha] said to him [Meir], "With what were you engaged?"

    F. He said to him, "'So the Lord blessed the latter end of Job more than his beginning' (Job 42:12)."

    G. He said to him, "And what do you have to say about it?"

    H. He said to him, "'blessed' means that he gave him twice as much money as he had before."

    I. He said to him, "Aqiba, your master, did not explain it in that way. This is how he explained it: "'So the Lord blessed the latter end of Job more than his beginning': it was on account of the repentance and the good deeds that were in his hand to begin with.'"

    J. He said to him, "And what else did you say?"

    K. He said to him, "'Better is the end of a thing than the beginning thereof' (Qoh. 7:8)."

    L. He said to him, "And what do you have to say about it?"

    M. He said to him, "You have the case of someone who buys merchandise in his youth and loses on it, while in his old age he profits through it.

    N. "Another matter: 'Better is the end of a thing than the beginning thereof' (Qoh. 7:8): you have the case of someone who does wicked deeds in his youth, but in his old age he does good deeds.

O. "Another matter: 'Better is the end of a thing than the beginning thereof' (Qoh. 7:8): you have the case of someone who studies Torah in his youth but forgets it, and in his old age it comes back to him. [Since Elisha was an apostate who had earlier been a great master of the Torah, these interpretations bear a personal message to him from his disciple, Meir.]

P. "Thus 'Better is the end of a thing than the beginning thereof' (Qoh. 7:8)."

Q. He said to him, "Aqiba, your master, did not explain matters in this way.

R. "Rather, 'Better is the end of a thing than the beginning thereof' (Qoh. 7:8): the end of a matter is good when it is good from the very beginning.'

S. "And there is this case [which illustrates Aqiba's view]: Abbuyah, my father, was one of the leading figures of the generation, and when the time came to circumcise me, he invited all the leading men of Jerusalem, and he invited R. Eliezer and R. Joshua with them.

T. "And when they had eaten and drunk, these began to say psalms, and those began to say [Rabinowitz, p. 77:] alphabetical acrostics.

U. "Said R. Eliezer to R. Joshua, 'These are engaged with what matters to them, so should we not devote ourselves to what matters to us?'

V. "They began with [verses of] the Torah, and from the Torah, they went on to the prophets, and from the prophets to the writings. And the matters gave as much joy as when they were given from Sinai, so fire leapt round about them.

W. "For was not the very act of giving them through fire? 'And the mountain burned with fire to the heart of heaven' (Dt. 4:11).

X. "[My father] said, 'Since such is the great power of Torah, this son, if he survives for me, lo, I shall give him over to the Torah.'

Y. "But since his true intentionality was not for the sake of Heaven [but for the ulterior motive of mastering the supernatural power of the Torah], my Torah did not endure in me.

Z. [Elisha continues in his talk with Meir:] "And what [else] did you say?"

AA. [Meir said to Elisha,] "'Gold and glass cannot equal it' (Job 28:17)."

BB. He said to him, "And what did you have to say about it?"

CC. He said to him, "This refers to teachings of the Torah, which are as hard to acquire as golden utensils and as easy to break as glass."

DD. He said to him, "Aqiba, your master, did not explain matters in this way.

EE. "Rather: 'just as golden and glass utensils, should they break, can be repaired, so a disciple of the sages who loses his master of the Mishnah can regain it.'"

FF. [Meir said to Elisha,] "Turn back."

GG. He said to him, "Why?"

HH. [Elisha] said to [Meir], "Up to here is the Sabbath limit [and within this space alone are you permitted to walk about]."

II. [Meir] said to him, "How do you know?"

JJ.	[Elisha] said to him, "It is from the hooves of my horse, for the horse has already travelled two thousand cubits."
KK.	[Meir] said to [Elisha], "And all this wisdom is in your possession, and yet you do not return?"
LL.	He said to him, "I don't have the power to do so."
MM.	He said to him, "Why not?"
NN.	He said to him, "I was riding on my horse and sauntering past the synagogue on the Day of Atonement that coincided with the Sabbath. I heard an echo floating in the air: '"Return, O backsliding children" (Jer. 3:14), "Return to me and I will return to you" (Mal. 3:7) – except for Elisha b. Abbuyah.
OO.	"'For he knew all my power, but he rebelled against me.'"

2.	A.	And how did he come to do such a deed? They tell the following:
	B.	One time he was sitting and repeating [Torah-sayings] in the valley of Gennesaret.
	C.	He saw a man climb up a palm tree on the Sabbath, take the dam with the offspring, and climb down whole and in one piece. Then at the end of the Sabbath he saw another man climb up a palm tree and take the offspring but send away the dam, and he came down, and a snake bit him and he died.
	D.	He said, "It is written, 'You shall in any manner let the dam go, but the young you may take for yourself, that it may be well with you and that you may live a long time' (Dt. 22:7).
	E.	"Now where is the goodness and the long life of this man?"
	F.	But he did not know that R. Aqiba had expounded in a public address: "'that it may be well with you': in the world that is entirely good.
	G.	"'and that you may live a long time': in the world that lasts for ever."
3.	A.	And some say that it was because he saw the tongue of R. Judah the baker being carried out in the mouth of a dog.
	B.	He said, "If this tongue, which has labored in the Torah throughout the man's life, is treated in this way, a tongue of one who does not know and does not labor in the Torah – all the more so!"
	C.	He said, "If so, then there is no granting of a reward for the righteous and no resurrection of the dead."
4.	A.	And some say that it was because when his mother was pregnant with him, she passed by temples of idolatry and smelled the odor,
	B.	and they gave her some of [the offering to the idol] to eat, and she ate it, and it diffused in her like the poison of an insect.
5.	A.	After some time Elisha b. Abbuyah fell ill.
	B.	They came and told R. Meir, "Elisha, your master, is sick."
	C.	He came to him.
	D.	He said to him, "Repent."
	E.	He said to him, "Even to this point do they accept [repentance]?'
	F.	He said to him, "Is it not written, 'You turn man to contrition' (Ps. 90:3) – until the very crushing of the spirit."
	G.	At that moment Elisha b. Abbuyah wept, and died.
	H.	And R. Meir rejoiced, saying, "It appears that it was from the midst of repentance that my master has gone away."

6. A. And when they buried him, a fire came to burn up his grave.
    B. They came and told R. Meir, "The grave of your master is burning."
    C. He came and spread his cloak over it.
    D. He said to him, "'Remain this night': in this world, the whole of which is night.
    E. "'and in the morning, if he will redeem you [lit.: do the part of the next of kin for you], well; let him do it':
    F. "'and in the morning': in the world that is wholly good.
    G. "'if he will redeem you, well and good, he will redeem you': this refers to the Holy One, blessed be He: 'The Lord is good to all' (Ps. 145:9).
    H. "'but if he is not willing to redeem you, you, then, as the Lord lives, I will redeem you. Lie down until the morning.'"
    I. [Rabinowitz:] And the fire subsided.
7. A. They said to him, "My lord, in the world to come, if they say to you, whom do you want, your father or your master, what will you say?"
    B. He said to them, "Father, then my master."
    C. They said to him, "Will they listen [when you ask for Elisha, who was an apostate]?"
    D. He said to them, "Is it not an explicit teaching of the Mishnah? **The case of a scroll may on the Sabbath may be saved from a fire together with the scroll, and the case of tefillin together with the tefillin [M. Shab. 16:1].**
    E. "They will save Elisha because of the merit of his Torah-learning."
8. A. After some time, his daughters came and begged for charity from our lord [Judah the Patriarch].
    B. He said, "'Let there be none to extend kindness to him, neither let there be any to be gracious to his orphaned children' (Ps. 109:12)."
    C. They said, "My lord, do not focus upon his deeds, focus upon his Torah."
    D. At that moment our lord wept and made the decree concerning them that they were to receive their requirements.
    E. He said, "If one whose mastery of Torah was not for the sake of Heaven has produced such as these, one whose Torah is for the sake of Heaven how much the more so!"

This entire composition is parachuted down because of the appeal to our base verse as a prooftext at one point in the narrative. The whole has been assembled – much of it a sustained, unitary and flowing story – to make the points at the end about the power of repentance and of Torah study. But the exposition of the relationship between the sinning master and the disciple transcends the requirement of an exemplary account of virtue. Our interest is of course limited; but the selection of a powerful and enormous piece of writing, obviously composed for its own purposes, shows us how the compilers of the document broadened the conception of what a compilation should, and need not, encompass. The impact upon their recasting of the book of Ruth is at once nearly nil and also profound and encompassing.

Now to a passage composed with a document in mind, but not the document in which the passage now appears. The base verse is here subordinated; there are three cases to prove a point. Hence a document that wished to present syllogistic arguments in behalf of propositions can have been served by what follows, but a document meant to form a commentary to the book of Ruth is not well served. The following falls into the second of the four classes of materials set forth earlier.

LXXII:iii.

1. A   Said R. Yosé, "There were three who were tempted by their inclination to do evil, but who strengthened themselves against it in each case by taking an oath: Joseph, David, and Boaz.

B.   "Joseph: 'How then can I do this great wickedness and sin against God' (Gen. 39:9).

C.   [Yosé continues, citing] R. Hunia in the name of R. Idi: 'Does Scripture exhibit defects? What Scripture here says is not, "and sin against the Lord," but "and sin against God."

D.   "'For he had sworn [in the language of an oath] to his evil inclination, saying, "By God, I will not sin or do this evil."'

E.   "David: 'And David said, 'As the Lord lives, no, but the Lord shall smite him' (1 Sam. 26:10).

F.   "To whom did he take the oath?

G.   "R. Eleazar and R. Samuel b. Nahman:

H.   "R. Eleazar said, 'It was to his impulse to do evil.'

I.   "R. Samuel b. Nahman said, 'It was to Abishai b. Zeruiah. He said to him, "As the Lord lives, if you touch him, I swear that I will mix your blood with his."'

J.   "Boaz: 'as the Lord lives, I will do the part of the next of kin for you. Lie down until the morning.'

K.   "R. Judah and R. Hunia:

L.   "R. Judah said, 'All that night his impulse to do evil was besieging him and saying to him, "You are a free agent and on the make, and she is a free agent and on the make. Go, have sexual relations with her, and let her be your wife!"

M.   "'And so he took an oath against his inclination to do evil, saying, "'as the Lord lives."'

N.   "'And to the woman he said, "Remain this night and in the morning, if he will do the part of the next of kin for you, well; let him do it; but if he is not willing to do the part of the next of kin for you, then...I will do the part of the next of kin for you. Lie down until the morning."'

O.   "And R. Hunia said, 'It is written, "A wise man is strong [*beoz*]. Yes, a man of knowledge increases strength" (Prov. 24:5).

P.   "'Read the word for strong [*beoz*] as Boaz:

Q.   "'A wise man is Boaz.

R.   "'"and a man of knowledge increases strength," because he strengthened himself with an oath.'"

Now we see what a passage serving our base verse can accomplish. But even here, of course, our base verse is made to address the interest of a proposition not particular to the passage at hand. The proposition of Yosé is that one should strengthen himself against temptation by taking an oath, and he gives three examples of that fact, of which ours is third only by reason of the redactional requirement of our compilers. Otherwise any order will serve as well. I have represented matters as though the whole were Yosé's statement, but of course, that is hardly required. In fact each item is autonomous of the others, with its independent exposition of its case. Thus B-D form an independent statement on Joseph, then D-E on David, with the appended expansion of F-I. J then stands on its own, with the appended and essential materials of Kff. An alternative theory is that to Yosé are to be attributed only the barebones of the proposition, consisting of B, E, and J, with the rest inserted to expand on his point; that seems to me entirely plausible. In this treatment of the base verse, therefore, we find three quite distinct compositions. LXII:i is particular to the base verse, but only a minor gloss; LXII:ii is an astonishing composition on its own, formed around the figure of Elisha b. Abbuyah. LXII:iii assembles three cases to establish a proposition.

iv. What Is at Stake: The Three Stages of Literary Formation and the Formation of a New Hermeneutics

Once we recognize, as I have shown we must, that the rabbinic documents constitute texts, not merely scrapbooks or random compilations of ad hoc and episodic materials, both the hermeneutics and the (theoretical) history of the texts are recast. For our criteria for interpreting a passage is now the program of the document. Our interest in philology – meanings of words scattered over a variety of documents – correspondingly diminishes. The context now predominates; meanings of words and phrases, while interesting, move away from center stage. And the texts now are seen to have histories – the texts, that is, the completed documents, and not merely the materials that the texts (happen, adventitiously, to) contain. And yet, we recognize, within these same thirteen well-crafted documents, sizable selections of materials did circulate from one document to another. The documentary hypothesis affects the itinerant compositions, for it identifies what writings are extra-documentary and non-documentary and imposes upon the hermeneutics and history of these writings a set of distinctive considerations too. For these writings serve the purposes not of compilers (or authors or authorships) of distinct compilations, but those of a variety of compilers; that means some writings are particular to a document and immediately express the purposes of a distinct authorship or group of compilers, while other writings work well for two or more documents.

Let me expand on this point, since the movement of materials from compilation to compilation has always enjoyed prominence in such literary history and theory as have been shaped for the canon before us. By definition, according to the results of the present experiment, these other writings have been made up not with a given document's requirements in mind, but within a different theory altogether of the purpose and meaning of writing. Not only so, but, as we saw, there is a class of writings, associated with the kind in Ruth Rabbah LXII:iii in its independence of existing documentary compilations, that clearly means to serve the purposes of compilers of a document – but not the document(s) in which these writings now find their place. Writings of this class permit us to speculate on the existence of compilations now no longer in our hands, or, more to the point, *types* of compilations we (no longer) possess.

v. The Priority of Documentary Hermeneutics

Before proceeding, let me restate the premise of the whole. The analysis of the types of compositions of which rabbinic compilations are made up rests upon one fundamental premise. It is that rabbinic documents are texts and not scrapbooks,[5] that we moreover may identify the traits that characterize one piece of compilation and distinguish those traits from the ones that mark another compilation within the canon of the Judaism of the Dual Torah. My argument in favor of the documentary integrity of rabbinic compilations can stand reiteration.

In my study of Leviticus Rabbah I proposed to demonstrate in the case of that compilation of exegeses of Scripture that a rabbinic document constitutes a text, not merely a scrapbook or a random compilation of episodic materials. A text is a document with a purpose, one that exhibits the traits of the integrity of the parts to the whole and the fundamental autonomy of the whole from other texts. I showed

---

[5]But it must be said that some of the compilations, e.g., Leviticus Rabbah and Genesis Rabbah and Sifra, exhibit much more cogency than do others, e.g., Lamentations Rabbah and Esther Rabbah. However, I am not inclined to dismiss even Lamentations Rabbah, Esther Rabbah, and Ruth Rabbah as no more than scrapbooks. There is considerable attention among their compilers devoted to formal patterns, for one thing, and a well-crafted propositional program emerges in each of these compilations, for another. I find them admirable in their documentary cogency, but it is a different kind of coherence from that exhibited in the great Sifra or the two Sifrés. And, I hasten to add, formally we do not deal with the decadence of the form defined by Genesis Rabbah and Leviticus Rabbah, but in a revision of that form.

that the document at hand therefore falls into the classification of a cogent composition, put together with purpose and intended as a whole and in the aggregate to bear a meaning and state a message.

I therefore disproved the claim, for the case before us, that a rabbinic document serves merely as an anthology or miscellany or is to be compared only to a scrapbook, made up of this and that. In that exemplary instance I pointed to the improbability that a document has been brought together merely to join discrete and ready-made bits and pieces of episodic discourse. A document in the canon of Judaism thus does not merely define a context for the aggregation of such already completed and mutually distinct materials. Rather, I proved, that document constitutes a text. So at issue in my study of Leviticus Rabbah is what makes a text a text, that is, the textuality of a document. At stake is how we may know when a document constitutes a text and when it is merely an anthology or a scrapbook.

The importance of that issue for the correct method of comparison is clear. If we can show that a document is a miscellany, then traits of the document have no bearing on the contents of the document – things that just happen to be preserved there, rather than somewhere else. If, by contrast, the text possesses its own integrity, then everything in the text must first of all be interpreted in the context of the text, then in the context of the canon of which the text forms a constituent. Hence my stress on the comparison of whole documents, prior to the comparison of the results of exegesis contained within those documents, rests upon the result of the study of Leviticus Rabbah. Two principal issues frame the case. The first is what makes a text a text. The textuality of a text concerns whether a given piece of writing hangs together and is to be read on its own The second is what makes a group of texts into a canon, a cogent statement all together. At issue is the relationship of two or more texts of a single, interrelated literature to the worldview and way of life of a religious tradition viewed whole.

Now it may be claimed by proponents of the view that redactional, hence documentary, considerations are of negligible importance that powerful evidence contradicts my emphasis on the documentary origin of much writing now located in midrash compilations.[6] They point to the fact that stories and exegeses move from document to document. The

---

[6]These proponents are not fictive. David Weiss Halivni concentrates on sayings and their solitary journeys through various pericopes, scarcely attending to the traits of documents at all. I have dealt with his contrary approach to literary history in *Making the Classics in Judaism: The Three Stages of Literary Formation* (Atlanta, 1990: Scholars Press for Brown Judaic Studies).

travels of a given saying or story or exegesis of Scripture from one document to another validate comparing what travels quite apart from what stays home. And that is precisely what comparing exegeses of the same verse of Scripture occurring in different settings does. Traveling materials enjoy their own integrity, apart from the texts – the documents – that quite adventitiously give them a temporary home. The problem of *integrity* therefore is whether a rabbinic document stands by itself or right at the outset forms a scarcely differentiated segment of a larger and uniform canon, one made up of materials that travel everywhere and take up residence indifferent to the traits of their temporary abode.

The reason one might suppose that, in the case of the formative age of Judaism, a document does not exhibit integrity and is not autonomous is simple. The several writings of the rabbinic canon of late antiquity, formed from the Mishnah, ca. A.D. 200, through the Talmud of Babylonia, ca. A.D. 600, with numerous items in between, do share materials – sayings, tales, protracted discussions. Some of these shared materials derive from explicitly cited documents. For instance, passages of Scripture or of the Mishnah or of the Tosefta, cited verbatim, will find their way into the two Talmuds. But sayings, stories, and sizable compositions not identified with a given, earlier text and exhibiting that text's distinctive traits will float from one document to the next.

That fact has so impressed students of the rabbinic canon as to produce a firm consensus of fifteen hundred years' standing. It is that one cannot legitimately study one document in isolation from others, describing its rhetorical, logical, literary, and conceptual traits and system all by themselves. To the contrary, all documents contribute to a common literature, or, more accurately, religion – Judaism. In the investigation of matters of rhetoric, logic, literature, and conception, whether of law or of theology, all writings join equally to given testimony to the whole. For the study of the formative history of Judaism, the issue transcends what appears to be the simple, merely literary question at hand: when is a text a text? In the context of this book: when do the interests of the framers of a text participate in the writing of their text? and when do they merely compile from ready-made materials whatever suits their purpose? In the larger context of that question we return to the issue of the peripatetic sayings, stories, and exegeses.

vi. The Three Stages of Literary Formation Revisited

When I frame matters of literary theory, including literary history ("the three stages of literary formation") in terms of the problem of the rabbinic document, I ask what defines a document as such, the text-ness, the textuality, of a text. How do we know that a given book in the canon of Judaism is something other than a scrapbook? The choices are clear. One theory is that a document serves solely as a convenient repository of prior sayings and stories, available materials that will have served equally well (or poorly) wherever they took up their final location. In accord with that theory it is quite proper in ignorance of all questions of circumstance and documentary or canonical context to (to take the example of Comparative Midrash as presently performed) compare the exegesis of a verse of Scripture in one document with the exegesis of that verse of Scripture found in some other document.

The other theory is that a composition exhibits a viewpoint, a purpose of authorship distinctive to its framers or collectors and arrangers. Such a characteristic literary purpose – by this other theory – is so powerfully particular to one authorship that nearly everything at hand can be shown to have been (re)shaped for the ultimate purpose of the authorship at hand, that is, collectors and arrangers who demand the title of authors. In accord with this other theory context and circumstance form the prior condition of inquiry, the result, in exegetical terms, the contingent one. To resort again to a less than felicitous neologism, I thus ask what signifies or defines the "document-ness" of a document and what makes a book a book. I therefore wonder whether there are specific texts in the canonical context of Judaism or whether all texts are merely contextual. In framing the question as I have, I of course lay forth the mode of answering it. We have to confront a single rabbinic composition, and ask about its definitive traits and viewpoint.

vii. Itinerancy and Documentary Integrity: The Problem of the Peripatetic Composition

But we have also to confront the issue of the traveling sayings, the sources upon which the redactors of a given document have drawn. For there are sayings that do travel from one document to another without exhibiting much wear from the journey, and, as I shall show in Part Three, there also are sources that are equally at home everywhere because they belong nowhere. And such sources call into question the documentary theory of the making of the classics in Judaism that I present in this book. So let us turn to the matter of what is called "the sources."[7]

By "sources" I mean (for the purposes of argument here) simply passages in a given book that occur, also, in some other rabbinic book. Such sources – by definition prior to the books in which they appear – fall into the classification of materials general to two or more compositions and by definition not distinctive and particular to any one of them. The word "source" therefore serves as an analogy to convey the notion that two or more sets of authors have made use of a single, available item. About whether or not the shared item is prior to them both or borrowed by one from the other at this stage we cannot speculate.[8]

Let me now summarize this phase of the argument. We ask about the textuality of a document – is it a composition or a scrapbook? – so as to determine the appropriate foundations for comparison, the correct classifications for comparative study. We seek to determine the correct context of comparison, hence the appropriate classification. My claim is simple: once we know what is unique to a document, we can investigate the traits that characterize all the document's unique and so definitive materials. We ask about whether the materials unique to a document also cohere, or whether they prove merely miscellaneous. If they do cohere, we may conclude that the framers of the document have followed a single plan and a program. That would in my view justify the claim that the framers carried out a labor not only of conglomeration, arrangement and selection, but also of genuine authorship or composition in the narrow and strict sense of the word. If

---

[7]This is defined at great length in my treatment of Halivni's theory of sources and traditions cited above. I redefine "sources" and "traditions" at the end of that paper, in terms that I think far more suitable.

[8]To state the consequences for Comparative Midrash, which has received attention in its own terms: These shared items, transcending two or more documents and even two or more complete systems or groups, if paramount and preponderant, would surely justify the claim that we may compare [3] exegeses of verses of Scripture without attention to [2] context. Why? Because there is no context defined by the limits of a given document and its characteristic plan and program. All the documents do is collect and arrange available materials. The document does not define the context of its contents. If that can be shown, then *Comparative Midrash* may quite properly ignore the contextual dimension imparted to sayings, including exegeses of Scripture, by their occurrence in one document rather than some other. In this connection, see my *Comparative Midrash: The Plan and Program of Genesis Rabbah and Leviticus Rabbah.* (Atlanta, 1986: Scholars Press for Brown Judaic Studies.) *Comparative Midrash* II. *The Plan and Program of Lamentations Rabbah, Esther Rabbah, Ruth Rabbah, and Song of Songs Rabbah* is planned.

so, the document emerges from authors, not merely arrangers and compositors. For the same purpose, therefore, we also take up and analyze the items shared between that document and some other or among several documents. We ask about the traits of those items, one by one and all in the aggregate. In these stages we may solve for the case at hand the problem of the rabbinic document: do we deal with a scrapbook or a cogent composition? A text or merely a literary expression, random and essentially promiscuous, of a larger theological context? That is the choice at hand.

Since we have reached a matter of fact, let me state the facts as they are. To begin with, I describe the relationships among the principal components of the literature with which we deal. The several documents that make up the canon of Judaism in late antiquity relate to one another in three important ways.

First, all of them refer to the same basic writing, the Hebrew Scriptures. Many of them draw upon the Mishnah and quote it. So the components of the canon join at their foundations.

Second, as the documents reached closure in sequence, the later authorship can be shown to have drawn upon earlier, completed documents. So the writings of the rabbis of the talmudic corpus accumulate and build from layer to layer.

Third, as I have already hinted, among two or more documents some completed units of discourse, and many brief, discrete sayings, circulated, for instance, sentences or episodic homilies or fixed apophthegms of various kinds. So in some (indeterminate) measure the several documents draw not only upon one another, as we can show, but also upon a common corpus of materials that might serve diverse editorial and redactional purposes.

The extent of this common corpus can never be fully known. In my exemplary materials, Ruth Rabbah LXII:ii and iii present what can have formed a common corpus. But we know only what we have, not what we do not have. So we cannot say what has been omitted, or whether sayings that occur in only one document derive from materials available to the editors or compilers of some or all other documents. That is something we never can know. We can describe only what is in our hands and interpret only the data before us. Of indeterminates and endless speculative possibilities we need take no account. In taking up documents one by one, do we not obscure their larger context and their points in common?

In fact, shared materials proved for Leviticus Rabbah not many and not definitive. They form an infinitesimal proportion of Genesis Rabbah, under 3-5% of the volume of the *parashiyyot* for which I conducted probes.[9] Materials that occur in both Leviticus Rabbah and some other document prove formally miscellany and share no single viewpoint or program; they are random and brief. What is unique to Leviticus Rabbah and exhibits that document's characteristic formal traits also predominates and bears the message of the whole. So much for the issue of the peripatetic exegesis. To date I have taken up the issue of homogeneity of "sources," in a limited and mainly formal setting, for the matter of how sayings and stories travel episodically from one document to the next.[10] The real issue is not the traveling, but the unique, materials: the documents, and not what is shared among them. The variable – what moves – is subject to analysis only against the constant: the document itself.

viii. Theology and Hermeneutics:
The Unacknowledged Participant in the Debate

To describe and analyze documents one by one violates the lines of order and system that have characterized all earlier studies of these same documents. Until now, just as people compared exegeses among different groups of a given verse of Scripture without contrasting one circumstance to another, so they tended to treat all of the canonical texts as uniform in context, that is, as testimonies to a single system and structure, that is, to Judaism. What sort of testimonies texts provide varies according to the interest of those who study them. That is why, without regard to the source of the two expositions of the same verse, people would compare one *midrash*, meaning the interpretation of a given verse of Scripture, with another *midrash* on the same verse of Scripture. True enough, philologians look for meanings of words and phrases, better versions of a text. For them all canonical documents equally serve as a treasury of philological facts and variant readings. Theologians study all texts equally, looking for God's will and finding testimonies to God in each component of the Torah of Moses our Rabbi. Why so? Because all texts ordinarily are taken to form a common

---

[9] There were two kinds of exceptions. First, entire *parashiyyot* occur in both Leviticus Rabbah and, verbatim, in Pesiqta deR. Kahana. Second, Genesis Rabbah and Leviticus Rabbah share sizable compositions. The former sort always conform to the formal program of Leviticus Rabbah. They in no way stand separate from the larger definitive and distinctive traits of the document. The latter sort fit quite comfortably, both formally and programmatically, into both Genesis Rabbah and Leviticus Rabbah, because those two documents themselves constitute species of a single genus.

[10] *The Peripatetic Saying. The Problem of the Thrice-Told Tale in Talmudic Literature* (Chico, 1985: Scholars Press for Brown Judaic Studies).

statement, "Torah" in the mythic setting, "Judaism" in the theological one.

But comparison cannot be properly carried out on such a basis. The hermeneutical issue dictated by the system overall defines the result of description, analysis, and interpretation.   Let me give a single probative example. From the classical perspective of the theology of Judaism the entire canon of Judaism ("the one whole Torah of Moses, our rabbi") equally and at every point testifies to the entirety of Judaism. Why so? Because all documents in the end form components of a single system. Each makes its contribution to the whole. If, therefore, we wish to know what "Judaism" or, more accurately, "the Torah," teaches on any subject, we are able to draw freely on sayings relevant to that subject wherever they occur in the entire canon of Judaism. Guided only by the taste and judgment of the great sages of the Torah, as they have addressed the question at hand, we thereby describe "Judaism." And that same theological conviction explains why we may rip a passage out of its redactional context and compare it with another passage, also seized from its redactional setting. It goes without saying that the theological *apologia* for doing so has yet to reach expression; and there can be no other than a theological *apologia*. In logic I see none; epistemologically there never was one. The presence of a theological premise has yet to be acknowledged, or even recognized, by exponents of the anti-documentary hermeneutic and theory of literary history alike.

ix. Autonomy, Connection, Continuity

In fact documents stand in three relationships to one another and to the system of which they form part, that is, to Judaism, as a whole. The specification of these relationships constitutes the principal premise of this inquiry and validates the approach to the formation of compositions and composites that I offer here.

[1] Each document is to be seen all by itself, that is, as autonomous of all others.

[2] Each document is to be examined for its relationships with other documents universally regarded as falling into the same classification, as Torah.

[3] And, finally, in the theology of Judaism (or, in another context, of Christianity) each document is to be allowed to take its place as part of the undifferentiated aggregation of documents that, all together, constitute the canon of, in the case of Judaism, the "one whole Torah revealed by God to Moses at Mount Sinai."

Simple logic makes self-evident the proposition that, if a document comes down to us within its own framework, as a complete book with a beginning, middle, and end, in preserving that book, the canon presents us with a document on its own and not solely as part of a larger composition or construct. So we too see the document as it reaches us, that is, as autonomous.

If, second, a document contains materials shared verbatim or in substantial content with other documents of its classification, or if one document refers to the contents of other documents, then the several documents that clearly wish to engage in conversation with one another have to address one another. That is to say, we have to seek for the marks of connectedness, asking for the meaning of those connections. It is at this level of connectedness that we labor. For the purpose of comparison is to tell us what is like something else, what is unlike something else. To begin with, we can declare something unlike something else only if we know that it is like that other thing. Otherwise the original judgment bears no sense whatsoever. So, once more, canon defines context, or, in descriptive language, the first classification for comparative study is the document, brought into juxtaposition with, and contrast to, another document.

Finally, since the community of the faithful of Judaism, in all of the contemporary expressions of Judaism, concur that documents held to be authoritative constitute one whole, seamless "Torah," that is, a complete and exhaustive statement of God's will for Israel and humanity, we take as a further appropriate task, if one not to be done here, the description of the whole out of the undifferentiated testimony of all of its parts. These components in the theological context are viewed, as is clear, as equally authoritative for the composition of the whole: one, continuous system. In taking up such a question, we address a problem not of theology alone, though it is a correct theological conviction, but one of description, analysis, and interpretation of an entirely historical order.

In my view the various documents of the canon of Judaism produced in late antiquity demand a hermeneutic altogether different from the one of homogenization and harmonization, the ahistorical and anti-contextual one definitive for the prevailing hermeneutic and theory of literary history. It is one that does not harmonize but that differentiates. It is a hermeneutic shaped to teach us how to read the compilations of exegeses first of all one by one and in a particular context, and second, in comparison with one another.

Let me review in this context out the method I applied to both Rabbah compilations[11] and plan to apply to the four final Rabbah compilations later on: Lamentations Rabbah, Esther Rabbah, Ruth Rabbah, and Song of Songs Rabbah.[12] It is not complicated and rests upon what seem to me self-evident premises. I have to prove that the document at hand rests upon clear-cut choices of formal and rhetorical preference, so it is, from the viewpoint of form and mode of expression, cogent. I have to demonstrate that these formal choices prove uniform and paramount. So for the several compilations I have analyzed large *parashiyyot* (systematic and sustained compositions of exegeses) to show their recurrent structures. These I categorize. Then, I proceed to survey all *parashiyyot* of each of the complete compilations and find out whether or not every *parashah* of the entire document finds within a single cogent taxonomic structure suitable classifications for its diverse units of discourse. If one taxonomy serves all and encompasses the bulk of the units of discourse at hand, I may fairly claim that Leviticus Rabbah or Genesis Rabbah, or Lamentations Rabbah, Esther Rabbah, and Ruth Rabbah, respectively, do constitute a cogent formal structure, based upon patterns of rhetoric uniform and characteristic throughout.

My next step, for the several probes and documents, is to ask whether the framers of the document preserved a fixed order in arranging types of units of discourse, differentiated in accord with the forms I identified. In both documents I am able to show that, in ordering materials, the framers or redactors paid much attention to the formal traits of their units of discourse. They chose materials of one formal type for beginning their sustained exercises of argument or syllogism, then chose another formal type for the end of their sustained exercises of syllogistic exposition. This seems to me to show that the framers or redactors followed a set of rules which we are able to discern. Finally, in the case of the several documents, I outline the program and show the main points of emphasis and interest presented in each. In this way I characterize the program as systematically as I described the plan. In this way I answer the question, for the documents under study, of whether or not we deal with a text, exhibiting traits of composition, deliberation, proportion, and so delivering a message on its own. Since we do, then Leviticus Rabbah or Genesis Rabbah, on the one side, and Lamentation Rabbah, Esther Rabbah, Ruth Rabbah, and

---

[11]Reference is made to *The Integrity of Leviticus Rabbah* (Chico, 1985), and *Comparative Midrash: The Program and Plan of Genesis Rabbah and Leviticus Rabbah* (Atlanta, 1985).

[12]This will be *Comparative Midrash II.*

Song of Songs Rabbah, on the other, do demand description, analysis, and interpretation first of all each compilation on its own, as an autonomous statement. It then requires comparison and contrast with other compositions of its species of the rabbinic genus, that is to say, it demands to be brought into connection with, relationship to, other rabbinic compositions.[13]

x. The Next Stage

My "three stages" in ordinal sequence correspond, as a matter of fact, to three types of writing. The first – and last in assumed temporal order – is writing carried out in the context of the making, or compilation, of a classic. That writing responds to the redactional program and plan of the authorship of a classic. The second, penultimate in order, is writing that can appears in a given document but better serves a document other than the one in which it (singularly) occurs. This kind of writing seems to me not to fall within the same period of redaction as the first. For while it is a type of writing under the identical conditions, it also is writing that presupposes redactional programs in no way in play in the ultimate, and definitive, period of the formation of the canon: when people did things this way, and not in some other. That is why I think it is a kind of writing that was done prior to the period in which people limited their redactional work and associated labor of composition to the program that yielded the books we now have.

The upshot is simple: whether the classification of writing be given a temporal or merely taxonomic valence, the issue is the same: have these writers done their work with documentary considerations in mind? I believe I have shown that they have not. Then where did they expect their work to makes its way? Anywhere it might, because, so they assumed, fitting in nowhere in particular, it found a suitable locus everywhere it turned up. But I think temporal, not merely taxonomic, considerations pertain. Let me say why.

The third kind of writing seems to me to originate in a period prior to the other two. It is carried on in a manner independent of all redactional considerations such as are known to us. Then it should derive from a time when redactional considerations played no

---

[13]The quite separate question of the use and meaning of Scripture in Judaism is addressed in my *Judaism and Scripture: The Evidence of Leviticus Rabbah* (Chicago, 1986: University of Chicago Press). The beginning of my theological path is marked by *Writing with Scripture: The Authority and Uses of the Hebrew Bible in the Torah of Formative Judaism* (Minneapolis, 1989: Fortress Press) [with William Scott Green].

paramount role in the making of compositions. A brief essay, rather than a sustained composition, was then the dominant mode of writing.

Do I place a priority, in the framing of a hypothesis, over taxonomy or temporal order? Indeed I do. I could have spoken to three types of writing, rather than speaking of the sequence of in which these types of writing took shape. Accordingly, I am inclined to suppose that non-documentary compositions took shape not only separated from, but in time before, the documentary ones did. My reason for thinking so is worth rehearsing, even though it is not yet compelling. The kinds of non-documentary writing I have assembled in Ruth Rabbah LXII:ii (and, I hasten to add, a good case can be made for the inclusion of the non-extant-documentary writing in LXII:iii) focus on matters of very general interest.

These matters may be assembled into two very large rubrics: virtue, on the one side, reason, on the other. Stories about sages fall into the former category; all of them set forth in concrete form the right living that sages exemplify. Essays on right thinking, the role of reason, the taxonomic priority of Scripture, the power of analogy, the exemplary character of cases and precedents in the expression of general and encompassing rules – all of these intellectually coercive writings set forth rules of thought as universally applicable, in their way, as are the rules of conduct contained in stories about sages, in theirs. A great labor of generalization is contained in both kinds of non-documentary and extra-documentary writing. And the results of that labor are then given concrete expression in the documentary writings in hand; for these, after all, do say in the setting of specific passages or problems precisely what, in a highly general way, emerges from the writing that moves hither and yon, never with a home, always finding a suitable resting place.

Now, admittedly, that rather general characterization of the non-documentary writing is subject to considerable qualification and clarification. But it does provide a reason to assign temporal priority, not solely taxonomic distinction, to the non-documentary compositions I have assembled for exemplary purposes in Ruth Rabbah LXII:ii and iii. We can have had commentaries of a sustained and systematic sort on (to take one example not portrayed here) the book of Chronicles, on the one side, treatises on virtue, on the second, gospels, on the third – to complete the triangle. But we do not have these kinds of books.

The books we do have not only preserve the evidences of the possibility of commentaries and biographies. More than that, they also bring to rich expression the messages that such books will have set forth. And most important, they also express in fresh and unanticipated contexts those virtues and values that commentaries and biographies ("gospels") meant to bring to realization, and they do so in accord with the modes of thought that sophisticated reflection on right thinking has exemplified in its way as well. So when people went about the work of making documents, they did something fresh with something familiar. They made cogent compositions, documents, texts enjoying integrity and autonomy. But they did so in such a way as to form of their distinct documents a coherent body of writing, of books, a canon, of documents, a system. And this they did in such a way as to say, in distinctive and specific ways, things that, in former times, people had expressed in general and broadly applicable ways. We have moved beyond the wild storms of inchoate speculation, but have yet to reach the safe harbor of established fact. But the course is true, the destination in sight, the journey's end not at all in doubt.

EPILOGUE

11

The Documentary History
of Judaism

Or:

Why Schechter, Moore, and Urbach
Are Irrelevant to Scholarship Today

We began with the great Max Kadushin, whom we must continue to read. Let us conclude with less interesting figures and their results, which we may henceforward ignore as simply baseless. When we investigate the history of the formative stage of the Judaism of the Dual Torah, what can we now learn from the generations of scholarship that began with Solomon Schechter and concluded with Ephraim E. Urbach? For, during that long period, the premises of learning in the rabbinic literature of late antiquity joined new historical interest with a received theological conviction. The former wished to describe in context ideas that had formerly been assigned no context at all: they were "Torah," and now were to be the history of ideas. The latter maintained that the documents of the rabbinic corpus were essentially seamless and formed one vast Dual Torah, oral and written; and that all attributions were valid, so that if a given authority was supposed to have made a statement, he really made it. On the basis of that received conviction, imputing inerrancy to the attributions (as well as to the storytellers) just as had many generations of the faithful, but asking questions of context and development that were supposed to add up to history, Schechter, Moore, Kadushin, Urbach, and all the other great figures of the first three-quarters of the twentieth century set forth their accounts.

But what if we recognize that documentary formulations play a role in the representation of compositions, so that the compositors' formulation of matters takes a critical place in the making of the documentary evidence? And what if, further, we no longer assume the inerrancy of the Oral Torah's writings, so that attributions are no longer taken at face value, stories no longer believed unless there are grounds for disbelief (as the Jerusalem canard has it)? Then the fundamental presuppositions of the writing of Schechter, Moore, Kadushin, Urbach, and lesser figures prove null. And that fact bears in its wake the further problem: since we cannot take their answers at face value, can we pursue their questions any more? In my judgment, the answer is negative. The only reason nowadays to read Schechter, Moore, Kadushin, Urbach and others is to see what they have to say about specific passages upon which, episodically and unsystematically, they have comments to make. All work in the history of the formative age of the Judaism of the Dual Torah that treats documentary lines as null and attributions as invariably valid must be dismissed as a mere curiosity; a collection and arrangement of this and that, bearing no compelling argument or proposition to be dealt with by the new generation.[1]

---

[1]William Horbury, reviewing my *Vanquished Nation, Broken Spirit* (*Epworth Review*, May, 1989), correctly observes: "Emotional attitudes form a traditional moral topic, and the recommendations on them in rabbinic ethics have often been considered, for example, in the *Rabbinic Anthology* of C. G. Montefiore and H. Loewe...This historical inquiry is closely related to the author's other work, and it is written on his own terms; he does not mention other writers on rabbinic ethics, and he gives no explicit criticism or development of modern study by others of the rabbinic passages and ideas with which he deals. He cannot be said to have fulfilled his obligation to his readers." Horbury does not seem to know my extensive writings on others who have worked on the formative history of Judaism, even though these have been collected and set forth in a systematic way, both as book reviews and as methodological essays, time and again. My *Ancient Judaism: Disputes and Debates* (Chico, 1986: Scholars Press for Brown Judaic Studies) is only one place in which I have indeed done just what Horbury asks, addressing Urbach and Moore and some of their most recent continuators in a systematic and thorough way. I am amazed that he can imagine I have not read the literature of my field; I not only have read and repeatedly criticized it, but I have done so in every accessible medium. His reviews of my work are simply uninformed and captious. His treatment of my *Incarnation of God* in *Expository Times*, which makes the same point in a more savage manner, shows the real problem; he does not find it possible to state more than the topic (the title!) of the book and

Let me now reframe the question in a manner which will make clear the right way in which to work. For when we grasp how we must now investigate the formative history of Judaism, we shall also see why Schechter, Moore, and Urbach no longer compel attention for any serious and important purpose.

The question that demands a response before any historical issues can be formulated is this: How are we to determine the particular time and circumstance in which a writing took shape, and how shall we identify the generative problems, the urgent and critical questions, that informed the intellect of an authorship and framed the social world that nurtured that same authorship? Lacking answers to these questions, we find our work partial, and, if truth be told, stained by sterile academicism. Accordingly, the documentary method requires us to situate the contents of writings into particular circumstances, so that we may read the contents in the context of a real time and place. How to do so? I maintain that it is by reference to the time and circumstance of the closure of a document, that is to say, the conventional assignment of a piece of writing to a particular time and place, that we proceed outward from context to matrix.

Everyone down to Urbach, including Montefiore and Loewe, Schechter, Moore, and the rest, simply take at face value attributions of sayings to particular authorities and interpret what is said as evidence of the time and place in which the cited authorities flourished. When studying topics in the Judaism of the sages of the rabbinic writings from the first through the seventh centuries, people routinely cite sayings categorized by attribution rather than by document. That is to say, they treat as one group of sayings whatever is assigned to Rabbi X. This is without regard to the time of redaction of the documents in which those sayings occur or to similar considerations of literary context and documentary circumstance. The category defined by attributions to a given authority furthermore rests on the premise that the things given in the name of Rabbi X really were said by him. No other premise would justify resort to the category deriving from use of a name, that alone. Commonly, the next step is to treat those sayings as evidence of ideas held, if not by that particular person, then by

---

cannot tell his readers what thesis or proposition is set forth in the book. Given those limitations of intellect, one can hardly find surprising his inability to grasp why Urbach, Schechter, Moore, Kadushin, and others by contemporary standards simply have nothing to teach us about the formative history of Judaism. Horbury wants us to do chemistry by appeal to not the oxygen but the phlogiston theory, and he wants geography to be carried out in accord with the convictions of the flat-earthers. But the latter have a better sense of humor about themselves.

people in the age in which the cited authority lived. Once more the premise that the sayings go back to the age of the authority to whom they are attributed underpins inquiry. Accordingly, scholars cite sayings in the name of given authorities and take for granted that those sayings were said by the authority to whom they were attributed and, of course, in the time in which that authority flourished. By contrast, in my method of the documentary study of Judaism, I treat the historical sequence of sayings only in accord with the order of the documents in which they first occur. Let me expand on why I have taken the approach that I have, explain the way the method works, and then, as before, set forth an example of the method in action.[2]

---

[2]My example is drawn from a whole series of books in which I worked on the histories of specific conceptions or problems, formulated as I think correct, out of the sequence of documents. These are in the following works of mine:

The Idea of Purity in Ancient Judaism. The Haskell Lectures, 1972-1973. (Leiden, 1973: E. J. Brill). [This was a most preliminary work, which made me aware of the problems to be addressed later on. The documentary theory of the history of ideas was worked out only in the earlier 1980s.]

Judaism and Story: The Evidence of The Fathers According to Rabbi Nathan. (Chicago, 1990: University of Chicago Press).

The Foundations of Judaism. Method, Teleology, Doctrine. (Philadelphia, 1983-5: Fortress Press). I-III. I. *Midrash in Context. Exegesis in Formative Judaism.* (Second printing: Atlanta, 1988: Scholars Press for Brown Judaic Studies).

The Foundations of Judaism. Method, Teleology, Doctrine. (Philadelphia, 1983-5: Fortress Press). I-III. II. *Messiah in Context. Israel's History and Destiny in Formative Judaism.* (Second printing: Lanham, 1988: University Press of America). Studies in Judaism series.

The Foundations of Judaism. Method, Teleology, Doctrine. (Philadelphia, 1983-5: Fortress Press). I-III. III. *Torah: From Scroll to Symbol in Formative Judaism.* (Second printing: Atlanta, 1988: Scholars Press for Brown Judaic Studies).

The Foundations of Judaism. (Philadelphia, 1988: Fortress). Abridged edition of the foregoing trilogy.

Vanquished Nation, Broken Spirit. The Virtues of the Heart in Formative Judaism. (New York, 1987: Cambridge University Press). Jewish Book Club selection, 1987.

Editor: *Judaisms and their Messiahs in the beginning of Christianity.* (New York, 1987: Cambridge University Press). [Edited with William Scott Green and Ernest S. Frerichs.]

Judaism in the Matrix of Christianity. (Philadelphia, 1986: Fortress Press). (British edition, Edinburgh, 1988: T. & T. Collins).

Judaism and Christianity in the Age of Constantine. Issues of the Initial Confrontation. (Chicago, 1987: University of Chicago Press).

Judaism and its Social Metaphors. Israel in the History of Jewish Thought. (New York, 1988: Cambridge University Press).

Since many sayings are attributed to specific authorities, why not lay out the sayings in the order of the authorities to whom they are attributed, rather than in the order of the books in which these sayings occur, which forms the documentary method for the description of the matrix of texts in context? It is because the attributions cannot be validated, but the books can. The first of the two principles by which I describe the matrix that defines the context in which texts are framed is that we compose histories of ideas of the Judaism of the Dual Torah in accord with the sequence of documents that, in the aggregate, constitute the corpus and canon of the Judaism of the Dual Torah. And those histories set forth dimensions of the matrix in which that Judaism, through its writings, is to be situated for broader purposes of interpretation. Documents reveal the system and structure of their authorships, and, in the case of religious writing, out of a document without named authors we may compose an account of the authorship's religion: a way of life, a worldview, a social entity meant to realize both. Read one by one, documents reveal the interiority of intellect of an authorship, and that inner-facing quality of mind inheres even when an authorship imagines it speaks outward, toward and about the world beyond. Even when set side by side, moreover, documents illuminate the minds of intersecting authorships, nothing more.

Then why not simply take at face value a document's *own* claims concerning the determinate situation of its authorship? Readers have already noted innumerable attributions to specific authorities. One obvious mode of determining the matrix of a text, the presently paramount way, as I said, is simply to take at face value the allegation that a given authority, whose time and place we may identify, really said what is attributed to him, and that if a writing says something happened, what it tells us is not what its authorship thought happened, but what really happened. That reading of writing for purposes of not only history, but also religious study, is in fact commonplace. It characterizes all accounts of the religion, Judaism, prior to mine, and it remains a serious option for all those outside of my school and circle.[3] Proof of that fact is to be shown, lest readers who

---

The Incarnation of God: The Character of Divinity in Formative Judaism. (Philadelphia, 1988: Fortress Press).

Edited: *The Christian and Judaic Invention of History.* [Edited with William Scott Green]. (Atlanta, 1989: Scholars Press for American Academy of Religion). Studies in Religion series. [All of the papers in this collection are worked out within the basic thesis of the documentary history of ideas.]

[3]That is why people can still read Urbach or Moore as though we learned anything of historical and not merely ad hoc exegetical interest from their

find accommodation in more contemporary intellectual worlds, where criticism and the active intellect reign, doubt my judgment of competing methods and differing accounts. Accordingly, let me characterize the prevailing way of determining the historical and religious matrix of texts, and then proceed to explain my alternate mode for answering the question of what is to be learned, from within a piece of writing, about the religious world beyond.

In historical study, we gain access to no knowledge a priori. All facts derive from sources correctly situated, e.g., classified, comprehensively and completely described, dispassionately analyzed, and evaluated. Nothing can be taken for granted. What we cannot show, we do not know. These simple dogmas of all historical learning derive not from this writer but go back to the very beginnings of Western critical historical scholarship, to the age of the Renaissance. But all historical and religions-historical scholarship on the documents of the Judaism of the Dual Torah in its formative age, except for mine and for that of a very few others, ignores the canons of criticism that govern academic scholarship. Everyone in the past and many even now take for granted that pretty much everything they read is true – except what they decide is not true.

They cannot and do not raise the question of whether an authorship knows what it is talking about, and they do not address the issue of the purpose of a text: historical or imaginative, for example. For them the issue always is history, namely, what really happened, and that issue was settled, so to speak, at Sinai: it is all true (except, on an episodic basis, what is not true, which the scholars somehow know instinctively). They exhibit the credulity characteristic of the believers, which in the circle of piety is called faith, and rightly so, but in the center of academic learning is mere gullibility. The fundamentalists in the talmudic academies and rabbinical seminaries and Israeli universities take not only as fact but at face value everything in the holy books. "Judaism" is special and need not undergo description, analysis, and interpretation in accord with a shared and public canon of rules of criticism. "We all know" how to do the work, and "we" do not have to explain to "outsiders" either what the work is or why it is important. It is a self-evidently important enterprise in

---

compilations of sayings under their various rubrics. In this regard Urbach's various asides are quite interesting, even though not a single account of the history and context of an idea can stand; and the straight historical chapters — e.g., on the social role of sages, on the life of Hillel, on the history of the time — are not only intellectually vulgar, they are a travesty of scholarship, even for the time and within the premises in which they were written.

the rehearsal of information. Knowing these things the way "we" know them explains the value of knowing these things.

Scholarship formed on the premise that the sources' stories are to be believed at face value does not say so; rather, it frames questions that implicitly affirm the accuracy of the holy books, asking questions, for example, that can only be answered in the assumption that the inerrant Scriptures contain the answers – therefore, as a matter of process, do not err. By extension holy books that tell stories produce history through the paraphrase of stories into historical language: this is what happened, this is how it happened, and here are the reasons why it happened. If the Talmud says someone said something, he really said it, then and there. That premise moreover dictates their scholarly program, for it permits these faithful scholars to describe, analyze and interpret events or ideas held in the time in which that person lived. Some of these would deny the charge, and all of them would surely point, in their writing, to evidence of a critical approach. But the premise remains the old gullibility. Specifically, the questions they frame to begin with rest on the assumption that the sources respond. The assumption that, if a story refers to a second century rabbi, then the story tells us about the second century, proves routine. And that complete reliance merely on the allegations of sayings and stories constitutes perfect faith in the facticity of fairy tales.

The operative question facing anyone who proposes to translate writing into religion – that is, accounts of "Judaism," as Moore claims to give, or "The Sages," that Urbach imagines he has made for us, is the historical one: How you know exactly what was said and done, that is, the history that you claim to report about what happened long ago? Specifically, how do you know he really said it? And if you do not know that he really said it, how can you ask the questions that you ask, which has as its premise the claim that you can say what happened or did not happen?

The wrong, but commonplace, method is to assume that if a given document ascribes an opinion to a named authority the opinion actually was stated in that language by that sage. On this assumption a much richer history of an idea, not merely of the literary evidences of that idea, may be worked out without regard only to the date of the document at hand. Within this theory of evidence, we have the history of what individuals thought on a common topic. I have already set forth the reason that we cannot proceed to outline the sequence of ideas solely on the basis of the sequence of the sages to whom ideas are attributed. We simply cannot demonstrate that a given authority really said what a document assigns to him. Let me list the range of uncertainty that necessitates this fresh approach, which I have invented.

First, if the order of the documents were fully sound and the contents representative of rabbinical opinion, then the result would be a history of the advent of the idea at hand and the development and articulation of that idea in formative Judaism. We should then have a fairly reliable picture of ideas at hand as these unfolded in orderly sequence. But we do not know that the canonical history corresponds to the actual history of ideas. Furthermore, we cannot even be sure that the order of documents presently assumed in scholarly convention is correct. Second, if a rabbi really spoke the words attributed to him, then a given idea would have reached expression within Judaism *prior* to the redaction of the document. Dividing things up by documents will tend to give a later date and thus a different context for interpretation to opinions held earlier than we can presently demonstrate. Third, although we are focusing upon the literature produced by a particular group, again we have no clear notion of what people were thinking outside of that group. We therefore do not know how opinions held by other groups or by the Jewish people in general came to shape the vision of rabbis. When, for example, we note that there also existed poetic literature and translations of Scriptures characteristic of the synagogue worship, we cannot determine whether the poetry and most translations spoke for rabbis or for some quite different group.

For these reasons I have chosen to address the contextual question within the narrow limits of the canon. That accounts for my formulation of the episteme as "the canonical history of ideas," and explains, also, why I have carefully avoided claiming that a given idea was broadly held only at a given time and place. All I allege is that a given document underscores the presence of an idea for that authorship – that alone. Obviously, if I could in a given formulation relate the appearance of a given idea to events affecting rabbis in particular or to the life of Israel in general, the results would be exceedingly suggestive. But since we do not know for whom the documents speak, how broadly representative they are, or even how comprehensive is their evidence about rabbis' views, we must carefully define what we do and do not know. So for this early stage in research the context in which a given idea is described, analyzed, and interpreted is the canon. But this first step alone carries us to new territory. I hope that in due course others will move beyond the limits which, at the moment, seem to me to mark the farthest possible advance. Now let us turn to the specific case meant to illustrate the method.

Let me now explain in some greater detail the alternative, which I call the documentary history of ideas. It is a mode of relating writing to religion through history through close attention to the circumstance in which writing reached closure. It is accomplished, specifically, by assessing shifts exhibited by a sequence of documents and appealing to the generally accepted dates assigned to writings in explaining those shifts. In this way I propose to confront questions of cultural order, social system and political structure, to which the texts respond explicitly and constantly. Confronting writings of a religious character, we err by asking questions of a narrowly historical character: what did X really say on a particular occasion, and why. These questions not only are not answerable on the basis of the evidence in hand. They also are trivial, irrelevant to the character of the evidence. What strikes me as I review the writings just now cited is how little of real interest and worth we should know, even if we were to concede the historical accuracy and veracity of all the many allegations of the scholars we have surveyed. How little we should know – but how much we should have *missed* if that set of questions and answers were to encompass the whole of our inquiry.

If we are to trace the unfolding, in the sources of formative Judaism, of a given theme or ideas on a given problem, the order in which we approach the several books, that is, components of the entire canon, gives us the sole guidance on sequence, order, and context, that we are apt to find. As is clear, we have no way of demonstrating that authorities to whom, in a given composition, ideas are attributed really said what is assigned to them. The sole fact in hand therefore is that the framers of a given document included in their book sayings imputed to named authorities. Are these dependable? Unlikely on the face of it. Why not? Since the same sayings will be imputed to diverse authorities by different groups of editors, of different books, we stand on shaky ground indeed if we rely for chronology upon the framers' claims of who said what. More important, attributions by themselves cannot be shown to be reliable.

What we cannot show we do not know.[4] Lacking firm evidence, for example, in a sage's own, clearly assigned writings, or even in writings redacted by a sage's own disciples and handed on among them in the

---

[4]It should be underlined that a British scholar, Hyam Maccoby, maintains exactly the opposite, alleging in a letter to the editor of *Commentary* and in various other writings that there is historical knowledge that we possess a priori. We must be thankful to him for making explicit the position of the other side. No historical scholarship known to me concurs with his position on a priori historical knowledge; all modern learning in history begins with sources, read *de novo*.

discipline of their own community, we have for chronology only a single fact. It is that a document, reaching closure at a given time, contains the allegation that Rabbi X said statement Y. So we know that people at the time of the document reached closure took the view that Rabbi X said statement Y. We may then assign to statement Y a position, in the order of the sequence of sayings, defined by the location of the document in the order of the sequence of documents. The several documents' dates, as is clear, all constitute guesses. But the sequence explained in the prologue, Mishnah, Tosefta, Yerushalmi, Bavli for the exegetical writings on the Mishnah is absolutely firm and beyond doubt. The sequence for the exegetical collections on Scripture Sifra, the Sifrés, Genesis Rabbah, Leviticus Rabbah, the Pesiqtas and beyond is not entirely sure. Still the position of the Sifra and the two Sifrés at the head, followed by Genesis Rabbah, then Leviticus Rabbah, then Pesiqta deR. Kahana and Lamentations Rabbati and some related collections, seems likely.

What are the canonical mainbeams that sustain the history of ideas as I propose to trace that history? A brief reprise of the information given in the Prologue suffices. The formative age of Judaism is the period marked at the outset by the Mishnah, taking shape from sometime before the Common Era and reaching closure at ca. 200 C.E., and at the end by the Talmud of Babylonia, ca. 600 C.E. In between these dates, two streams of writings developed, one legal, explaining the meaning of the Mishnah, the other theological and exegetical, interpreting the sense of Scripture. The high points of the former come with tractate Abot which is the Mishnah's first apologetic, the Tosefta, a collection of supplements ca. 300 C.E., the Talmud of the Land of Israel ca. 400 C.E., followed by the Babylonian Talmud. The latter set of writings comprise compositions on Exodus, in Mekilta attributed to R. Ishmael and of indeterminate date, Sifra on Leviticus, Sifre on Numbers, and another Sifre, on Deuteronomy at a guess to be dated at ca. 300 C.E., then Genesis Rabbah ca. 400 C.E., Leviticus Rabbah ca. 425 C.E., and at the end, Pesiqta deRab Kahana, Lamentations Rabbati, and some other treatments of biblical books, all of them in the fifth or sixth centuries. These books and some minor related items together form the canon of Judaism as it had reached its definitive shape by the end of late antiquity.

If we lay out these writings in the approximate sequence in which they reached closure beginning with the Mishnah, the Tosefta, then Sifra and its associated compositions, followed by the Talmud of the Land of Israel, and alongside Genesis Rabbah and Leviticus Rabbah, then Pesiqta deRab Kahana and its companions, and finally the Talmud of Babylonia, we gain what I call "canonical history." This is, specifically, the order of the appearance of ideas when the documents, read in the outlined sequence, address a given idea or topic. The consequent history consists of the sequence in which a given statement on the topic at hand was made (early, middle, or late) in the unfolding of the canonical writings. To illustrate the process, what does the authorship of the Mishnah have to say on the theme? Then how does the compositor of Abot deal with it? Then the Tosefta's compositor's record comes into view, followed by the materials assembled in the Talmud of the Land of Israel, alongside those now found in the earlier and middle ranges of compilations of scriptural exegeses, and as always, the Talmud of Babylonia at the end. In the illustrative exercise that follows we shall read the sources in exactly the order outlined here. I produce a picture of how these sources treat an important principle of the Judaism of the Dual Torah We shall see important shifts and changes in the unfolding of ideas on the symbol under study.

So, in sum, this story of continuity and change rests upon the notion that we can present the history of the treatment of a topical program in the canonical writings of that Judaism. I do not claim that the documents represent the state of popular or synagogue opinion. I do not know whether the history of the idea in the unfolding official texts corresponds to the history of the idea among the people who stand behind those documents. Even less do I claim to speak about the history of the topic or idea at hand outside of rabbinical circles, among the Jewish nation at large. All these larger dimensions of the matter lie wholly beyond the perspective of this book. The reason is that the evidence at hand is of a particular sort and hence permits us to investigate one category of questions and not another. The category is deigned by established and universally held conventions about the order in which the canonical writings reached completion. Therefore we trace the way in which matters emerge in the sequence of writings followed here.

We trace the way in which ideas were taken up and spelled out in these successive stages in the formation of the canon. Let the purpose of the exercise be emphasized. *When we follow this procedure, we discover how, within the formation of the rabbinical canon of writings, the idea at hand came to literary expression and how it was then shaped to serve the larger purposes of the nascent canonical system as a whole.* By knowing the place and uses of the topic under study within the literary evidences of the rabbinical system, we gain a better understanding of the formative history of that system. What do we not learn? Neither the condition of the people at large nor the full range and power of the rabbinical thinkers' imagination comes to the fore.

About other larger historical and intellectual matters we have no direct knowledge at all. Consequently we claim to report only what we learn about the canonical literature of a system evidenced by a limited factual base. No one who wants to know the history of a given idea in all the diverse Judaisms of late antiquity, or the role of that idea in the history of all the Jews in all parts of the world in the first seven centuries of the Common Era will find it here.

In order to understand the documentary method we must again underline the social and political character of the documentary evidence presented. These are public statements, preserved and handed on because people have adopted them as authoritative. The sources constitute a collective, and therefore official, literature. All of the documents took shape and attained a place in the canon of the rabbinical movement as a whole. None was written by an individual in such a way as to testify to personal choice or decision. Accordingly, we cannot provide an account of the theory of a given individual at a particular time and place. We have numerous references to what a given individual said about the topic at hand. But these references do not reach us in the authorship of that person, or even in his language. They come to us only in the setting of a *collection* of sayings and statements, some associated with names, other unattributed and anonymous. The collections by definition were composed under the auspices of rabbinical authority – a school or a circle. They tell us what a group of people wished to preserve and hand on as authoritative doctrine about the meaning of the Mishnah and Scripture. The compositions reach us because the larger rabbinical estate chose to copy and hand them on. Accordingly, we know the state of doctrine at the stages marked by the formation and closure of the several documents.

We follow what references we find to a topic in accord with the order of documents just now spelled out. In this study we learn the order in which ideas came to expression in the canon. We begin any survey with the Mishnah, the starting point of the canon. We proceed systematically to work our way through tractate Abot, the Mishnah's first apologetic, then the Tosefta, the Yerushalmi, and the Bavli at the end. In a single encompassing sweep, we finally deal with the entirety of the compilations of the exegeses of Scripture, arranged, to be sure, in that order that I have now explained. Let me expand on the matter of my heavy emphasis on the order of the components of the canon. The reason for that stress is simple. We have to ask not only what documents viewed whole and all at once ("Judaism") tell us about our theme. In tracing the order in which ideas make their appearance, we ask about the components in sequence ("history of Judaism") so far as we can trace the sequence. Then and only then shall we have access to issues of *history*, that is, of change and development. If our theme makes its appearance early on in one form, so one set of ideas predominate in a document that reached closure in the beginnings of the canon and then that theme drops out of public discourse or undergoes radical revision in writings in later stages of the canon, that fact may make considerable difference. Specifically, we may find it possible to speculate on where, and why a given approach proved urgent, and also on the reasons that that same approach receded from the center of interest.

In knowing the approximate sequence of documents and therefore the ideas in them (at least so far as the final point at which those ideas reached formal expression in the canon), a second possibility emerges. What if – as is the case – we find pretty much the same views, treated in the same proportion and for the same purpose, yielding the same message, early, middle, and late in the development of the canon? Then we shall have to ask why the literature remains so remarkably constant. Given the considerable shifts in the social and political condition of Israel in the land of Israel as well as in Babylonia over a period of more than four hundred years, that evident stability in the teachings for the affective life will constitute a considerable fact for analysis and interpretation. History, including the history of religion, done rightly thus produces two possibilities, both of them demanding sustained attention. Things change. Why? Things do not change. Why not? We may well trace the relationship between the history of ideas and the history of the society that holds those same ideas. We follow the interplay between society and system – worldview, way of life, addressed to a particular social group – by developing a theory of the relationship between contents and context, between the world in which people live and the world which people create in their shared social and imaginative life. When we can frame a theory of how a system in substance relates to its setting, of the interplay between the social matrix and the mode and manner of a society's worldview and way of life, then we may develop theses of general intelligibility, theories of why this, not that, of why, and why no and how come.

The story of continuity and change rests upon the notion that we can present the history of the treatment of a topical program in the canonical writings of that Judaism. I do not claim that the documents represent the state of popular or synagogue opinion. I do not know whether the history of the idea in the unfolding official texts corresponds to the history of the idea among the people who stand behind those documents. Even less do I claim to speak about the history of the topic or idea at hand outside of rabbinical circles, among the Jewish nation at large. All these larger dimensions of the matter lie wholly beyond the perspective of this book. The reason is that the evidence at hand is of a particular sort and hence permits us to investigate one category of questions and not another. The category is defined by established and universally held conventions about the order in which the canonical writings reached completion. Therefore we trace the way in which matters emerge in the sequence of writings followed here. We trace the way in which ideas were taken up and spelled out in these successive stages in the formation of the canon. When we follow this procedure, we discover how, within the formation of the rabbinical canon of writings, the idea at hand came to literary expression and how it was then shaped to serve the larger purposes of the nascent canonical system as a whole.

My documentary method for the study of Judaism yields concrete results, and I have published extensive accounts of them. Here I give an example of the result of the method I have outlined. For that example, I take the documentary history of the single critical symbol of the Judaism of the Dual Torah, namely, (the) Torah. That documentary history traces the story of how "the Torah" lost its capital letter and definite article and ultimately became "torah." What for nearly a millennium had been a particular scroll or book came to serve as a symbol of an entire system. When a rabbi spoke of torah, he no longer meant only a particular object, a scroll and its contents. Now he used the work to encompass a distinctive and well-defined worldview and way of life. Torah had come to stand for something one does. Knowledge of the Torah promised not merely information about what people were supposed to do, but ultimate redemption or salvation.

In the Judaism of the Dual Torah as it emerged from its formative age., everything was contained in that one thing, "Torah." When we speak of "torah," or "the Torah," in rabbinical literature of late antiquity, we no longer denote a particular book, on the one side, or the contents of such a book, on the other. Instead, we connote a broad range of clearly distinct categories of noun and verb, concrete fact and abstract relationship alike. "Torah" stands for a kind of human being. It connotes a social status and a sort of social group. It refers to a type of social relationship. It further denotes a legal status and differentiates among legal norms. As symbolic abstraction, the word encompasses things and persons, actions and status, points of social differentiation and legal and normative standing, as well as "revealed truth." In all, the main points of insistence of the whole of Israel's life and history come to full symbolic expression in that single word. If people wanted to explain how they would be saved, they would use the word Torah. If they wished to sort out their parlous relationships with gentiles, they would use the word Torah. Torah stood for salvation and accounted for

Israel's this-worldly condition and the hope, for both individual and national alike, of life in the world to come. For the kind of Judaism under discussion, therefore, the word Torah stood for everything. The Torah symbolized the whole, at once and entire. When, therefore, we wish to describe the unfolding of the definitive doctrine of Judaism in its formative period, the first exercise consists in paying close attention to the meanings imputed to a single word. Every detail of the religious system at hand exhibits essentially the same point of insistence, captured in the simple notion of the Torah as the generative symbol, the total, exhaustive expression of the system as a whole.

If we start back with the Mishnah, which later on formed the oral part of the one whole Torah, written and oral, revealed by God to Moses at Sinai, we look in vain for a picture of the Mishnah as (part of) the Torah. For the Mishnah provided no account of itself. Unlike biblical law codes, the Mishnah begins with no myth of its own origin. It ends with no doxology. Discourse commences in the middle of things and ends abruptly. What follows from such laconic mumbling is that the exact status of the document required definition entirely outside the framework of the document itself. The framers of the Mishnah gave no hint of the nature of their book, so the Mishnah reached the political world of Israel without a trace of self-conscious explanation or any theory of validation. The framers of the Mishnah nowhere claim, implicitly or explicitly, that what they have written forms part of the Torah, enjoys the status of God's revelation to Moses at Sinai, or even systematically carries forward secondary exposition and application of what Moses wrote down in the wilderness. Later on, I think two hundred years beyond the closure of the Mishnah, the need to explain the standing and origin of the Mishnah led some to posit two things. First, God's revelation of the Torah at Sinai encompassed the Mishnah as much as Scripture. Second, the Mishnah was handed on through oral formulation and oral transmission from Sinai to the framers of the document as we have it.

As for the Mishnah itself, however, it contains not a hint that anyone has heard any such tale. The earliest apologists for the Mishnah, represented in Abot and the Tosefta alike, know nothing of the fully realized myth of the Dual Torah of Sinai. Only the two Talmuds reveal that conception – alongside their mythic explanation of where the document came from and why it should be obeyed. So the Yerushalmi marks the change. In any event, the absence of explicit expression of such a claim in behalf of the Mishnah requires little specification. It is just not there. A survey of the uses of the word Torah in the Mishnah, to be sure, provides us with an account of what the framers of the Mishnah, founders of what would emerge as rabbinic

Judaism, understood by that term. But it will not tell us how they related their own ideas to the Torah, nor shall we find a trace of evidence of that fully articulated way of life – the use of the word Torah to categorize and classify persons, places, things, relationships, all manner of abstractions – that we find fully exposed in some later redacted writings.

The next document in sequence beyond the Mishnah, Abot, The Fathers, draws into the orbit of Torah-talk the names of authorities of the Mishnah. But Abot does not claim that the Mishnah forms part of the Torah, any more than the document imputes supernatural standing to sages, as we saw in Chapter Seven. Nor, obviously, does the tractate know the doctrine of the two Torahs. Only in the Talmuds do we begin to find clear and ample evidence of that doctrine. Abot, moreover, does not understand by the word Torah much more than the framers of the Mishnah do. Not only does the established classification scheme remain intact, but the sense essentially replicates already familiar usages, producing no innovation. On the contrary, I find a diminution in the range of meanings. Yet Abot in the aggregate does differ from the Mishnah. The sixty-two tractates of the Mishnah contain Torah sayings here and there. But they do not fall within the framework of Torah discourse. They speak about other matters entirely. Abot, by contrast, says a great deal about Torah study. The claim that Torah study produces direct encounter with God forms part of Abot's thesis about the Torah. In Abot, Torah is instrumental. The figure of the sage, his ideals and conduct, forms the goal, focus and center. To state matters simply: Abot regards study of Torah as what a sage does. The substance of Torah is what a sage says. That is so whether or not the saying relates to scriptural revelation. The content of the sayings attributed to sages endows those sayings with self-validating status. The sages usually do not quote verses of Scripture and explain them, nor do they speak in God's name. Yet, it is clear, sages talk Torah. What follows? It is this: if a sage says something, what he says is Torah. More accurately, what he says falls into the classification of Torah. Accordingly Abot treats Torah learning as symptomatic, an indicator of the status of the sage, hence, as I said, as merely instrumental. The instrumental status of the Torah, as well as of the Mishnah, lies in the net effect of their composition: the claim that through study of the Torah sages enter God's presence. So study of Torah serves a further goal, that of forming sages. The theory of Abot pertains to the religious standing and consequence of the learning of the sages. To be sure, a secondary effect of that theory endows with the status of revealed truth things sages say. But then it is because they say them, not because they have heard them in an endless chain back to Sinai. The fundament of truth is passed on through sagacity, not through already formulated and carefully memorized truths. That is shy the single most important word in Abot also is the most common, the word "says."

The Mishnah is held in the Yerushalmi to be equivalent to Scripture (Y. Hor. 3:5). But the Mishnah is not called Torah. Still, once the Mishnah entered the status of Scripture, it would take but a short step to a theory of the Mishnah as part of the revelation at Sinai – hence, Oral Torah. In the Yerushalmi we find the first glimmerings of an effort to theorize in general, not merely in detail, about how specific teachings of Mishnah relate to specific teachings of Scripture. The citing of scriptural prooftexts for Mishnah propositions, after all, would not have caused much surprise to the framers of the Mishnah; they themselves included such passages, though not often. But what conception of the Torah underlies such initiatives, and how Yerushalmi sages propose to explain the phenomenon of the Mishnah as a whole? The following passage gives us one statement. It refers to the assertion at M. Hag. 1:8D that the laws on cultic cleanness presented in the Mishnah rest on deep and solid foundations in the Scripture.

Y. Hagigah 1:7

[V A]   The laws of the Sabbath [M. 1:8B]: R. Jonah said R. Hama bar Uqba raised the question [in reference to M. Hag. 1:8D's view that there are many verses of Scripture on cleanness], "And lo, it is written only, 'Nevertheless a spring or a cistern holding water shall be clean; but whatever touches their carcass shall be unclean' (Lev. 11:36). And from this verse you derive many laws. [So how can M. 8:8D say what it does about many verses for laws of cultic cleanness?]"

[B]   R. Zeira in the name of R. Yohanan: "If a law comes to hand and you do not know its nature, do not discard it for another one, for lo, many laws were stated to Moses at Sinai, and all of them have been embedded in the Mishnah."

The truly striking assertion appears at B. The Mishnah now is claimed to contain statements made by God to Moses. Just how these statements found their way into the Mishnah, and which passages of the Mishnah contain them, we do not know. That is hardly important, given the fundamental assertion at hand. The passage proceeds to a further, and far more consequential, proposition. It asserts that part of the Torah was written down, and part was preserved in memory and transmitted orally. In context, moreover, that distinction must encompass the Mishnah, thus explaining its origin as part of the Torah. Here is a clear and unmistakable expression of the distinction between two forms in which a single Torah was revealed and handed on at Mount Sinai, part in writing, part orally.

While the passage below does not make use of the language, Torah-in-writing and Torah-by-memory, it does refer to "the written" and "the oral." I believe myself fully justified in supplying the word Torah in square brackets. The reader will note, however, that the word Torah likewise does not occur at K, L. Only when the passage reaches its climax, at M, does it break down into a number of categories – Scripture, Mishnah, Talmud, laws, lore. It there makes the additional point that everything comes from Moses at Sinai. So the fully articulated theory of two Torahs (not merely one Torah in two forms) does not reach final expression in this passage. But short of explicit allusion to Torah-in-writing and Torah-by-memory, which (so far as I am able to discern) we find mainly in the Talmud of Babylonia, the ultimate theory of Torah of formative Judaism is at hand in what follows.

Y. Hagigah 1:7

[V D]   R. Zeirah in the name of R. Eleazar: "'Were I to write for him my laws by ten thousands, they would be regarded as a strange thing' (Hos. 8:12). Now is the greater part of the Torah written down? [Surely not. The oral part is much greater.] But more abundant are the matters which are derived by exegesis from the written [Torah] than those derived by exegesis from the oral [Torah]."

[E]   And is that so?

[F]   But more cherished are those matters which rest upon the written [Torah] than those which rest upon the oral [Torah]....

[J]   R. Haggai in the name of R. Samuel bar Nahman, "Some teachings were handed on orally, and some things were handed on in writing, and we do not know which of them is the more precious. But on the basis of that which is written, "And the Lord said to Moses, Write these words; in accordance with these words I have made a covenant with you and with Israel' (Ex. 34:27), [we conclude] that the ones which are handed on orally are the more precious."

[K]   R. Yohanan and R. Yudan b. R. Simeon – One said, "If you have kept what is preserved orally and also kept what is in writing, I shall make a covenant with you, and if not, I shall not make a covenant with you."

[L]   The other said, "If you have kept what is preserved orally and you have kept what is preserved in writing, you shall receive a reward, and if not, you shall not receive a reward."

[M]   [With reference to Deut. 9:10: "And on them was written according to all the words which the Lord spoke with you in the mount,"] said R. Joshua b. Levi, "He could have written, 'On them,' but wrote, 'And on them.' He could have written, 'All,' but wrote, 'According to all.' He could have written, 'Words,' but wrote 'The words.' [These then serve as three encompassing clauses, serving to include] Scripture, Mishnah, Talmud, laws, and lore. Even what an experienced student in the future is going to teach before his master already has been stated to Moses at Sinai."

[N]   What is the scriptural basis for this view?

[O]   "There is no remembrance of former things, nor will there be any remembrance of later things yet to happen among those who come after" (Qoh. 1:11).

[P]   If someone says, "See, this is a new thing," his fellow will answer him, saying to him, "this has been around before us for a long time."

Here we have absolutely explicit evidence that people believed part of the Torah had been preserved not in writing but orally. Linking that part to the Mishnah remains a matter of implication. But it surely comes fairly close to the surface, when we are told that the Mishnah contains Torah traditions revealed at Sinai. From that view it requires only a small step to the allegation that the Mishnah is part of the Torah, the oral part. To define the category of the Torah as a source of salvation, as the Yerushalmi states matters, I point to a story that explicitly states the proposition that the Torah constitutes a source of salvation. In this story we shall see that because people observed the rules of the Torah, they expected to be saved. And if they did not observe, they accepted their punishment. So the Torah now stands for something more than revelation and life of study, and (it goes without saying) the sage now appears as a holy, not merely a learned, man. This is because his knowledge of the Torah has transformed him. Accordingly, we deal with a category of stories and sayings about the Torah entirely different from what has gone before.

Y. Taanit 3:8

[II A]   As to Levi ben Sisi: troops came to his town. He took a scroll of the Torah and went up to the roof and said, "Lord of the ages! If a single word of this scroll of the Torah has been nullified [in our town], let them come up against us, and if not, let them go their way."

[B]   Forthwith people went looking for the troops but did not find them [because they had gone their way].

[C]   A disciple of his did the same thing, and his hand withered, but the troops went their way.

[D]   A disciple of his disciple did the same thing. His hand did not wither, but they also did not go their way.

[E]   This illustrates the following apophthegm: You can't insult an idiot, and dead skin does not feel the scalpel.

What is interesting here is how taxa into which the word Torah previously fell have been absorbed and superseded in a new taxon. The Torah is an object: "He took a scroll...." It also constitutes God's revelation to Israel: "If a single word...." The outcome of the revelation is to form an ongoing way of life, embodied in the sage himself: "A disciple of his did the same thing...." The sage plays an intimate part in the supernatural event: "His hand withered...." Now can we categorize this story as a statement that the Torah constitutes a particular object, or a source of divine revelation, or a way of life? Yes and no. The Torah here stands not only for the things we already have catalogued. It represents one more thing which takes in all the others. Torah is a source of salvation. How so? The Torah stands for, or constitutes, the way in which the people Israel saves itself from marauders. This straightforward sense of salvation will not have surprised the author of Deuteronomy.

In the canonical documents up to the Yerushalmi, we look in vain for sayings or stories that fall into such a category. True, we may take for granted that everyone always believed that, in general, Israel would be saved by obedience to the Torah. That claim would not have surprised any Israelite writers from the first prophets down through the final redactors of the Pentateuch in the time of Ezra and onward through the next seven hundred years. But, in the rabbinical corpus from the Mishnah forward, the specific and concrete assertion that by taking up the scroll of the Torah and standing on the roof of one's house, confronting God in heaven, a sage in particular could take action against the expected invasion – that kind of claim is not located, so far as I know, in any composition surveyed so far.

Still, we cannot claim that the belief that the Torah in the hands of the sage constituted a source of magical, supernatural, and hence salvific power, simply did not flourish prior, let us say, to ca. 400 C.E. We cannot show it, hence we do not know it. All we can say with assurance is that no stories containing such a viewpoint appear in any rabbinical document associated with the Mishnah. So what is critical here is not the generalized category – the genus – of conviction that the Torah serves as the source of Israel's salvation. It is the concrete assertion – the speciation of the genus – that in the hands of the sage and under conditions specified, the Torah may be utilized in pressing circumstances as Levi, his disciple, and the disciple of his disciple, used it. That is what is new. This stunningly new usage of Torah found in the Yerushalmi emerges from a group of stories not readily classified in our established categories. All of these stories treat the word Torah (whether scroll, contents, or act of study) as source and guarantor of salvation. Accordingly, evoking the word Torah forms the centerpiece of a theory of Israel's history, on the one side, and an account of the teleology of the entire system, on the other. Torah indeed has ceased to constitute a specific thing or even a category or classification when stories about studying the Torah yield not a judgment as to status (i.e., praise for the learned man) but promise for supernatural blessing now and salvation in time to come.

The key to the first Talmud's theory of the Torah lies in its conception of the sage, to which that theory is subordinate. Once the sage reaches his full apotheosis as Torah incarnate, then, but only then, the Torah becomes (also) a source of salvation in the present concrete formulation of the matter. That is why we traced the doctrine of the Torah in the salvific process by elaborate citation of stories about sages, living Torahs, exercising the supernatural power of the Torah, and serving, like the Torah itself, to reveal God's will. Since the sage embodied the Torah and gave the Torah, the Torah naturally came to stand for the principal source of Israel's salvation, not merely a scroll, on the one side, or a source of revelation, on the other. The history of the symbolization of the Torah proceeds from its removal from the framework of material objects, even from the limitations of its own contents, to its transformation into something quite different and abstract, quite distinct from the document and its teachings. The Torah stands for this something more, specifically, when it comes to be identified with a living person, the sage, and endowed with those particular traits that the sage claimed for himself. While we cannot say that the process of symbolization leading to the pure abstraction at hand moved in easy stages, we may still point to the stations that had to be passed in sequence. The word Torah reached the apologists for the Mishnah in its long-established meanings: Torah scroll, contents of the Torah scroll. But even in the Mishnah itself, these meanings provoked a secondary development, status of Torah as distinct from other (lower) status, hence, Torah teaching in contradistinction to scribal teaching. With that small and simple step, the Torah ceased to denote only a concrete and material thing – a scroll and its contents. It now connoted an abstract matter of status. And once made abstract, the symbol entered a secondary history beyond all limits imposed by the concrete object, including its specific teachings, the Torah scroll.

I believe that Abot stands at the beginning of this process. In the history of the word Torah as abstract symbol, a metaphor serving to sort out one abstract status from another regained concrete and material reality of a new order entirely. For the message of Abot, as we saw, was that the Torah served the sage. How so? The Torah indicated who was a sage and who was not. Accordingly, the apology of Abot for the Mishnah was that the Mishnah contained things sages had said. What sages said formed a chain of tradition extending back to Sinai. Hence it was equivalent to the Torah. The upshot is that words of sages enjoyed the status of the Torah. The small step beyond, I think, was to claim that what sages said was Torah, as much as what Scripture said was Torah. And, a further small step (and the steps need not have been taken separately or in the order here suggested) moved matters to the position that there were two forms in which the Torah reached Israel: one [Torah] in writing, the other [Torah] handed on orally, that is, in memory. The final step, fully revealed in the Talmud at hand, brought the conception of Torah to its logical conclusion: what the sage said was in the status of the Torah, was Torah, because the sage was Torah incarnate. So the abstract symbol now became concrete and material once more. We recognize the many, diverse ways in which the Talmud stated that conviction. Every passage in which knowledge of the Torah yields power over this world and the next, capacity to coerce to the sage's will the natural and supernatural worlds alike, rests upon the same viewpoint. The first Talmud's theory of the Torah carries us through several stages in the processes of the symbolization of the word Torah. First transformed from something material and concrete into something abstract and beyond all metaphor, the word Torah finally emerged once more in a concrete aspect, now as the encompassing and universal mode of stating the whole doctrine, all at once, of Judaism in its formative age.

The documentary history of the symbol, Torah, raises more questions than it settles. For once we recognize that shifts and turnings in the treatment of a fixed topic or symbol characterize the movement from one writing to the next, we want to explain change. And, in the nature of things, we wonder what has happened in the world beyond that has led to the reconsideration of the generative symbol of a system such as this one. Identifying the documentary matrix of an idea or a symbol directs our attention not to, but beyond, the sequence of writings. We want to ask about the world beyond the system. In other studies I have addressed that question; it would carry me far afield to deal with it here. It suffices at this point simply to observe that, in light of what has been said, any account of an idea, myth, issue, conception – emotions, incarnation, for example – that takes for granted all sources exist on a timeless plain and takes at face value all attributions simply has nothing of value to teach for those interested in the history of religion and of religious ideas. I repeat, that does not mean bibliographical studies will omit all reference to these works, even though they now form mere curiosities. But it does mean that we no longer have to take seriously and argue with results that derive from premises that no longer hold true. So no, we no longer have to read Moore or Urbach or Schechter.

Index

Aaron 58, 59, 80, 87, 88, 94-96, 135, 150

Abagtha 96

Abba b. Kahana 54, 57, 111

Abbahu 78, 105

Abbuyah 176

Abishai b. Zeruiah 179

Abot 206-208, 211-213, 217

Abraham 19, 78, 92, 129, 132

Absalom 56, 76

Adam 75, 93, 96, 156

Adkins, A. S. H. 35, 36

Admatha 90-92

Aha 57, 86, 100, 110, 125

Ahasuerus 89, 90, 93, 96

Ahijah the Shilonite 78

Ahitophel 76

Aibu 107, 109

Alexandri 106

Allan, D. J. 35, 38

altar 25, 79, 86, 92, 113, 124, 125, 127

Amalek 116, 117

Amminadab 65

Ammonite 62, 64, 65, 94

Amos 86, 87, 95, 127

Aqiba 19, 108, 149, 150, 153, 154, 175-177

Aristotle 23, 32-36, 38, 39

Armstrong, A. H. 35, 40-42

Artaxerxes 87

Assyria 57

Athaliah 64

atonement 16, 27, 30, 69, 128, 139, 141, 156, 177

Attribute of Justice 110

Augustine 1

Azariah 64, 77, 135, 137, 139

Babylonia 3, 4, 7, 81, 85, 86, 122, 149, 174, 183, 206, 207, 209, 214

Bar Qamsa 113

Barnes, Jonathon 35

base verse, base-verse 55, 59, 60, 74, 80, 89, 91, 99, 101, 107, 115, 126, 129, 141, 154, 174, 178-180

Bavli 3, 147, 149-151, 155, 168, 174, 206, 208

Belshazzar 87, 89, 95, 96

Benjamin 95, 96, 108, 128

Berekhiah 58, 63, 78, 79, 97, 116, 122, 132, 137, 140

Beth El 98

Bigtha 96

Boaz 54, 55, 58, 59, 62-67, 102, 179

Bonsirven 9

Buber, Martin 116

Caleb 127

canon 1, 2, 9, 10, 13, 145, 147, 150, 152, 155, 158, 163, 166, 172, 174, 181-184, 186, 188, 189, 191, 193, 201, 202, 204-210

canonical 2-5, 19, 49, 146, 150, 159, 163, 165, 168, 174, 184, 187, 204, 206-210, 216

Carshena 90-92

Chaldeans 136

Cherniss, Harold 35

Christ Jesus 45

Christian, Christianity 2, 40-42, 149, 175, 188, 200

Chronicles (1 Chr., 2 Chr., Chr.) 57, 66, 74, 112, 165, 192

Church 40-42

classification 23-26, 28, 31-42, 52, 157, 161, 163, 182, 185, 188, 189, 191, 212, 216

cogent discourse, logic of 168

Cohen 105, 106, 108, 111, 115, 116

commandment 25, 76, 96-98

covenant 52, 53, 69, 85, 214

creation 38, 40, 42, 75, 76

Creator 42, 127

Daniel 64, 123, 135, 136

Daniel (Dan.) 58, 86, 95, 122, 133

Darius the Mede 95

Davar aher, Davar-aher 8, 73, 74, 76, 79, 82, 85, 87, 91, 97, 105, 119

David 54-56, 59, 62-67, 69, 76, 77, 88, 89, 119, 121, 179, 180, 182

Day of Atonement 27, 30, 128, 139, 177

Deuteronomy (Deut., Dt.) 25, 57, 64, 65, 69, 75, 79, 93, 94, 100, 116, 132, 136, 137, 150, 155, 176, 177, 206, 214, 216

Dillon, J. M. 34

divorced 107-109

Doeg 76

Dual Torah 39, 41, 211

Dura synagogue 150

Edom 78, 79, 86, 116, 117

Egypt 53, 66, 85, 101, 106, 119, 126-128, 130, 131

Egyptians 117

Elasa 139

Eleazar 88, 161, 179, 214

Eleazar b. Azariah 77

Eleazar b. R. Simeon 78

Eliezer 161, 176

Eliezer b. Hyrcanus 150

Eliezer b. Jacob 130

Elijah 59, 98, 99, 135, 137

Elimelech 61

Elisha b. Abbuyah 177, 180

epistemology 37

Esau 77-79, 100, 101, 110

Esther 66

Esther Rabbah 1, 4, 6-8, 68, 69, 74, 85-87, 90, 93, 181, 185, 190

Ethiopians 127

Eve 75, 93, 96

Evil-merodach 89

exegetical 48, 59, 65, 131, 132, 134, 184, 201, 206

Exodus (Ex.) 53, 55, 58, 59, 62, 64, 82, 92, 106, 110, 114, 119, 120, 127, 130-135, 136, 138, 140, 150, 206, 214

Ezekiel (Ezek.) 75, 110, 111, 127

Ezra 87, 92, 135-137, 216

Feldman, Louis H. 35

Festival of Tabernacles 80

fixed association, logic of 52

fixed associative 48, 65

Freedman 78, 79

Garden of Eden 74-76

Gehenna 75, 76

Genesis Rabbah 8, 73, 74, 76, 77, 80, 150, 166, 181, 185-187, 190, 206

gentiles 45, 156, 160, 210

God 2-5, 10, 15, 16, 23, 24, 31, 32, 39-42, 52, 53, 55, 60-64, 66-70, 74-76, 78, 79, 82, 85, 86, 89, 93, 95, 98, 99, 101, 102, 107, 109, 111, 116, 117, 122, 125-129, 131, 132, 179, 187, 188, 198, 200, 211-213, 216

Goodenough, Erwin R. 35

Gospel 149, 175

Greco-Roman heritage 2

Greece, Greek 34-36, 81, 85-87

Green, William Scott 8, 70, 191, 200

guilt-offering 26-29

Hadrian 88

Haggadah 19

Haggai 133, 214

halakhic tradition 3

Halivni, David Weiss 182

Ham 94

Hama 80

Hama b. Hanina 86, 111

Hama b. Uqba 108, 213

Haman 85, 87, 92, 93, 110

Hanania b. Hakhinai 25

Hananiah 64, 113

Hanina son of R. Aha 87

Harbona 96

heaven 52, 59, 63, 88, 114, 117, 138, 176, 178, 216

Hebrew 8, 16, 156, 186, 191

hermeneutic(s) 9, 50, 70, 163, 167-169, 180, 181, 187, 188, 189

Heschel, Abraham J. 19

Hezekiah 56, 59, 64, 79

Hezron 54, 65

hierarchy, hierarchical, hierarchized 23, 24, 29, 31, 32, 36, 40, 41

Hillel b. Berekhiah 109

Hinena 125

Hinena b. R. Pappa 124

Hiyya 85, 111, 115

Hiyya b. R. Abba 138

Holiness 14

Holy of Holies 30

Holy One 54, 57-59, 64, 77, 78, 88, 92, 95, 97-101, 106-108, 110, 116, 117, 120-122, 124, 129-134, 140, 178

Holy Spirit 80, 98, 99, 123, 125

Holy stones 111, 112

Holy Things 25-27, 30, 87

Horbury, William 198

Horeb 127, 128

Hoshiah 80

Hoshaiah (Hos.) 58, 100, 107, 109, 130, 134, 214

human 14, 35, 36, 40, 42, 153, 210

Huna of Sepphoris 111

Hunia 130, 179

Idi 179

idol 57, 62, 102, 108, 177

intersecting verse 55, 74, 77, 87, 89, 91, 98, 99, 101, 107, 116, 123, 124

Isaac 64, 77-79, 116, 131, 133, 137, 154

Isaac b. Marion 59

Isaac b. Qaseratah 58

Isaac b. R. Merion 58, 134

Isaiah 56, 92, 117

Isaiah (Isa.) 56, 58, 63, 78, 79, 92, 93, 95, 108, 114, 117, 121, 129, 133, 137-140

Ishmael 19, 94, 153, 154, 206

Ishmael b. Elisha 114

Islamic 3

Israel 2, 3, 8, 10, 16, 23, 34, 46-48, 52-54, 56, 60, 61, 63, 64, 68, 69, 75-77, 80-83, 97, 100, 101, 106-111, 114, 117, 122, 126-128, 136-141, 147, 152, 160, 189, 200, 204, 206, 207, 209, 211, 215-217

Israel, Community of 116, 127, 132, 133

Israel, Congregation of 131

Israel, Land of 53, 81, 97, 106, 122, 136, 147, 206, 207, 209

Israelite 42, 46, 50, 54, 60-63, 67, 68, 70, 81, 82, 102, 110, 129, 135, 156, 216

Issachar 90, 91

Jacob 8, 83, 88, 90, 98, 114, 140

Japheth 94

Jastrow 131-133

Jeremiah 111, 112, 117

Jeroboam 78

Jerusalem 27, 34, 57, 58, 63, 95, 109, 110, 112-114, 116, 121, 126, 127, 138, 176, 198

Jerusalemites 112, 115

Jesse 65

Jesus Christ 41, 149

Jethro 120

Jew 55, 62, 105, 140

Job 55, 58, 62, 77, 111, 134, 175, 176

Jonah 58, 134, 213

Jonathan 58

Joseph 35, 39, 66, 120, 122, 123, 179, 180

Joshua 60, 75, 97-99, 127, 128, 136, 176

Joshua b. Abin 117

Joshua b. Hananiah 113

Joshua b. Levi 117, 122, 138, 214

Joshua of Sikhnin 59, 138

Judah 55, 58, 64, 95, 96, 107-109, 120, 128, 129, 134, 160, 177-179

Judah b. Ezekiel 122

Judah b. R. Ilai 93

Judah b. R. Simon 62, 86, 122, 139

Judah b. Rabbi 133

Judah the Patriarch 110, 178

"Judaism" 3, 5, 6, 9, 34, 80, 126, 183, 188, 201-203, 208

Judaism 1-10, 13-15, 18-21, 23, 24, 32-35, 40-43, 45-47, 49, 60, 62, 65, 80, 83, 96, 126, 145-147, 149-151, 155, 157, 159, 165-170, 172-175, 181-184, 186-189, 191, 197-212, 214, 218

Judaism of the Dual Torah 1-5, 7, 9, 10, 13-15, 18-20, 45, 46, 49, 60, 96, 126, 146, 149, 150, 167, 173, 181, 197, 198, 201, 202, 207, 210

Judges 100, 130

justice 16, 81, 82, 107-110

Kadushin, Max 5, 8-10, 13-20, 119, 197, 198

kingdom of heaven 138

Kings (1 Kgs., 2 Kgs., Kgs.) 56, 69, 78, 80, 98, 110, 121, 122

Kohen 59

Lamentations (Lam.) 64, 107, 108, 109-112, 116, 117, 139

Lamentations Rabbah 1, 4, 6-8, 68, 74, 105, 181, 185, 190

Lamentations Rabbati 206

Levi 57-59, 63, 86, 87, 94, 117, 122, 136, 138, 140, 214-216

Levi b. R. Haita 128

Levi bar Hayyata 57

Levi ben Sisi 215

Levites 82, 89

Leviticus (Lev.) 13, 16, 25, 26, 29, 85, 87, 89, 93, 95, 96, 111, 117, 139, 150, 154-156, 160, 166, 181, 182, 185-187, 190, 191, 206, 213

Listenwissenschaft 33

Loewe, Raphael 47, 198, 199

logic 1, 2, 10, 13, 14, 16, 17, 19, 29, 31, 38, 39, 48, 52, 65, 119, 145, 150, 153, 155, 157, 161, 168, 183, 188, 189

logics, propositional 48

Long, A. A. 34

Lord 56, 57, 59, 61, 62, 64, 65, 75-77, 79, 85-89, 94, 95, 98, 100, 110, 114, 116, 117, 120, 121, 127, 129, 130, 132, 133, 136-138, 140, 152, 156, 160, 174, 175, 178, 179, 214, 215

Lot 94, 96, 98

love 16, 76, 77, 86, 124, 131-133, 135-137

Luther 1

Maccoby, Hyam 205

Mal. 59, 75, 177

Manasseh 57, 59

Marsena 90-92

media 4, 5, 33, 45, 81, 85, 86, 90, 91

Mehuman 96

Meir 26, 27, 124, 125, 160, 175-178

Mekilta 16

Mekilta attributed to R. Ishmael 206

Melchizedek 137

Memucan 90-92

mercy 77, 79, 108

Merlan, P. 35

Merses 90-92

Messiah 45-47, 53, 56, 57, 59-61, 63, 64, 68, 69, 74, 112, 119, 130, 135, 137, 138, 200

Messiah-sage 54, 67

midrash 21, 50, 126, 147, 166, 187, 200

midrash compilation(s) 1, 5-7, 45, 48-50, 51, 52, 60, 67, 151, 152, 159, 164, 169, 170, 172, 182

midrash exegetes 47, 49

midrash, comparative 184, 185, 190

Minio-Paluello, Lorenzo 35, 37

Miriam 80

Mishael 64

Mishnah 1, 5, 6, 21, 23-25, 29, 31, 33, 35, 36, 38, 39, 41, 42, 62, 81, 91, 139, 147-151, 155, 159, 162, 163, 166, 168, 172, 174, 176, 178, 183, 186, 206-208, 211-217

Moab, Moabite 46, 47, 53, 54, 55, 60-65, 67, 68, 70, 94, 128

Moabite Messiah 45, 67, 74

Montefiore, C. G. 198, 199

Moore, George F. 10, 197-199, 201, 203, 218

Mordecai 69, 136

Moriah 78, 79

Moses 2, 43, 58, 64, 70, 75, 80, 117, 120, 123, 125, 127, 129-131, 133, 135, 136, 149, 150, 152, 160, 187, 188, 211, 213, 214

Muslim 2

Nahman b. Samuel b. Nahman 76

Nahshon 65

Naomi 61-64, 102

narrative 9, 70, 79, 167, 173, 175, 178

Nathan 110, 124

Nazir, Nazirite 25

Nebuchadnezzar 86, 89, 95, 109, 136

Nebuzaradan 109

neo-Platonic 166

neo-Platonism 32, 33, 35

Neusner, Jacob 8

Noah 55, 64, 76, 77, 94, 96, 100

Numbers (Num.) 25, 26, 80, 106, 107, 109, 125, 127, 128, 133, 136, 140

oath(s) 29-31, 66, 130, 134, 179, 180

Obadiah (Obad.) 78, 137

Obed 65

offering 26-28, 30, 31, 61, 156, 177

Old Testament 48

Omnipresent 62

ontological 24, 26, 28, 34, 40, 41

Oral Torah 213

Orpah 61

Owens, Joseph 35, 39

pagan, paganism 40-42, 93, 135

parable 49, 78, 79, 158

Parker, G. F. 35

Passover 107, 127

Paul 1, 9

Pentateuch 150, 216

Perez 54, 65

Persia 90, 91, 137

Pesiqta deR. Kahana 187, 206

Pesiqta Rabbati 147

Pesiqtas 206

Pharaoh 110, 120

Philo 33, 35

philosophy 4, 5, 21, 23-25, 28, 32-36, 38-43, 47, 48, 166

philosophy, Greek 34, 35

Phineas 76, 86, 94, 120

Platonism, *see also* neo-Platonism 34, 35, 40

Platonism, Middle 34, 40

Plotinus 34, 35

Potiphar 120

prayer 16, 129

Presence of God 24, 63, 78, 82, 125, 129

prophecy 24, 98, 99

proposition 2-6, 23, 24, 28-30, 32-35, 39, 47, 52, 59, 65, 66, 68, 69, 93, 108, 155, 156, 158, 167, 172-174, 180, 189, 198, 213, 215

proselytes 61, 62, 67, 102, 140

Proverbs (Prov.) 77, 79, 90, 93-95, 97, 98, 100, 101, 103, 116, 120, 121, 123, 139, 179

Psalms (Ps.) 53, 54, 56, 63, 64, 74-77, 86-89, 92, 97, 102, 105-107, 116, 121, 122, 124, 127, 128, 132, 133, 176, 177, 178

punishment 26, 29, 30, 53, 91, 93, 116, 117, 215

Qamsa 113

Qohelet (Qoh.) 56, 58, 123, 175, 176, 215

Rabban Gamaliel 124, 125

Rabbi 70, 110, 149-151, 187, 188, 199, 200, 203, 204, 206, 210

rabbinic 1, 6, 8-10, 13-20, 70, 145, 147, 150, 152, 158, 169, 172-174, 180-186, 191, 197-199, 211

Rabinowitz 58, 59, 98, 176, 178

Ram 65

Reale, Giovanni 35

Rebecca 78

redeemer 58, 63, 133

Rehum 87

repentance 14, 16, 57, 60, 99, 175, 177, 178

resurrection 77, 177

Reuben 59

rhetoric, rhetorical 29, 31, 48, 73, 123, 145, 148, 168, 183, 190

Rome, Romans 78, 85, 101, 113, 117

Ruth 54, 55, 61-64

Ruth, Book of 47, 49-52, 65, 66, 68, 69, 171, 173, 174, 178, 179

Ruth Rabbah 1, 4, 6-8, 45-48, 50-52, 67-70, 74, 97, 100-102, 173, 174, 181, 185, 186, 190, 192

Sabbath 27-30, 63, 105, 106, 128, 175-178, 213

sacrifices 26, 27, 102, 113, 156

sage(s) 9, 19, 26, 28, 33, 38, 41, 46-49, 51, 52, 54, 55, 67-69, 81, 83, 111, 112, 121, 149-151, 162, 165, 166, 170, 174-176, 188, 192, 199, 201, 203, 212, 213, 215-218

Salmon 65

Sambursky, S. 34

Samuel 57, 85, 111

Samuel (1 Sam., 2 Sam., Sam.) 56, 62, 65, 76, 77, 179

Samuel b. Nahman 115, 179, 214

Samuel bar Abba 120

sanctuary 26, 27, 30, 87, 107, 121, 122, 134, 160

Schechter, Solomon 10, 15, 18, 19, 197-199, 218

scribe 73, 87

Scripture 8, 23, 26, 39-42, 45-50, 52, 57, 59, 61, 62, 65-70, 79, 85-87, 93, 94, 96, 97, 105, 106, 111, 112, 115, 116, 120, 131, 132, 139, 149, 150, 152-162, 165, 174, 179, 181, 183-185, 187, 191, 192, 206, 208, 211-214, 217

Seventh Year 25, 105, 106

Shem 55, 64, 94

Shema 129, 132

Shethar 90-92

Shimshai 87

Sifra 39, 41, 155, 156, 158-160, 181, 206

Sifra to Leviticus 150

Simeon b. Gamaliel 27, 114

Simeon b. Judah of Kefar Akum 82

Simeon b. Laqish 132, 139

Simeon b. Yohai 88, 90

Simon 88, 90-92, 98, 123, 124, 131-133, 137

sin-offering 26-28

Sinai 2, 76, 82, 83, 106, 110, 119, 124-126, 131-133, 135, 148, 176, 188, 202, 211-215, 217

sins 26, 31, 56, 62, 69, 111, 139, 141

slothfulness 97-99

Solomon 9, 56, 59, 62, 63, 67, 119-125, 127, 197

Song of Songs 83, 123, 126, 135

Song of Songs Rabbah 1, 4, 6-8, 74, 85, 119, 120, 124, 127-129, 131, 135, 138, 185, 190, 191

Steinsaltz, Adin 19

Stoic 34

syllogistic 1, 4, 37, 48, 83, 147, 179, 190

synagogue 82, 83, 132, 133, 150, 177, 204, 207, 209

tabernacle 120, 127, 129

Talmud of Babylonia 4, 7, 149, 174, 183, 206, 207, 214

Talmuds 1, 159, 164, 183, 211, 212

Tamar 55, 64

Tanhuma 58, 133

Tannaite 94, 124

Tarshish 90-92

taxic indicator 31, 34

taxon, taxa 15, 24, 25, 27, 31, 155, 215

taxonomy, taxonomic 25, 31, 33, 35, 37-39, 147, 151, 155, 159, 163-165, 169, 172, 190-192

teleology 25, 200, 216

Temple 29, 57, 68, 80, 81, 83, 86, 89, 92, 93, 95, 102, 107, 108, 112, 113, 115, 121, 123, 125, 126, 133, 135-137

Ten Commandments 82, 129

Ten Tribes 95, 96, 108, 128

The Fathers According to Rabbi Nathan 150, 151, 200

theology 2-7, 9, 10, 14-16, 18-21, 23, 42, 43, 45, 69, 74, 102, 119, 126, 135, 183, 187-189

Titus 109

Tosefta 150, 162, 183, 206, 208, 211

tradition 3, 19, 24, 32, 34, 40, 42, 147, 182, 217

Trajan 85

transgression(s) 25-28, 139

uncleanness 26, 30, 31, 152-154

Urbach, E. E. 10, 19, 197-199, 201, 203, 218

valuation 160-162

Vashti 89, 90, 96

Vespasian 85, 109

Weiss, J. G. 47

West, Western 2, 3, 8, 19, 36, 39, 202

Wolfson, Harry A. 35

woman 26, 27, 46, 54, 55, 59, 60, 63, 64, 67, 70, 78, 108, 112, 149, 162, 175, 179

Written Torah 46, 52

Yerushalmi 3, 150, 155, 206, 208, 211, 213, 215, 216

Yohai b. R. Hanina 56

Yohanan 56, 59, 82, 86, 98, 110, 111, 124-126, 134, 136, 137, 213, 214

Yohanan ben Zakkai 150

Yosé 113, 153, 154, 179, 180

Yosé b. R. Hanina 132, 133

Yudan 130

Yudan b. R. Simeon 214

Yudan b. R. Simon 123

Zechariah (Zech.) 58, 63, 98, 137, 138

Zechariah b. Eucolus 113

Zeira 213

Zeirah 214

Zethar 96

Zion 80, 81, 112-115, 135, 137, 138

Zoroastrian 3

Brown Judaic Studies

140001	*Approaches to Ancient Judaism I*	William S. Green
140002	*The Traditions of Eleazar Ben Azariah*	Tzvee Zahavy
140003	*Persons and Institutions in Early Rabbinic Judaism*	William S. Green
140004	*Claude Goldsmid Montefiore on the Ancient Rabbis*	Joshua B. Stein
140005	*The Ecumenical Perspective and the Modernization of Jewish Religion*	S. Daniel Breslauer
140006	*The Sabbath-Law of Rabbi Meir*	Robert Goldenberg
140007	*Rabbi Tarfon*	Joel Gereboff
140008	*Rabban Gamaliel II*	Shamai Kanter
140009	*Approaches to Ancient Judaism II*	William S. Green
140010	*Method and Meaning in Ancient Judaism*	Jacob Neusner
140011	*Approaches to Ancient Judaism III*	William S. Green
140012	*Turning Point: Zionism and Reform Judaism*	Howard R. Greenstein
140013	*Buber on God and the Perfect Man*	Pamela Vermes
140014	*Scholastic Rabbinism*	Anthony J. Saldarini
140015	*Method and Meaning in Ancient Judaism II*	Jacob Neusner
140016	*Method and Meaning in Ancient Judaism III*	Jacob Neusner
140017	*Post Mishnaic Judaism in Transition*	Baruch M. Bokser
140018	*A History of the Mishnaic Law of Agriculture: Tractate Maaser Sheni*	Peter J. Haas
140019	*Mishnah's Theology of Tithing*	Martin S. Jaffee
140020	*The Priestly Gift in Mishnah: A Study of Tractate Terumot*	Alan. J. Peck
140021	*History of Judaism: The Next Ten Years*	Baruch M. Bokser
140022	*Ancient Synagogues*	Joseph Gutmann
140023	*Warrant for Genocide*	Norman Cohn
140024	*The Creation of the World According to Gersonides*	Jacob J. Staub
140025	*Two Treatises of Philo of Alexandria: A Commentary on De Gigantibus and Quod Deus Sit Immutabilis*	David Winston/John Dillon
140026	*A History of the Mishnaic Law of Agriculture: Kilayim*	Irving Mandelbaum
140027	*Approaches to Ancient Judaism IV*	William S. Green
140028	*Judaism in the American Humanities*	Jacob Neusner
140029	*Handbook of Synagogue Architecture*	Marilyn Chiat
140030	*The Book of Mirrors*	Daniel C. Matt
140031	*Ideas in Fiction: The Works of Hayim Hazaz*	Warren Bargad
140032	*Approaches to Ancient Judaism V*	William S. Green
140033	*Sectarian Law in the Dead Sea Scrolls: Courts, Testimony and the Penal Code*	Lawrence H. Schiffman
140034	*A History of the United Jewish Appeal: 1939-1982*	Marc L. Raphael
140035	*The Academic Study of Judaism*	Jacob Neusner
140036	*Woman Leaders in the Ancient Synagogue*	Bernadette Brooten
140037	*Formative Judaism: Religious, Historical, and Literary Studies*	Jacob Neusner
140038	*Ben Sira's View of Women: A Literary Analysis*	Warren C. Trenchard
140039	*Barukh Kurzweil and Modern Hebrew Literature*	James S. Diamond

140040	*Israeli Childhood Stories of the Sixties: Yizhar, Aloni,Shahar, Kahana-Carmon*	Gideon Telpaz
140041	*Formative Judaism II: Religious, Historical, and Literary Studies*	Jacob Neusner
140042	*Judaism in the American Humanities II: Jewish Learning and the New Humanities*	Jacob Neusner
140043	*Support for the Poor in the Mishnaic Law of Agriculture: Tractate Peah*	Roger Brooks
140044	*The Sanctity of the Seventh Year: A Study of Mishnah Tractate Shebiit*	Louis E. Newman
140045	*Character and Context: Studies in the Fiction of Abramovitsh, Brenner, and Agnon*	Jeffrey Fleck
140046	*Formative Judaism III: Religious, Historical, and Literary Studies*	Jacob Neusner
140047	*Pharaoh's Counsellors: Job, Jethro, and Balaam in Rabbinic and Patristic Tradition*	Judith Baskin
140048	*The Scrolls and Christian Origins: Studies in the Jewish Background of the New Testament*	Matthew Black
140049	*Approaches to Modern Judaism I*	Marc Lee Raphael
140050	*Mysterious Encounters at Mamre and Jabbok*	William T. Miller
140051	*The Mishnah Before 70*	Jacob Neusner
140052	*Sparda by the Bitter Sea: Imperial Interaction in Western Anatolia*	Jack Martin Balcer
140053	*Hermann Cohen: The Challenge of a Religion of Reason*	William Kluback
140054	*Approaches to Judaism in Medieval Times I*	David R. Blumenthal
140055	*In the Margins of the Yerushalmi: Glosses on the English Translation*	Jacob Neusner
140056	*Approaches to Modern Judaism II*	Marc Lee Raphael
140057	*Approaches to Judaism in Medieval Times II*	David R. Blumenthal
140058	*Midrash as Literature: The Primacy of Documentary Discourse*	JacobNeusner
140059	*The Commerce of the Sacred: Mediation of the Divine Among Jews in the Graeco-Roman Diaspora*	Jack N. Lightstone
140060	*Major Trends in Formative Judaism I: Society and Symbol in Political Crisis*	Jacob Neusner
140061	*Major Trends in Formative Judaism II: Texts, Contents, and Contexts*	Jacob Neusner
140062	*A History of the Jews in Babylonia I: The Parthian Period*	Jacob Neusner
140063	*The Talmud of Babylonia: An American Translation. XXXII: Tractate Arakhin*	Jacob Neusner
140064	*Ancient Judaism: Debates and Disputes*	Jacob Neusner
140065	*Prayers Alleged to Be Jewish: An Examination of the Constitutiones Apostolorum*	David Fiensy
140066	*The Legal Methodology of Hai Gaon*	Tsvi Groner
140067	*From Mishnah to Scripture: The Problem of the Unattributed Saying*	Jacob Neusner
140068	*Halakhah in a Theological Dimension*	David Novak

140069	*From Philo to Origen: Middle Platonism in Transition*	Robert M. Berchman
140070	*In Search of Talmudic Biography: The Problem of the Attributed Saying*	Jacob Neusner
140071	*The Death of the Old and the Birth of the New: The Framework of the Book of Numbers and the Pentateuch*	Dennis T. Olson
140072	*The Talmud of Babylonia: An American Translation. XVII: Tractate Sotah*	Jacob Neusner
140073	*Understanding Seeking Faith: Essays on the Case of Judaism. Volume Two: Literature, Religion and the Social Study of Judiasm*	JacobNeusner
140074	*The Talmud of Babylonia: An American Translation. VI: Tractate Sukkah*	Jacob Neusner
140075	*Fear Not Warrior: A Study of 'al tira' Pericopes in the Hebrew Scriptures*	Edgar W. Conrad
140076	*Formative Judaism IV: Religious, Historical, and Literary Studies*	Jacob Neusner
140077	*Biblical Patterns in Modern Literature*	David H. Hirsch/ Nehama Aschkenasy
140078	*The Talmud of Babylonia: An American Translation I: Tractate Berakhot*	Jacob Neusner
140079	*Mishnah's Division of Agriculture: A History and Theology of Seder Zeraim*	Alan J. Avery-Peck
140080	*From Tradition to Imitation: The Plan and Program of Pesiqta Rabbati and Pesiqta deRab Kahana*	Jacob Neusner
140081	*The Talmud of Babylonia: An American Translation. XXIIIA: Tractate Sanhedrin, Chapters 1-3*	Jacob Neusner
140082	*Jewish Presence in T. S. Eliot and Franz Kafka*	Melvin Wilk
140083	*School, Court, Public Administration: Judaism and its Institutions in Talmudic Babylonia*	Jacob Neusner
140084	*The Talmud of Babylonia: An American Translation. XXIIIB: Tractate Sanhedrin, Chapters 4-8*	Jacob Neusner
140085	*The Bavli and Its Sources: The Question of Tradition in the Case of Tractate Sukkah*	Jacob Neusner
140086	*From Description to Conviction: Essays on the History and Theology of Judaism*	Jacob Neusner
140087	*The Talmud of Babylonia: An American Translation. XXIIIC: Tractate Sanhedrin, Chapters 9-11*	Jacob Neusner
140088	*Mishnaic Law of Blessings and Prayers: Tractate Berakhot*	Tzvee Zahavy
140089	*The Peripatetic Saying: The Problem of the Thrice-Told Tale in Talmudic Literature*	Jacob Neusner
140090	*The Talmud of Babylonia: An American Translation. XXVI: Tractate Horayot*	Martin S. Jaffee
140091	*Formative Judaism V: Religious, Historical, and Literary Studies*	Jacob Neusner
140092	*Essays on Biblical Method and Translation*	Edward Greenstein
140093	*The Integrity of Leviticus Rabbah*	Jacob Neusner
140094	*Behind the Essenes: History and Ideology of the Dead Sea Scrolls*	Philip R. Davies

140095	*Approaches to Judaism in Medieval Times, Volume III*	David R. Blumenthal
140096	*The Memorized Torah: The Mnemonic System of the Mishnah*	Jacob Neusner
140098	*Sifre to Deuteronomy: An Analytical Translation. Volume One: Pisqaot One through One Hundred Forty-Three. Debarim, Waethanan, Eqeb*	Jacob Neusner
140099	*Major Trends in Formative Judaism III: The Three Stages in the Formation of Judaism*	Jacob Neusner
140101	*Sifre to Deuteronomy: An Analytical Translation. Volume Two: Pisqaot One Hundred Forty-Four through Three Hundred Fifty-Seven. Shofetim, Ki Tese, Ki Tabo, Nesabim, Ha'azinu, Zot Habberakhah*	Jacob Neusner
140102	*Sifra: The Rabbinic Commentary on Leviticus*	Jacob Neusner/ Roger Brooks
140103	*The Human Will in Judaism*	Howard Eilberg-Schwartz
140104	*Genesis Rabbah: Volume 1. Genesis 1:1 to 8:14*	Jacob Neusner
140105	*Genesis Rabbah: Volume 2. Genesis 8:15 to 28:9*	Jacob Neusner
140106	*Genesis Rabbah: Volume 3. Genesis 28:10 to 50:26*	Jacob Neusner
140107	*First Principles of Systemic Analysis*	Jacob Neusner
140108	*Genesis and Judaism*	Jacob Neusner
140109	*The Talmud of Babylonia: An American Translation. XXXV: Tractates Meilah and Tamid*	Peter J. Haas
140110	*Studies in Islamic and Judaic Traditions*	William Brinner/Stephen Ricks
140111	*Comparative Midrash: The Plan and Program of Genesis Rabbah and Leviticus Rabbah*	Jacob Neusner
140112	*The Tosefta: Its Structure and its Sources*	Jacob Neusner
140113	*Reading and Believing*	Jacob Neusner
140114	*The Fathers According to Rabbi Nathan*	Jacob Neusner
140115	*Etymology in Early Jewish Interpretation: The Hebrew Names in Philo*	Lester L. Grabbe
140116	*Understanding Seeking Faith: Essays on the Case of Judaism. Volume One: Debates on Method, Reports of Results*	Jacob Neusner
140117	*The Talmud of Babylonia. An American Translation. VII: Tractate Besah*	Alan J. Avery-Peck
140118	*Sifre to Numbers: An American Translation and Explanation, Volume One: Sifre to Numbers 1-58*	Jacob Neusner
140119	*Sifre to Numbers: An American Translation and Explanation, Volume Two: Sifre to Numbers 59-115*	Jacob Neusner
140120	*Cohen and Troeltsch: Ethical Monotheistic Religion and Theory of Culture*	Wendell S. Dietrich
140121	*Goodenough on the History of Religion and on Judaism*	Jacob Neusner/ Ernest Frerichs
140122	*Pesiqta deRab Kahana I: Pisqaot One through Fourteen*	Jacob Neusner
140123	*Pesiqta deRab Kahana II: Pisqaot Fifteen through Twenty-Eight and Introduction to Pesiqta deRab Kahana*	Jacob Neusner
140124	*Sifre to Deuteronomy: Introduction*	Jacob Neusner

140126	*A Conceptual Commentary on Midrash Leviticus Rabbah:*	
	Value Concepts in Jewish Thought	Max Kadushin
140127	*The Other Judaisms of Late Antiquity*	Alan F. Segal
140128	*Josephus as a Historical Source in Patristic Literature*	
	through Eusebius	Michael Hardwick
140129	*Judaism: The Evidence of the Mishnah*	Jacob Neusner
140131	*Philo, John and Paul: New Perspectives on Judaism*	
	and Early Christianity	Peder Borgen
140132	*Babylonian Witchcraft Literature*	Tzvi Abusch
140133	*The Making of the Mind of Judaism: The Formative Age*	Jacob Neusner
140135	*Why No Gospels in Talmudic Judaism?*	Jacob Neusner
140136	*Torah: From Scroll to Symbol Part III: Doctrine*	Jacob Neusner
140137	*The Systemic Analysis of Judaism*	Jacob Neusner
140138	*Sifra: An Analytical Translation Vol. 1*	Jacob Neusner
140139	*Sifra: An Analytical Translation Vol. 2*	Jacob Neusner
140140	*Sifra: An Analytical Translation Vol. 3*	Jacob Neusner
140141	*Midrash in Context: Exegesis in Formative Judaism*	Jacob Neusner
140143	*Oxen, Women or Citizens? Slaves in the System of*	
	Mishnah	Paul V. Flesher
140144	*The Book of the Pomegranate*	Elliot R. Wolfson
140145	*Wrong Ways and Right Ways in the Study of Formative*	
	Judaism	Jacob Neusner
140146	*Sifra in Perspective: The Documentary Comparison of the*	
	Midrashim of Ancient Judaism	Jacob Neusner
140148	*Mekhilta According to Rabbi Ishmael: An Analytical*	
	Translation Volume I	Jacob Neusner
140149	*The Doctrine of the Divine Name: An Introduction to*	
	Classical Kabbalistic Theology	Stephen G. Wald
140150	*Water into Wine and the Beheading of John the Baptist*	Roger Aus
140151	*The Formation of the Jewish Intellect*	Jacob Neusner
140152	*Mekhilta According to Rabbi Ishmael: An Introduction to Judaism's*	
	First Scriptural Encyclopaedia	Jacob Neusner
140153	*Understanding Seeking Faith. Volume Three*	Jacob Neusner
140154	*Mekhilta According to Rabbi Ishmael: An Analytical Translation*	
	Volume Two	Jacob Neusner
140155	*Goyim: Gentiles and Israelites in Mishnah-Tosefta*	Gary P. Porton
140156	*A Religion of Pots and Pans?*	Jacob Neusner
140157	*Claude Montefiore and Christianity*	Maurice Gerald Bowler
140158	*The Philosopical Mishnah Volume III*	Jacob Neusner
140159	*From Ancient Israel to Modern Judaism Volume 1: Intellect in Quest of*	
	Understanding	Neusner/Frerichs/Sarna
140160	*The Social Study of Judaism Volume I*	Jacob Neusner
140161	*Philo's Jewish Identity*	Alan Mendelson
140162	*The Social Study of Judaism Volume II*	Jacob Neusner
140163	*The Philosophical Mishnah Volume I : The Initial Probe*	Jacob Neusner
140164	*The Philosophical Mishnah Volume II : The Tractates Agenda: From Abodah*	
	Zarah Through Moed Qatan	Jacob Neusner
140166	*Women's Earliest Records*	Barbara S. Lesko

140167	*The Legacy of Hermann Cohen*	William Kluback
140168	*Method and Meaning in Ancient Judaism*	Jacob Neusner
140169	*The Role of the Messenger and Message in the Ancient Near East*	
		John T. Greene
140171	*Abraham Heschel's Idea of Revelation*	Lawerence Perlman
140172	*The Philosophical Mishnah Volume IV: The Repertoire*	Jacob Neusner
140173	*From Ancient Israel to Modern Judaism Volume 2: Intellect in Quest of Understanding*	Neusner/Frerichs/Sarna
140174	*From Ancient Israel to Modern Judaism Volume 3: Intellect in Quest of Understanding*	Neusner/Frerichs/Sarna
140175	*From Ancient Israel to Modern Judaism Volume 4: Intellect in Quest of Understanding*	Neusner/Frerichs/Sarna
140176	*Translating the Classics of Judaism: In Theory and In Practice*	Jacob Neusner
140177	*Profiles of a Rabbi: Synoptic Opportunities in Reading About Jesus*	Bruce Chilton
140178	*Studies in Islamic and Judaic Traditions II*	William Brinner/Stephen Ricks
140179	*Medium and Message in Judaism: First Series*	Jacob Neusner
140180	*Making the Classics of Judaism: The Three Stages of Literary Formation*	Jacob Neusner
140181	*The Law of Jealousy: Anthropology of Sotah*	Adriana Destro
140182	*Esther Rabbah I: An Analytical Translation*	Jacob Neusner
140183	*Ruth Rabbah: An Analytical Translation*	Jacob Neusner
140184	*Formative Judaism: Religious, Historical and Literary Studies*	Jacob Neusner
140185	*The Studia Philonica Annual*	David T. Runia
140186	*The Setting of the Sermon on the Mount*	Davies
140187	*The Midrash Compilations of the Sixth and Seventh Centuries Volume One*	Jacob Neusner
140188	*The Midrash Compilations of the Sixth and Seventh Centuries Volume Two*	Jacob Neusner
140189	*The Midrash Compilations of the Sixth and Seventh Centuries Volume Three*	Jacob Neusner
140190	*The Midrash Compilations of the Sixth and Seventh Centuries Volume Four*	Jacob Neusner
140191	*The Religious World of Contemporary Judaism: Observations and Convictions*	Jacob Neusner
140192	*Approaches to Ancient Judaism: Volume VI*	Jacob Neusner/ Ernest S. Frerichs
140193	*Lamentations Rabbah: An Analytical Translation*	Jacob Neusner
140194	*Early Christian Texts on Jews and Judaism*	Robert S. MacLennan
140195	*Lectures on Judaism*	Jacob Neusner
140196	*Torah and the Chronicler's History Work*	Judson R. Shaver
140197	*Song of Songs Rabbah: An Analytical Translation Volume One*	Jacob Neusner
140198	*Song of Songs Rabbah: An Analytical Translation Volume Two*	Jacob Neusner
140199	*From Literature to Theology in Formative Judaism*	Jacob Neusner

Brown Studies on Jews and Their Societies

145001   *American Jewish Fertility*   Calvin Goldscheider
145003   *The American Jewish Community*   Calvin Goldscheider
145004   *The Naturalized Jews of the Grand Duchy of Posen in 1834 and 1835*   Edward David Luft
145005   *Suburban Communities: The Jewishness of American Reform Jews*   Gerald L. Showstack
145007   *Ethnic Survival in America*   David Schoem

Brown Studies in Religion

147001   *Religious Writings and Religious Systems Volume 1*   Jacob Neusner, et al
147002   *Religious Writings and Religious Systems Volume 2*   Jacob Neusner, et al
147003   *Religion and the Social Sciences*   Robert Segal

DATE DUE

HIGHSMITH   # 45220